XX

D0231694

DALKEY
An Anthology

Leabharlanna Bhaile Thormod / Tel. 6269324/
Ballyfermot Library

Withdrawn from Stock
Dublin City Public Libraries

Compiled by FRANK MULLEN

Edited by PADRAIG YEATES

First published by Frank Mullen 2008

© Copyright 2008

Frank Mullen

ISBN No. Paperback: 184055131-3

ISBN No. Hardback: 184055130-5

All rights reserved. No part of this book may be reproduced
or utilised in any form or by any means without prior written
permission from the author.

Typesetting and design
Mullen Print
Unit B1, Centrepoint,
Rosemount Business Park,
Blanchardstown, Dublin 11,
Ireland.

Edited by Padraig Yeates

Cover design: Donal Smyth

All proceeds from the sale of this book will go to Dalkey United Development Fund.

Acknowledgements

I would like to gratefully acknowledge the advice and assistance of many people who directly or indeed indirectly helped me in the production of this book.

My long time friend and well known historian and writer Padraig Yeates for the giving of his time not just in the editing of this book but for all his professional advice and patience.

The staff of the National Library, the Gilbert Library, the UCD Library and the various archives that I visited. As I am not computer literate without their professionalism and good humour at all times I would not have succeeded in getting so much information.

To many local people for supplying materials, old photographs and for providing the names of people in those photos, Margaret Smith, Dynphna Redmond, Sheila Farrell, Des McWilliams, Pat O'Brien, Mary Byrne and her son Alan, Pat Kavanagh, Sean Thomas, Fergus Smyth, Joe and Andy O'Rourke, Michael Hayde Jnr., Hugh McCann, Harry Byrne, Noel Kavanagh, Mary Coyle, Marie Thorpe, Ged Pierse, Dan Finnegan, Michael Mullen, John Cunningham and Marian Holden.

To Canon Ben Neill, Rector of St. Patrick's Church of Ireland and Very Rev. John McDonagh P.P. Dalkey for supplying very interesting material from their respective church records. To the staff of Harold Boys, Castlepark and St. Patrick's Schools for their help.

To Ger Coakley, editor Comunity Council Newsletter for his assistance.

To all who have written, gave permission to publish previously published articles that are so important in compiling an anthology including families of writers who have passed on, for allowing us to publish such interesting items.

To Sean O'Gorman, Ciaran Coleman and their families for their help in proof reading.

To Penny Lannin of Dalkey Business Centre for her truly invaluable help in typing and emailing so much over the last 3 years or so. Her professionalism was matched only by her courtesy. I also want to express my thanks to Lorraine Cameron, Pauline Seymour, Barbara McMahon, Analiese Dolan.

To all who have supplied the photographs that appear in the book and who have reprinted so many, Sam Caren, Aindreas Scholz and David McMahon of Dalkey Photo Centre. Stephen Crowzier, Alan Spellman, George Stuart photographers.

To Bert Wright for his professional advice which was so important.
To Mullen Print Ltd., Bernard Adderley, Tony Mullen & staff for their usual professionalism and their help in so many different ways.

A very important person in the production of this book which I never envisaged would involve so much work was Donal Smyth who designed the production. Donals' family have been involved with Dalkey United since its foundation and his service and expertise has been so willingly forthcoming that it is not possible to quantify its importance.

Finally to my wife Ellen, without her help and invaluable support not just indeed in the compiling of this book but at all times has been such that without her I would never have completed it. When difficulties or problems arose she helped me as she has done in all of our married life together by being a true stalwart, a person with great inner strength and yet always positive, unstinting in her support.

Dedication

This book is dedicated to all who offered their support and services voluntarily, to improve the quality of life and give enjoyment to so many in our beloved town, in memory of all who have done so in the past and with best wishes and Gods blessings to all who will continue the good work in the future

and

To my wife Ellen
who is the personification of kindness and whom I love dearly

Table of Contents

Preface

During my adult life, I have written reports, pamphlets and brochures on various subjects but I never contemplated writing a book.

I presume because of my involvement in various organisations, I have been asked on several occasions to write books on different subjects. I have always declined the requests. Some of these offers were for monetary rewards, others on a voluntary basis. I never hesitated in refusing the requests although I considered it an honour that some people thought I was competent to undertake such a task. I believe their confidence to say the least, was misplaced, perhaps my efforts to write this book will prove this to be true.

Since I wrote a recent publication for our beloved Dalkey United Football Club, Golden Jubilee Brochure, followed by our 2003/04 Year Book, I have been subjected to significant pressure to write a history of our club. I refused these requests until one day a few years ago I met a lady on Convent Road, whom I know all my life, who asked me to write a book. Dympna Redmond, who during her lifetime has contributed in a very significant way to the well being of the people in Dalkey in the various groups that she is involved with, such as the Community Council, the Lady's Club and other voluntary organisations. After a lengthy discussion, I promised her I would give her suggestion serious consideration. Some days later, just by chance, I met her niece Noeleen Dunne and a similar conversation took place on Castle Street. One of the remarks Noeleen passed was: *"It would be a nice way to remember the lads who founded the club, my Dad (Paddy Larkin) who was chairman of the club for four years, from 1970 to 1974, and the others, who have now passed on, who gave great service to the club. It would also be a great record to give to all the young lads presently playing for the club, to hand on to their children and grandchildren in the years ahead."*

I told her that if the management committee agreed, I would do it and it would be an honour and a privilege. I told her Aunt Dymphna a few days later of my decision. I discussed the matter with my wife, Ellen, my family, the management committee of the club and others who had over the years been connected with the club. I also spoke to some of the writers referred to, whom I consider to be good, indeed in some cases, lifelong friends. The theme of their advice was very similar. It was: there is nobody who has been so close to the achievements of the club over the last fifty five years and that I never appeared reluctant to face up to a challenge in the past.

I felt that writing a book on the history of a football club over fifty five years would change its shape in the process of being written. This has been the case with this one. I worried if at the commencement it would change some day and it would fail to hold a reader's interest. I decided not just to write a history of Dalkey United, I would recall other interesting events that took place in Dalkey down through the years and for those who would not know Dalkey well, a description of our town, the changes, some of its personalities, its sports men and women and also some well-known local characters. I would endeavour to make it a mixture of an anthology, a diary, a type of miscellany. I hope I have gone some way in achieving this objective. As I have said so many times in the past, I am fortunate to have been born and reared in Dalkey and involved in such a great club for all of my adult life. I am also extremely lucky to have been helped and advised by so many wonderful people and great friends, not just in the club but throughout the sports world. I have endeavoured to produce an interesting anthology on Dalkey and if because of my passionate love of the club, the town and its people I departed from this objective by showing emotions, excitement or sadness in my efforts I hope I will be forgiven.

The problems faced in those days over fifty years ago in the running of a football club are similar in so many ways to the problems that those involved have to contend with today. To gain a fair idea of the significance of the contributions and effort that so many people made through the years to ensure that the club continued to exist, it is important to recall as many major developments in the distant past as it is to reflect on more recent ones. It is naturally easier to highlight recent events, such as successes, improvements of facilities and so forth but the events of far off years were the foundation stones on which the club was built into what it is today.

Shortly before going to print the management committee decided to concentrate exclusively on schoolboys and the growing popularity of schoolgirls football. This present season of 2008/09 we field 18 teams every weekend and run an academy for sixty young children under 7 years of age to prepare them for competitive football.

The cost of running the club is substantial and last season we converted the old dressing rooms area into a new modern complex at a cost in excess of €250,000 which we borrowed from the A.I.B. in Dalkey. We are now working to pay off this debt and all proceeds from the sale of this book will go in the building fund.

I believe the appeal of history is imaginative. It is to feel what life was really like in the past, to hear the voices of those long gone and to see how they looked as we gaze intensely at old photographs. In trying to create a picture of the past fifty five years in Dalkey United and further back for Dalkey Town as GM Trevelyan in his English social history stated: '*Consider that all lies in that one word past! What a pathetic, sacred in every sense poetic meaning is employed in it. History is after all true poetry and reality, if rightly interpreted, is grander than fiction*". "Stranger than fiction", some might say. I hope I have gone a distance with the help of many, in interpreting past events in a manner acceptable to any readers of the book. Believe me, I have tried.

Thanks,
Frank Mullen.

Forward by Mr. Ged Pierse, Life President, Dalkey United F.C.

This publication, which has been 4 years in the making, records some of the events and characters which have graced Dalkey over a hundred years and which have added to its unique character.

The proceeds from this book go exclusively to Dalkey United Football Club to help finance the major improvements planned for their facilities at Hyde Road, Dalkey.

Dalkey United fields up to 18 teams each weekend from its 260 playing members whose ages range from 7 to 17 years. In addition, the club provides initial coaching for 60 children between 5 and 7 years of age.

The day-to-day running of such a large club is supported by local contributions and managed by volunteers drawn from the parents of the children involved and local, interested, stalwarts.

The assortment of articles included in this anthology will give the reader a flavour of what life and living in Dalkey was all about in the past hundred plus years. It was a vibrant community with small, healthy, sporting clubs.

Apart from Dalkey United Football Club, we had a swimming club, a rowing club, a boxing club, Dalkey sea scouts, a table tennis club, a Gaelic club, a fishing club, a debating society and, of course, our church "sodalities".

I grew up in Dalkey and enjoyed all of these facilities. I remember many, many, idyllic summers spent at Bulloch and Coliemore Harbours, Dalkey Island and White Rock Strand.   On reflection, it seemed we were really in paradise. When

Ged Pierse

I emigrated in 1963, I left Dalkey with a heavy heart and throughout my 15-year absence; I pined for the hills and coastline of my childhood. Happily I returned with wife Paule and our family in 1978, never to leave again.

The locals say that you may grow old in Dalkey but you will always remain "young at heart". This I can assure you is the infectious appeal of the town.

I congratulate Frank Mullen and his team for producing such an interesting memorial of Dalkey and its characters and hope you find it enjoyable.

Leabharlanna Poiblí Chathair Bhaile Átha Cliath
Dublin City Public Libraries

PATRONS

Ged Pierse

Mark Rehill

Peter Borza

Charlie Chawke

Geoff Sullivan

Tim Kerins

Tony Weir

Seamus Sheeran

Fitzpatricks Castle Hotel

Eamonn Walshe

St. Laurences Club

Brian Conroy

Michael James

Catragh Books

Mitchell & Son, Winemerchants, Glasthule

Dan Finnegan

Otronto Properties

Eithne Smyth, Little Acres

Gerry Garvan

Benitos, Castle St., Dalkey

Ray Dolan

Avril Byrne

Derry O'Hegarty

Noel Kavanagh, Glasthule

Eric Keating

Rossa McDermott

Brian S. Nolan

Brian Lynch

The photograph on the front cover was taken by the late Brian Lynch, who was a senior executive photographer with Bord Failte.

The photo of a snow covered Dalkey Island and Colimore Harbour was taken some years before he died at a relatively young age on the 29th November 2000.

Brian was a native of Dalkey and enjoyed taking photographs particularly for local voluntary groups which he did because of his great love of his home town. He never charged a fee for his services.

I am sure readers will agree that the unique photograph on the cover which is as far as we can ascertain never been published before now, is a tribute to his professionalism, a lasting memory of a truly great camerman and a very kind person.

All connected with the publication of this book are grateful to Brian's widow Pauline and their children Liz and David for agreeing to the use of this photograph in Dalkey An Anthology.

Padraig Yeates
Editor

A Part of Dalkey

I have been part of Dalkey just as long as Dalkey United have been. I wasn't born here but came the whole way, two miles, from Glenageary, when I was a schoolgirl. In those days, I foolishly thought it was a step in the wrong direction. We were all dying to move towards the brightish lights of Dun Laoghaire and the very bright lights of Dublin. Dalkey seemed dangerously restful in comparison.

But, as everywhere, there were compensations and my friends and I took to having a walk past the pitch now and then to see nice, leggy looking fellows playing football. But we thought that we were very sophisticated at fourteen, so we didn't pretend we were looking at them at all, so that meant that sadly we never got to know them.

Dalkey was very, very different fifty years ago. Everything closed for lunch and everything closed down completely by 6:00pm, apart from a sortie for fish and chips, the place was dead quiet. Women didn't go to pubs and there were no cafes or restaurants. Television hadn't arrived. You sat at home with your family and listened to the radio, you visited other people's houses and maybe once a week you went to the pictures in Dun Laoghaire or Glasthule. You could hear your feet-echoing coming along Castle Street when it was dark. Some people talk about the Good Old Days but I'm not one to wallow in nostalgia. I think in many ways they were Desperate Old Days and that we are much better off.

Obviously, of course, the old days were good days for us as a family because our parents were alive and happy and we had a great home on Knocnacree Road, where all our friends were welcome. Obviously, too, we remember, whether rightly or wrongly, that all the summers were gloriously hot and we swam every day from June to September and put on Nivea Crème to sit in the garden when we were meant to be studying for exams.

But, in general, Dalkey has become so marvellous and lively and better since then that

Maeve Binchy

I often wish I could bring my mother and father back, even just for a week, to show them the great place they chose for us to live. For one thing, they would be delighted that their children, who had all taken up very different jobs and married happily very different kinds of people, had all managed to live in or near Dalkey, where we see each other all the time and it sometimes feels as if no time has passed at all.

Thirty years later, I know my mother would love that Dalkey is covered in beautiful flowers and would look up admiringly at the arrangements high on the lampposts wondering exactly how they are fed and watered to look so well. My father would love the Heritage Centre and would be pleased that the litter has been brought so well under control and the streets kept so clean.

They would be amazed, and I think delighted, that lunches are served in every public house and that exotic foods, spices, vegetables and cheese are for sale in the shops. They would be bewildered by the range of restaurants and wonder where all the customers could possibly come from. Living as they did in a world where everyone went home to their tea at half past six, that would be one of the biggest changes. I would like to show them other changes for the better too, I don't believe that people have become hard and materialistic.

I honestly think that as a society we care much more than we used to about the sick, the elderly, the handicapped and those to whom life or events have dealt a poor hand of cards. The social services have improved greatly for a start, special housing has been started.

There was a time when good people just knelt at prayer, with head in their hands, and talked to God about themselves. But nowadays they do much better good by caring for their fellow men and women and acknowledging that to answer with a generous heart the needs of a neighbour is one of the greatest commandments of all. Today there is far less hypocrisy around than when I was young. It is realistic to hope that every baby born in Dalkey is a welcome baby who will have a family friend and a community to welcome the child. This was, sadly, not always the way in what people called the Good Old Days.

So I walk through the same streets as I walked half a century ago, I feel not a sense of regret for a vanished era and the ghosts of yesterday, instead I feel a sense of pride that so much has changed for the better. A feeling that the future will be better still and that nowadays we realise that it is up to us to ensure that it happens that way. Places don't get better or worse accidentally, we have been so lucky to live in this particular place so near a capital city and yet by the sea, near the mountains and with its own history and charm. We owe it to give something back to our neighbourhood. My wish and hope for Dalkey is that we take the name of our football club seriously and that we become Dalkey United in every sense of the word.

Proud of where we live, involved with those who share the place and giving our local club all the support in the world.

Maeve Binchy

Dalkey Island

Dalkey Island rises softly
From a churning tidal sea,
Undulating, springy grassland,
Grazing goatlife wanders free.

Granite boulders, ancient ruins,
Sheltered spots where one may rest.
Seagulls gliding, swooping, diving.
Fiercely guarding hidden nests.

Martello keeps its constant vigil
Waiting for Napoleon's fleet.
Alas the fort is now deserted
Where garrison was once complete.

St. Begnet's Church, another ruin,
Christians prayed there long ago,
When Dalkey was the port for Dublin
An island safe from mainland foe.

Now yachts and craft of all description
Slowly cruise this lovely sound
I anchor nearby, rocking gently
At one with beauty all around.

Betty Houton

The Recorder Of Dalkey

He was a tall man. With a brolly and that distinctive gait, he would walk from Fort Jamrud to Dalkey Railway Station each day on his way to the Bank in the City. Sometimes in the evening he would adjourn to John Searsons (now the Kings Inn) for convivial chat with his peers in the back room of the lounge, after meetings in the Town Hall. These meetings of the Dalkey Development Association provided an opportunity for him to express in a formal way issues that concerned him relating to Dalkey and its environs. Environmental issues were to come into vogue much later, but Frank 'Milo' O'Flanagan pursued singularly, matters relating to Dalkey in the fifties and sixties, long before

Community Councils and the latter day conversion of Dun Laoghaire Corporation to environmental protection.

His austere manner gave the impression that he had a rather gruff personality. On the contrary, he was affable and friendly, humorous and sensitive. He had an inquiring mind if his library was any indication of his intellectual prowess. His questioning attitude to local matters, together with his occasional letter to the Editor of the Irish Times revealed a man who was committed to the interests of Dalkey and relentless in voicing his concerns. An extract from his 'Dalkey Notes' illustrates his alertness to these concerns. '...C.I.E. decreed some time ago – much against the Dalkey traders and residents expressed wishes – that the Dalkey bus would not even enter Dalkey, but have its terminus far off in Ulverton Road. It is still there, and while the company insists on this venue, the Dalkey people should insist that adequate shelter be provided by C.I.E. at this exposed site.'

He was particularly interested in the protection of rights of way around Dalkey. Ever vigilant, as builders and greedy house owners attempted to close off local pathways and long established access routes, Frank would visit Dun Laoghaire Town Hall and consult old maps. Following his analysis, he would write letters to newspapers and Corporation Councillors, protest-

ing any infringements. In this regard, we owe a depth of gratitude to Frank O'Flanagan, for his leadership, citizenship and vision.

He was a man of vision in other respects. He regularly complained of the poor train service to Dalkey from the city, noting that the last train from Dublin was 7.30 p.m. He suggested trains on the hour comprising one or two carriages which would be more economical to operate whilst providing a more flexible and dependable service for Dalkey people. His letters to the Irish Times had little effect on the mandarins in C.I.E. He also proposed a local bus service (when the 'real' number 8 was operating) which would originate in Dun Laoghaire and serve Dalkey, the Vico Road and Killiney village. He felt this would appeal to tourists and provide Dalkey people with a reliable local service to Dun Laoghaire. That idea too was ignored.

Frank O'Flanagan also researched the history of Dalkey, and in his younger years presented papers to the Old Dublin Society. His well known 'Glimpses of old Dalkey' have recently been serialised in the Dalkey Community Newsletter. His research would later become the standard source on guides to Dalkey. He published a 'Guide to Dalkey' which included a map and index, costing one shilling and sixpence under the title 'The Recorder of Dalkey

Publications.' He also published a postcard of the Dalkey Town Commissioners' flag, 1869-1900. This flag measuring six feet by five feet was believed to be the only remaining flag of the Town Commissioners and he was proud to be the

Jack Carvill, President E. deVelera,
Frank Flanagan and John Bonas

sole owner.

Frank was a committee member of the Old Dublin Society, the Dalkey Development Association, Dalkey Literary, Historical and Debating Society, and the St. Dominic Savio Boys Club. The Boys Club published the 'Dalkey Sound', a news magazine between the years 1962-1966. This magazine was printed in the old presbytery on Fr. Brian Kelly's Gestetner without public acknowledgement of his kindness and generosity to the Boys Club over the years. Frank contributed to this publication by editing a Dalkey quiz, interviewing Dalkey people of some note, e.g. Milo O'Shea, Harry Webster, Norman Judd and Michael Spencer. He also wrote a column 'Dalkey Notes' under the pseudonym Sicnarf O'M. An extract from one of his columns on the crowning of the King of Dalkey in 1965 illustrates his humorous style of writing.

'Well the highlight of the Summer was the successful Revival of the crowning of the King of Dalkey. On Sunday, 6th June, 1965, "King Norman 1st King of Dalkey, Emperor of the Muglins, Cathoirleach of The Kish, etc. etc. in the formidable 20 stone presence of Councillor Norman Judd, landed in state by sea from the Dun Laoghaire Lifeboat at Bulloch Harbour to claim the ancient Kingdom of Dalkey, to be crowned in "Carrig-na-Greine", and to declare well and truly open a whole WEEK of Coronation Festivities.' A few of the enjoyable events that followed until Sunday, 13th June, 1965 may be mentioned – Coronation Banquet and Ball in "The Goat's Castle" (Town Hall to you), Coronation Ball in Cliff Castle Hotel, Football Matches (both Gaelic and Soccer), Boxing, Athletics, Waiters Races every evening in Castle Street, "King Fisher Contest" every day from Coliemore Harbour, Childrens' Art exhibition, Aeriocht, Teen-age Dance, and a host of others – all well patronised and successful. In addition the Dalkey "Dail Eireann" – the "Pimlico Parliament" dating back to the 1790's – was held in "The Goat's Castle" on 24th May, 1965 to "tidy up" Dalkey Legislation before the Coronation.' (Take note that the next sitting of the Ancient and August Assembly is scheduled for January, 1966 – the B.B.C. and Telefis Eireann are both understood to be interested!). Kings are rare things in the turbulent world of to-day, and little doubt exists that, of those that still survive King Norman First of Dalkey would win a Popularity Contest in the open field! Where else would you find "doctrinaire Republicans" shouting themselves hoarse with cries of "Long Live the King" '

He was proud that President Eamonn de Valera accepted the invitation of the Dalkey Literary Historical and Debating

Society to visit Dalkey on the occasion of a lecture by Dudley Edwards of U.C.D. He wrote

'The 19th January, 1966, will ever be a memorable day in Dalkey. At 7.45 p.m. that night the President of Ireland, His Excellency Eamonn de Valera, arrived in Castle Street on an official visit to Dalkey. Until 8.00 p.m. he graciously received some 50 members and guests of the Dalkey Literary Historical and Debating Society, in private audience in "The Regency Room" of "The Queens". At 8.00 p.m. – accompanied by his Aide – de-Camp and his personal Secretary – he entered the "Goat's Castle" (The Town Hall) to the strains of the Presidential salute rendered on a trumpet by Donal Cogan of Vico. He was enthusiastically greeted by the people – many of whom held different religious and political beliefs.(writer's amendment). The efficient stewards on the doors were N.C.O's in uniform of the local F.C.A., who earned universal praise for their appearance and their demeanour. Their attendance had been arranged through the everready co-operation of their Comdt. H.P. Ryan of Torca. The feature of the night was a paper entitled "1916, An Evaluation" by Dr. R. Dudley Edwards, Professor of Modern History in U.C.D. "Paper" is hardly the correct word, as the Lecturer spoke for an hour and a half to an enthralled and silent audience – and never used even a note! When leaving for Arus An Uachtarain, at the conclusion of a wonderful evening, President De Valera said to Councillor Norman Judd, President of the Dalkey Society, that "he had a most stimulating and interesting evening". And such was the unanimous opinion of the 450 people privileged to attend that night.'

Surprisingly, aside from all his many achievements, Frank, sought no accolades or prominence. He was simply a man who became endeared with the area in which he lived and its people. He rose to the challenge of preserving our heritage. He was also a man of justice and integrity. A man, too, who has not been given some tangible recognition which he rightly deserves by the people of Dalkey, or for that matter by Dun Laoghaire/Rathdown County Council.

Dr. Ciarán Coleman

"A Kind of Irish Brigadoon"

Soon after I had ended a ten year exile and returned to my native Dalkey, I wrote a television play called 'The Virgins' – an account of the exploits of three male celibates of this parish. In our town a secret is a crime against nature and a few days before the transmission date, one of the three lifted his face from the surface of a pint of Guinness and said to the barman, "I hear tell that Leonard has put the lads and me into a play on the gogglebox".

The barman, who already knew this but had the cunning of a papal nuncio, merely looked astonished and said, "Do you tell me?"

"True as God, next Sunday they're showing it." The man submerged his nose in the pint like a fish that has been too long out of water. When next heard his voice was wistful. "A pity we'll miss it. Sunday's our night for a jar in Finnegan's."

He never did see the play. Being a real Dalkey man – as distinct from a first-generation parvenu or runner-in – he will effortlessly set the world to rights, but is hanged if he will be at its beck and call. Discommoding yourself, he will tell you, is the kind of senseless jack-acting that gave Dinnie McCarthy the bad ticker and, in any case, watching yourself on television might be classified in the town as a form of affectation.

There is an elderly woman who whenever she sees me in the town, regards me with such venom that I cross the street. Last week, as I was collecting the newspapers, there was a growing noise at my elbow. She was muttering: "Look at him, standing there with the cigar stuck in his gob. I know the kick up the behind his mother would give him." I am, by the way, fifty-five.

The point of both anecdotes is that Dalkey seems to exist out of ordinary time; a kind of Irish Brigadoon without the mists, the feyness or the tendency to disappear. By rights, it should be off in the fastnesses of Kerry or in a fold of the Slieve Blooms; instead, it is on the southeast corner of Dublin Bay, nine miles from Grafton Street.

Hugh Leonard

A visitor, arriving first in Dublin, will ricochet from the Book of Kells to the mummies in St. Michan's Vault, then go tearing off pell-mell to the lakes of Killarney, pausing to plant a kiss on the Blarney Stone, before rampaging through Connemara and ending up at the Bunratty medieval banquet. If his aim is to see all of Ireland, he can do so at a fraction of the energy and expense. A microcosm exists.

You board a No. 8 bus at Eden Quay and go juddering out to Ballsbridge, past the red-bricked embassies and the front gardens where the flowers observe a discreet protocol and the trees blush for a week in May. Further on, the sea is in view, with the Hill of Howth across the bay and if the one-ring circus is in residence at Booterstown, a lone camel may be seen grazing on a patch of slobland. Just up the road is Blackrock Park where there was a production of 'Much Ado About Nothing' some years ago. It rained, allowing the local wags to apotheosize the occasion as 'Bad Day at Blackrock'. Another four miles and Dalkey Hill looms almost apologetically, with its castle – actually an old semaphore station that had delusions of grandeur – perched on the summit like holly on a pudding. The roads are decorously Edwardian. They amble sedately down to the sea, where James Joyce's Martello Tower overlooks the bathing place known as the Forty-Foot, which until recently had a sign saying: 'Forty Foot men only'. A final mile and the town is yours.

Dalkey's main, and only, street looks as if it had started out with the best of intentions, like a drunk walking past a policeman. For a hundred yards it is irreproachable, marching as straight as a die between two fifteenth century castles; then, perhaps distracted by Searson's pub to its right or The Queen's to its left, it lurches crookedly, tries to correct itself and staggers again. Finally, it pulls up short, dazed by the choice of The Club, The Arches or Dan Finnegan's. There are six pubs in all, which for an Irish small town is eremitical self-denial.

My own local, The Club, has an air of mild bohemianism, except at weekends, when it resembles a combination of Carnival time in Rio and Easter Sunday in St. Peter's Square. Even in quieter moments, its con- versationalists can be unpredictable. Only yesterday a lady sculptor told me, quite gratuitously, that she had tricked her Doctor into giving her a spinal x-ray and discovered that one of her vertebrae was missing. "Now" she said, "if only I can somehow cod him into doing a brain scan, I'll be on the pig's back." At this point, another lady made a flanking attack, told me not to mind that bloody bore and proceeded to hold forth on the merits of acupuncture. Her husband, a jazz trombonist, kept wondering aloud – to thin air and deaf ears – if Turk Murphy was still playing in Earthquake McGoon's in San Francisco.

Even to my eyes, which are afflicted with the belief that the past is yesterday, the town has changed. The aging corner boys, including my Uncle Sonny, no longer loaf at what was once Gilbey's Corner, their job-shy, begrudging eyes never missing the flick of a dog's tail the crooked length of Castle Street. They have gone to slouch against a celestial wall and spy on God.

There is an air of chic about the place, even if the only outward sign of change is that Findlater's, the family grocer, was taken over by Superquinn. The latter painted the clock on the front of the building a dingy orange and then had the temerity to be aggrieved when, quite properly, it self-destructed in disgust.

In what we call old God's time, dining out was unheard of. Now there are five restaurants tucked away behind the unchanged facades of what were hucksters' shops. These have given the town notoriety, for if you were brought up on spuds and back bacon, your conscience never quite takes in its stride the decadence of rack of spring lamb and chateau Lynch-Bagels by candlelight.

The sense of disquiet is at its most acute during the phenomena described – no one knows why – as safari dinners. These occur on Sunday evenings and consist of perhaps forty diners having appetisers in one restaurant, traipsing on foot to another for soup, to a third for a fish course, and so on. The procession, with everyone dressed to the nines, follows a piper winsomely attired in green jacket and saffron kilt. The chances are that between courses the gourmets will encounter a stream of worshipers leaving the church after evening devotions. You are surprised by an urge within yourself to look away from the Churchgoers; otherwise you might catch the faintly mocking glance that reminds you of how you once lived in the alley lane with the behind out of your trousers. The leap from a two-room cottage with a privy in the back yard to a trim all-mod-con bungalow on Avondale Road was a mighty one, but the past still has you in its pocket.

From Castle Street, narrow roads wander like tendrils around the hill or to the sea. The Town – or the village, as the Protestants call it – was, in my father's day, a stronghold of 'the quality', the Anglo-Irish, whose ivied houses moulder behind high walls or around the far bend of unkempt avenues. They moved out from Dublin when the railway came, more than a century ago, to enjoy a feudal existence thirty minutes away from their factories and counting houses. Storekeepers, gardeners, maids and cooks, roadmakers and masons followed them and were followed in their turn. Therefore, a town. The 'quality' died out, moved away or became integrated, lost among the mansions of the new affluence but you may still trace their spoor along Victoria Road and Trafalgar Terrace and past houses with names that sang of empire: Khyber Pass, Kalafat and Jamrud.

The native Irish, disinherited for so long, were quick to flourish their credentials: The house where my father worked for fifty-four years as a gardener ceased to be 'Enderley' and was re-christened 'Sancta Maria'.

Coliemore Road winds down to the harbour and a view to Dalkey Island, so theatrical as, at first sight, to resemble a backdrop. On second thought, you decide that it is an enormous floating set, built for a John Ford movie that was never made. A Martello Tower, one of a hundred along this coast, crowns the summit: a squat, granite pepper post still awaiting Bonaparte's men-o' war. Beneath it is a holy well – "fresh water in the middle of the sea" my father would brag, as if he himself had dug it that morning – which was once supposed to cure diseases of the throat. Now, judging from the colour of the water, it is more likely to cause them.

A few yards away are the ruins of a church supposedly built by the town's patron saint, St. Begnet. Like St. Patrick himself, St. Begnet may never have existed: There is even uncertainty as to whether he or she was male or female. No one bothers to argue about this: In Dalkey, when it is a question of sainthood, sex is hardly likely to have such relevance. The island, 400 yards offshore, is inhabited, year round, by wild goats and scuba divers.

As I write, in a house opposite and on a gray November day, the former stare down inscrutably at the bobbing heads of the latter. Instead of the summer yachts and power-boats, a trawler heads for home.

The name of Dalkey is Old Norse for 'island of thorns' – a reminder of the spiked barricades that warded off Viking invaders. For centuries, merchantmen found safe anchorage between the island and the tiny harbour, and seven castles, of which three still exist, were built to guard their cargoes from pirates. When the River Liffey was dredged, it became possible for ships to sail into Dublin, and Dalkey's hour of stardom was past. Unperturbed, the town went back to sleep.

A few hundred yards from the harbour, a mild schizophrenia sets in. The granite walls of the town are behind you; now there are palm trees and Mediterranean villas. Even the roads have such names as Sorrento, Nerano, Vico, in deference to a view that resembles a reversed negative of the Bay of Naples. Across Killiney Bay the Wicklow Mountains go tumbling out toward the sea: first, Carrick Gollogan, with its tower a disused smelting chimney; then the greater Sugarloaf, doubling for Vensuvius, and its lesser sibling; finally, Bray Head, its cliffs sheer to the water. In Ireland, all our cygnets are swans. These are mere foothills; other wilder mountains jostle from behind like less favoured guests in a wedding photograph. In between, there is the Vale of Shanganagh, hemmed by the long crescent moon of Killiney Strand. Closer to hand is the Vico Road, a cornice with pink and slate-blue houses clinging to the hillside and as the day ends the salt air carries the fragrance of night-scented stock.

Down to the left is what once gloried in the title of 'Gentle-men's bathing place'. Here, by way of proving the inviolability of the Victorian male, swimsuits were optional, and the tradition still persists. In my own youth, a brace of hussies – on a dare, perhaps – would peep down at us from the railway bank above the broken swimming pool and flee, shrieking at the horrendous sight of unclad males. Today, their daughters are likely to appear at the same vantage point but carrying either placards reading 'Segregated bathing unfair to women' or

cameras equipped with 200-millimetre lenses.

Further along the Vico, as it is called, there is a narrow and all-but-endless flight of stone steps known, because of their steepness, as the Cat's Ladder. The long toil upward is reminiscent of the Sisyphean climb of Laurel and Hardy toting a piano in 'The Music Box' but at the summit you are facing Torca Cottage, where Bernard Shaw spent his youthful summers. A plaque on the wall quotes him to the effect that whereas Ireland's men are mortal temporal, her hills are eternal.

The proof is all about. The climb continues along a grassy lane to the summit of Dalkey Hill and what is probably the most all-embracing view in Ireland. To the south are the fastnesses of Wicklow, where trout streams, mountain lakes, forests, miles of desolate bogland and the monastic ruins of Glendalough are an hour's car ride away. To the west – a dark pimple on Two Rock Mountain – is the burnt-out husk of the Hellfire Club, while to the north the two mile-long piers of Dun Laoghaire harbour are the arms of a gambler cradling his winnings, Dublin, blue under its smoke, is beyond.

Beneath one's feet is an amphitheatre of sheer cliff where a quarter of the hill was gouged to provide the granite for the piers two miles away. The stone was conveyed by an 'atmospheric railway'. A pumping station moved the wagons by air pressure and the route may be followed today along 'the metals', a lane-way that begins on the quarry floor and ends on the decorous tree-lines, sea-front of Dun Laoghaire.

There are other walks, trails that lead through rabbit woods and flowering gorse. The short, stubbly hill grass is so springy that it might be upholstered. You lie on it and see only the sky and a climbing 747 striking out for Shannon and New York. Then there is the stillness that comes at sunset and it is time to return at a half-trot – the road itself is down-hill – along Dalkey Avenue to the town. In short, it is a village for walkers and idlers. The traveller who merely likes to 'do' a place will be out of it in half a day and on his way to Killarney or Connemara, his visual appetite glutted and nothing else. To know the town, he must loiter along a moss-crowned road, stand on tiptoe to peer into an abandoned garden, sit for an hour by the harbour wall, or in Sorrento Park, or eavesdrop in Castle Street.

A real traveller does not go to a place: He bides his hour until it visits him. Dalkey is an anomaly, neither suburb nor country town. It is uniquely itself but typical of Ireland in one respect. Much disillusionment has been wreaked by travel brochures that rhapsodise over the friendliness of the Irish, when all the visitor is likely to receive is common civility. We keep our distance. Awareness of seeming quaint or putting on a free show for the tourist who has been weaned on the colleens and boisterous rustics out of 'The Quiet Man' has made us taciturn. The conversation in pubs, say the advertisement put out by the tourist board, is sparkling with epigrams. This is a fiction: What you get is one monologist waiting for another monologist to pause for breath. There are few aphorisms: mainly, there are anecdotes which become more maundering as the evening draws on. And the conversations are private.

If the visitor wishes to listen in, however, there is a way. An observation on the weather or the charms of the town will net him no more than hearty "Oh begod, you're right" and a view of several backs as ranks are closed against the interloper. What you must do is ask a question that invites an opinion: advice, for example, on a place to eat locally. At once, someone will off-handedly suggest the Baroque, say, just around the corner. This, as far as the others are concerned, is fighting talk. Not at all, Michael Duffy will retort, explaining that Americans are renowned trenchermen. "Leopold's is the place. Think of the amount of lamb they serve you. The plateful I got last week as near as dammit said baa to me."

Demarcation lines are now drawn. A bald accountant swears by Chez la Hiff. Mr Duffy snorts that you cannot get a drink there, not even on the sly. (Except for hotels, few Irish eating places are licensed to sell hard liquor.) "Look at the man," he says, waving at you. "He's banjaxed from seeing the sights. What good is a glass of bloody sherry to him?" A timid soul suggests yet a fourth restaurant and is shouted down. The food may be first-rate but the owner is regarded as pushy and having a smell of himself – a cardinal sin. The debate rages and if you never get a word in edgewise, you at least have the satisfaction of being the cause of it. That's Dalkey.

Hugh Leonard

A Tribute to John Wadham

Sunday Independent September 28, 2003

'*I was looking forward to playing with him but had received bad news myself three days earlier.*' **Professor Peter O'Brien** pays tribute to a legendary jazz drummer

Last Monday, at 8am, the great drummer and jazz musician, John Barker Wadham passed peacefully and gently away in St. Michael's Hospital, Dun Laoghaire, close by his beloved Barony of Dalkey, where he had spent the happiest years of his life.

He was just 66 years old and the news of his passing brought with it a very special and personal sadness to a great number of people who had known his unique character and talents from the world of jazz music and his many other interests such as the railways, the best of British Comedy and bird-watching.

John Wadham

John was the only and much-loved son of Cyril and Muriel Wadham. After school he attended Trinity College, where he got a degree in engineering.

He never practised as, by that time, he was already recognised as Ireland's foremost jazz drummer.

By the time I got to know him well, in the mid-Sixties, he had already acquired an international reputation and famous jazz visitors were always delighted to hear that 'the Wad', as he became known, would be directing rhythmic operations from his famous seat, an opinion shared by every single Irish jazz musician I know.

His inspired and perfect drumming, and presence always lifted a session into another and special dimension. Over the years he became known, too, as Ireland's leading drum teacher, and he must have put hundreds of pupils through their first paces – many of them going on to acquire international reputations – some with pop groups, where in the process, as John sometimes wryly remarked 'they became exceedingly rich men'. He was much loved by his pupils who always credited John with their success.

For 20 years I lived within half a mile of 'the Wad'. He lived with his parents in a beautiful house opposite Dalkey rail station. By coincidence his father Cyril was manager in Royal Irish Liver Insurance Company, a position previously occupied by my grandfather Percy Winder. Cyril had moved to Ireland to take up this job, but it was John who became your quintessential Englishman.

With his trademark, that wonderful handlebar moustache (which he would never remove despite film and other offers), and with his magical talents as a raconteur and storyteller, he became in time a much-loved figure in the hostelries of Dalkey, where he would astound the locals with his abilities with complex crosswords and his wit.

He was also a creature of habit and routine and when I first knew him, he would meet both his parents for lunch or an evening drink. In those days his bevy was modest half of shandy per session, a limit that increased in later years after his beloved parents died within a year of each other. Although he never said it, I believe he was lonely in the big house with its many memories.

For ten years John joined me in the band for the hugely popular revues with Des Keogh and Rosaleen Linehan and, as well as playing in all the big Dublin theatres, we would play country venues such as the Cork Opera House for runs of one of two weeks.

John made a big impact on these runs with his drumming and personality, but it was also a time to see a side of him outside music. For example he rose at 7 a.m. each morning to wash and polish his beautiful Granada car and as we were not working during the day, he would take the band on trips where we would learn about the birdlife of Cork in the rivers and lakes, listening to the Goons, or he would play rare recordings of stride piano masters such as James P and Fats of which, like his lifetime friend, Rock Fox, he had tremendous love and knowledge.

On May 26 last, a special testimonial concert was held for John Wadham in Fitzpatrick Castle Killiney County Dublin. I was looking forward to playing with him at this but had received bad news myself three days earlier. I would love to have been able to attend his funeral last Thursday and I was delighted to hear that it was a wonderful and festive occasion, and a fitting farewell to a man who fully deserved the title "doyen of the drums" for 50 special years.

And on any evening, if you would like to invite him back, just put on any one of his many CDs. You will always recognise the unique playing of John Barker Wadham, whom God preserve.

Professor Peter O'Brien

The Lungs of Dalkey

Bulloch Harbour is my favourite place in Dalkey. To me the Harbour and the Dalkey United/Cuala playing fields form part of the lungs and race memory of Dalkey and of Ireland. They provide an opportunity for local residents to breath, take exercise or simply relax and enjoy the time out we all need to survive.

Both amenities contain a warning for us to which I will return a little later.

Firth though may I point out that the two places form prime examples of the link between race memory and to-day's world. Cars pull up outside the playing fields disgorging players who wish to avail of the pitch facilities, or parents who will stand on the sidelines cheering on their six-year olds. As they do so, both parents and players mingle with the people boarding the Dalkey Flyer waiting to take them to Dublin Airport and on to the four corners of the earth.

At Bulloch Harbour, as you avail of the seats provided through a combination of an awakening civic pride, the memory of past loved ones, or the epic Atlantic voyage of the yacht Ituna, you are joined on the pier by international visitors. Poles wishing to hire the boats maintained by Christy Lawless and Dolores and Monica Smith, or Chinese coming to buy the crabs and mackerel landed by Harbour stalwarts like Tony Drummond.

Everyone, from whatever race or place, will be struck by the beauty of Bulloch. The view across the Bay towards Dun Laoghaire, or further out, towards Howth. The little boats at anchor, or coming and going to the Harbour's entrance.

If the weather is fine it's one of the loveliest spots in County Dublin. If it's bad it's still better than most places. I first began hiring boats there over fifty years ago, progressed to owning my own little yacht, a National Eighteen, and learned where all the best fishing places were from Dun Laoghaire Pier to the Muglins and Dalkey Island. Along the way I also discovered where all the best bowers for amatory excursions existed on Dalkey Island.

Tim Pat Coogan

In these matters I was self taught. My fishing instructor was Andrew 'Pa' Bradley. 'Pa' used to rule Bulloch Harbour from his shed where in the summer the local lads learned how to tie up boats, fix engines, catch fish, and to swear as only Andy could. They used to tell each other wonderingly that when Andy really got drunk it took not merely two gardai, but The Sergeant as well to get him to the station! There was even more wonderment one day when The Minister Paid a Visit. It was generally known that Andy had been in the old IRA and had come from the Six Counties, but what he did there nobody knew. Then, one summer's day, out of the blue, Frank Aiken, also from the Six Counties, a former Chief of Staff of the IRA and now Minister for Foreign Affairs was driven on to the quay.

He and Andy greeted each other warmly and then had a long intimate chat, the contents of which were never known but ever speculated on.

Andy was succeeded by another great character, Joe Lawless, under whose reign every one in the neighbourhood learned to row, fish and keep out of trouble albeit with vocabularies greatly enriched by words from a language which, as the song has it, the stranger does not know. Amongst them are outstanding citizens of Dalkey and the world (and as everyone knows the terms are interchangeable) such as Ian Flood, Joe Wildes, Ian McDonald, Brian Brennan, Hugo Hamilton and Denis Calthorpe.

Poor Joe and his gentle wife, Rose, have now left us but their son Christy carries on the tradition, having graduated along the way from coaxing sputtering Seagull engines into life as a boy, to keeping vintage cars running to-day. Joe's son-in-law, Peter O'Halloran, married to Joe's daughter Mary, is now the prime mover behind the display of flowers and annual events such as the Blessing of the Boats Festival which add to Bulloch's every increasing popularity.

To the great relief of Bulloch's patron Peter has also introduced Portaloos to the Harbour. This is an entirely congruent development as another of Joe's sons-in-law, Brian Brennan, married to Mary's elegant sister Catherine, and another graduate of the Bulloch College of Seagull Surgery, is justly renowned as Dalkey's Celebrity Plumber.

To me Bulloch Harbour ranks with the National Library as one of the best clubs in Ireland. As one enjoys its scenery, chats with Christy, Tony Drummond and the lads, or with Delores and Monica, you never know who will turn up. Every one from Frank Aiken, to a member of the U2 Group, to someone you last saw in America.

One doesn't have to talk if one doesn't wish to. Sometimes I sometimes simply sit on the pier and muse on its history. Originally built by monks as a herring port, it was the scene of one of the worst atrocities of 1798. Women and children, fleeing from the Yeomanry, in rowing boats were followed out to sea and drowned.

Drowned too in more recent times was Derry Smith, Monica's husband, who went out lobstering from Bulloch one day and never came back. Yacht dotted Dublin Bay, like the sea everywhere, has had its quota of hardship and tragedy.

But, mentions of yachts brings me back to the point I made at the outset about Bulloch and the Hyde Road playing fields being the lungs of Dalkey. They are, but they carry a future health warning. Unlike that on the cigarette package it is invisible. But it's there and you can see what I mean in Dun Laoghaire Harbour.

My father taught me how to swim and to fish from the West Pier. I fished and roamed the other piers at will, the Coal Quay, The East Pier. Canoed, and sailed little Dublin Bay Twelves and Fourteens, Mermaids even, all round the Harbour.

Where would you get a mooring to-day? Commercial marinas have blocked off much of the Harbour. Planned extensions of the marinas will block off more. Already there's a barrier across the Coal Quay, part of it is given over to a boat company, and there are signs up saying 'No Fishing'.

The all-devouring monster 'Development'

whose depredations lie behind so much of to-day's economic turmoil is increasingly taking Dun Laoghaire Harbour away from the ordinary man. Currently the monster has been halted in its tracks. But if the financial crisis is resolved, and in the history of either Bulloch, or indeed the playing fields, it is surely only a blip, then the monster will return. Freed is never permanently slain.

Seductive offers, such as that for Dun Laoghaire Golf Club, will resume: Cash, plus an alternative course. Keys and security barriers for the residents of luxury apartments. Marinas for the wealthy, or at least the debt shouldering. But what about the people who bring their kids to pay on the pitches or seek peace at Bulloch?

What about the quality of life in Dalkey?

We should treasure the playing fields and Bulloch Harbour now and for the future. When lungs are removed suffocation follows.

Tim Pat Coogan

Great seaman and community man, Joe Lawless

Bulloch Harbour Today and Times Past

Bulloch has always been a fishing harbour, and in most cases the fishermen fished in pairs. In the late 30's and early 40's my father Derry (Snowy) Smyth used to fish with Shiner Smyth (very distant relative), Joe Lawless did fish with Paddy Smyth, my Grandfather, who was the Quartermaster on the RMS Leinster, but had switched shifts the night before she sank off the Kish bank. George Williams and Mick Smyth, known as Nut always fished on their own. As in the old days, people still fish out of Bulloch to make a living. Charlie Mulvaney, James Cunningham, Chris Lawless (son of Joe), Tony Drummond and Jeremy Cunningham all fish the bay alone. Each one with his own style and area to fish. Sometimes encroachment does happen but this is normally accidental and can be sorted out peacefully. When a fisherman did employ a helper, he would normally give him 1/3 of the catch proceeds and keep 2/3 for himself. Lobster's and crabs in the 30's and 40's were plentiful so when they were brought to market in Dublin they got 50 shillings (about £2.50) for a lot (which consisted of 13 lobsters) and 30 shillings for a second lot. The price that they got for the crabs paid for their fare into Dublin on the tram.

To some people, helping a person is more important than the reward of receiving money, so a few people still, in this day and age use kudos as payment. Kudos is a form of payment which in plain English means, you scratch my back and I'll scratch yours, in other words, payment in kind. If someone does a job for someone else they will more than likely be rewarded with a favour in the future. Monica Smyth, James Cunningham, John Cunningham, Pete Carroll and Jeremy Cunningham (no relation to previous) use this form of payment daily, with great results.

In the 40's and 50's the two most common boats in the harbour were 18 ft yawls and 14 ft punts. These boats were mainly built in Athlone at a cost of £1 per foot including delivery. All the boats were clinker, meaning that the planks were overlapped, then nailed and roofed. The other type of wooden boat is called carvel. This is where the planks are placed side by side instead of overlapped. For hiring purposes, the punt was preferred as it was smaller and more easily manoeuvred and was less tiring to row over long periods. The cost of hiring a boat then was 2 shillings an hour and 2 and 6 pence if you wanted someone to row for you.

North Easterly gales lash the pier of Bulloch

Fishermans Huts

The huts on the right as you walk down to the pier, are known as "Fishermen's Huts" and have been ever present for over a hundred years. Of course renovations have been made, but the huts still stand where they were built. The first shed you come across is black and owned by the Dublin Port and Docks, now known as the Dublin

Port Company. It wasn't always the first shed, for if you look closely you will see a raised platform of concrete. This is where George Williams and Major Walker's hut stood. It was also the home of the Sea Scouts and Bulloch Rowing Club. Next is the black hut, which is presently used by the harbour caretaker. Many years ago, the hut was used by Shiner Smyth, and more recently it was from where the Sandycove Rowing Club, The St. Josephs, officially rowed from. The next shed was built in the late 50's/early 60's by the Dublin City Sea Anglers and is still owned and run by the anglers club. The last shed is Chris Lawless's, and has been the most used of them all. From talking to local people, Jim (Shiner) Smyth seems to be the earliest known fisherman of this century. Jim's brother Jack, who was Commodore of the Elderdempster Line, also fished from there when he retired from shipping. Billy Smyth, Pa Bradley and Joe Lawless also used this hut fishing.

Bulloch Today

Bulloch Harbour is approximately 8 miles South East from Dublin city centre. As you would expect, Bulloch has changed much since it was built in the early 1800's. Gone are the old coal yards, which were replaced by boat yards, which sadly are also gone. The only things that have lasted through

A painting of Bulloch by Thomas Serres in 1788

time, are the bollards which run along the main pier, and the shackle on the point which juts out from the pier. Both the bollards and the shackle were used in the early 1900's, to secure the coal and stone boats, which frequently used the harbour to land their goods. The goods were then either shipped up to Dublin via the pilots, or carted away to be distributed amongst the local population.

Whilst researching for this book, I found amongst other things that Bulloch had two main disadvantages. One was the fact that every time a North Easterly gale blows you have to literally batten down the hatches, that means that as long as the wind blows, Bulloch stands still. When the weather gets really bad, the sight of the pier being bashed by waves and the sea rising sometimes 20 ft into the air can be breathtaking. Most years the wind hits near the end of the summer and at night, this means that many of the private boats, which Bulloch is mainly used for now, are still moored in the harbour and have to be taken out before they are seriously damaged by the surge coming in and out of the harbour mouth. If there are too many boats in the harbour this causes problems, for as you take out the boats you have to find space on the pier to put them so they don't get further damaged. A few years ago, boulders taken from local building developments, were strategically placed at the most vulnerable spot, to the right of the old Dalkey Swimming Club clubhouse where the sea used to run up the rocks, like a runway and continue half way up the pier.

The other disadvantage that I spoke of is a rock which is about 100/150 yards out off the point. This rock can be clearly seen at spring tides, but is difficult to spot at any other time. To the locals it's like knowing the days of the week, but to visitors to Bulloch by sea it can prove very expensive. During the year, yachts tacking to get the best wind advantage have often come in too close and clipped the rock with their keels, which with the bigger yachts has proved very costly. Other boats such as speed boats, which aren't actually allowed near the pier at speed, have become croppers. Diving dinghies are other boats who year in year out get caught out by the rock. In captain Bligh's charter of the bay in 1800 he remarked on the rock and called it "Old Bulloch" which it's still called today. Another thing that has lasted a few years, though in bad disrepair, is the launch track and winch which is situated at the top of the slipway. Bad weather and general decay have meant the most of the original track had to be removed. The well at the top of the slip, which used to facilitate the rudders of the Dublin Bay 21 and 24 footers, was put in well after the original slip was built. The slip on the left as you look down into the harbour was built in October 1871, and the well was put in at the same time. The track and winch were used to launch the Dublin Bay boats and the same people were ever present, Derry Smyth and George Williams always seemed to be round when things were happening, and became very familiar with both the launching and hoisting of vessels via the slip. The only disadvantage of using the slip was that the track ended at the bottom, so when the tide was out the boats couldn't be launched. On the pier itself, there is a rectangular concrete structure. This was the home of Dalkey Swimming Club, but is now occupied by a scuba diving club. It was built in 1946 by the Dalkey club. The swimming club was unofficially formed in 1937/8 by Thomas Hamilton Ross (president), James J. Byrne (handicapper) and Jimmy McGlone (starter). In its day it averaged about 40 members. It was the members of this club, through their determination and 'hard labour', as one member put it, who built the point in 1942/43. It was constructed in just over a week. The swimming club was officially liquidated in February 1999. When it was built, the point was mainly used by the club for entering the water safely. Today it is used more than ever, because twice a day the tide goes out and on spring tides the water leaves the harbour totally. On some spring tides, the outer harbour could be left dry for between and hour and hour and a half. Without the point, the harbour would have been very inaccessible at low tides.

Beneath the road leading down to the pier, there is a shore, which during bad gales lets the water run from the back rocks into the harbour via a tunnel that runs beneath Western Marine. Without this shore the water that is trapped behind the houses would have nowhere to go, thus leaving the area to flooding, but thankfully sand bags came to the rescue. There is no doubt that without the shore, things could have been a lot worse.

Donal Smyth
Author of Bulloch Harbour Past &
Present. Published in 1999.

Voyage of Adventure

Ireland 50 years ago a could be a dispiriting place – there wasn't much money around and there were few chances of getting a job. Life for young people was drab and there was little prospect of adventure.

For people like Kevin O'Farrell, 23, Crosthwaite Park, who had served with the RAF at the end of WWII -"I joined up and, a few days later Hitler blew his brains out" – and later for a time in the Merchant Marine, the chance to take part in a journey into the unknown was particularly attractive.

Just down the road at Bulloch four students were preparing a boat, the Ituna, to sail to New York. Two of them, Tony Jacob 22, Wexford and Desmond Dalton, 20, Donnybrook had written to the famous American architect Frank Lloyd Wright and he had agreed to them taking their final course at his college in Wisconsin.

They were joined by an aeronautical engineer, Arthur Thompson who had to abandon the trip through ill-health and John Kenny 21, Nenagh another architectural student.

When Arthur Thompson left the crew he was replaced by Kevin O'Farrell, who described it at the time as a "a pier-head jump, bag in hand, just for the ride.

The Ituna, bought by Tony Jacob for £150 was then about 33 years old, 36 feet long, had a beam of 10 feet and a draft of five feet. When the students found it the boat was in poor condition, its name had been changed to 'Happy Days' and it had been used as a shrimper – there were no fittings, no accommodation, the decks were broken through, it lacked just about everything but the hull.

To raise the money to buy and repair the Ituna the students sold various possessions and one got a job at £6 a week, contributing £5 to the weekly kitty, while the other three worked on the boat.

Skipper Tony Jacob, although he had some sailing experience, had no knowledge of navigation and, in the interests of ever finding America at the end of their journey, he took a course at a Navigation School.

Jacob turned out to be a very good navigator; "We were particularly impressed when he brought us into Bermuda as it's a bloody difficult place to find. The highest point of the island is only about 100 feet – and that's the top of the lighthouse," says Kevin.

Provisions, as with almost everything else, were basic, potatoes and lots of tinned beans. "Someone had also got hold of a large supply of unripe bananas so we took them as well. It turned out to be a huge mistake as they all ripened on the same day, all went off within a few days and attracted every fly within a thousand miles. We had to dump them over the side."

Kevin O'Farrell at Bulloch Harbour.

On June 10, 1950 the Ituna left Bulloch Harbour in Dalkey for Rosslare where they stayed until June 15. Next scheduled stop was to be Madeira, but a fouled water tank compelled them to put into Brest, France. From there they stopped at Vigo and Funchal before beginning their Atlantic crossing on August 1 from Las Palmas.

They had a wireless on board, though not a transmitter and Kevin remembers they began listening to broadcasts of "The African Queen".

"We were very interested in it, but it kept fading away. We still managed to keep up with the plot day after day until the batteries finally gave out – just before the final broadcast."

It took four fairly uneventful weeks to reach Bermuda – the only moment of danger coming when skipper Tony Jacob was knocked overboard in a squall. But by the time the boat came round Tony was 500 yards away and, in the morning darkness, very difficult to see. But he was swimming strongly towards the vessel and was eventually brought to safety.

A few days later they were briefly joined by a whale which appeared just as interested in them as they were in it. "After carefully inspecting us, he decided we were harmless, blew a few spouts of water, as though in a farewell message, and turning on its side it slipped below," wrote John Kenny at the time.

After a month at sea they landed at Port Hamilton, Bermuda, where Kevin learned that his mother had died. He made arrangements to fly home but his father and other relatives advised him to continue on.

One of the first ambitions of the "piratical foursome" was to get shaved as they hadn't been able to shave because of the need to conserve water.

They left Bermuda on September 11, calculating to reach New York in seven days.

The weather was worsening and there were warnings of hurricanes. They knew the hurricane signs to look for, remembers Kevin, a rapidly falling barometer and rising swells. "But we hadn't been able to afford a barometer, we had bought along an old aircraft altimeter which made us so nervous with its highs and lows that we had to throw it overboard in the end."

The lads enjoy shooting for Harpers Bazaar.

After 14 days, the Ituna slipped quietly into New York and tied up at the 23rd Street boat dock at 2.20pm on September 24. They were greeted by Garth Healy, the Irish Consul General, and James O'Brien, representing the Mayor of New York. For a while the crew were in immense demand and even got paid by a fashion magazine shoot on the Ituna.

When the excitement in New York had died down John Des, and Tony travelled on to Wisconsin, the Irish Sweepstakes bought the Ituna and shipped it and Kevin back to Dublin on board the "Irish Pine". It remained moored on the Liffey for a time and, when the public had finally tired of the nine-day wonder, it was decided to raffle it off among all the Irish and British boat clubs.

Unfortunately, the winner turned out to be in Weymouth, Dorset, which hadn't enough draught to sail it.

It was sold on to a South African and sailed out of Cape Town for 25 years. Then it once again sailed to the USA where it went up for sale. Kevin being contacted at the time to see if he was interested. About 14 years ago, Kevin got a phone call from a young American couple who had bought the Ituna and were researching the history of the boat. He met them at Shannon. "they were hippies, guitar and all", dropped them off at a festival and then .....nothing. He believes the Ituna is still probably based somewhere around Annapolis. "If it is reasonably well maintained it could go on for a long time," he says.

A commemorative granite seat to mark the transatlantic voyage of Tony Jacob, Des Dalton, John Kenny and Kevin O'Farrell will be placed overlooking the sea at Bulloch on the anniversary of their departure, June 10th. According to Kevin, who now lives in Killaloe, the decision came as a surprise to him. "It was a big shock to me, but it is also a lovely gesture, particularly for the other guys. The story had a sad ending in some ways as John, Des and Tony all died young – I'm sure they would appreciate the memorial."

Ken Finlay
Southside Newspaper 31/5/2000

Atlantic Crossing Remembered

Saturday last in Bulloch Harbour was wet and miserable until just before 6.30 pm when the rain suddenly stopped and the sun shone brilliantly. The timing couldn't have been better as a small crowd gathered for the unveiling of a new granite seat at the side of the harbour in memory of an historic crossing of the Atlantic by four Irish students which started from Bulloch that day, June 10, in 1950.

Of the four just one, Kevin O'Farrell, 77, is still alive. He travelled from Killaloe for the event and met with members of the Dalton and Kenny families for what he described as a 'memorable and moving event.'

Billy Joe, Mary, Regina and Noreen Kenny with (front) Kevin O'Farrell.

The idea for the seat came through two local men, Pat Kavanagh and Frank Mullen, two years ago when, reminiscing about their football days, they came to the Ituna.

"I remember it all so vividly, the Ituna was moored for outfitting for a couple of weeks before she sailed. As kids we were always down in the harbour, there was a very active swimming club then," Frank Mullen told the People. "I remember the anxiety of the older people but we just thought it was a great adventure. It brought some excitement into what was a fairly dismal time in Dublin."

"All down through the years I thought there should be some visible form of recognition for the skill and courage of the four lads – Anthony Jacob, Desmond Dalton, John Kenny and Kevin O'Farrell.

Officially launching the new seat was local historian and 'man of the sea' Tim Pat Coogan who said he had the pleasure of knowing a number of leading characters from the drama of the Ituna as well as being a lifelong friend of the O'Farrell family.

Their story, he noted, was the kind of episode which adds colour to our local history.

Kevin O'Farrell thanked all those who attended on behalf of himself and his three shipmates, who, he said, were "surely here in spirit this evening."

After the ceremony The People spoke to Joe, Regina, Noreen, and Mary Kenny about their brother John.

"Our parents were worried, particularly when they were lost for weeks between Las Palmas and Bermuda. Then there was great excitement when they eventually arrived," they said.

Steve Dalton, son of Desmond, said that he had fond memories of his father who died when he was five. He presented Frank Mullen with an invitation to a Farewell Party held by the four crewmen in the Shangri-La Hotel, Dalkey, on May 31, 1950.

Steve, who is the holder of "countless clippings", says that he intends to put it all together and create a website in the near future to give everyone the chance to get all the information.

After the short ceremony a reception had been organised in Dalkey United Football Club. Speaking there Frank Mullen summed the occasion up by saying "It is our sincere hope and wish that the three lads will look down and consider that what we have done is appropriate."

Ken Finlay
The People 14/6/2000

Dalkey Man Recalls The Glen of Imaal Tragedy

On a June evening in 1940 on O'Connell Street, Mr. Eamon de Valera, as Taoiseach, addressed the largest meeting in the history of Dublin. That was what the Irish Press said the next day and it could not afford any liberties with facts when that tall gentleman was involved. On the platform during that golden evening of sunshine, when Europe's dark war clouds seemed on another planet, was Mr. Liam Cosgrave, Leader of the Opposition, and Mr. William Norton, Leader of the Labour Party.

The crowd applauded when they called for a united front in the greatest emergency in the life of the State and they called for "the nation's manhood" to join immediately, the army or one of the national services.

Mr. de Valera said: "I come to tell you the nation is in danger - a danger that is more menacing as the hours pass by". He did not say days. He knew that Reynaud of France was resigning, that the German army was within sixty miles of the Swiss frontier and that the Maginot Line, which the French considered an impregnable mechanised dyke against invasion, was being out-flanked.

A previous appeal had brought in 50,000 volunteers in a fortnight. Now there was a rush to the colours as patriotic lumps formed in the throats of young men who remembered the glorious dead of 1916 and all those rakes up near the rafters. And those who had been privileged to have a nodding acquaintance with the classics were whispering: Dulce et decorum est pro patria mori, or other Latin nonsense about the glories of dying for one's country.

The volunteers who shouted "bravos" and "aris" and such worthy phrases on that golden evening were to be among many who would discover that a peace-time army had ways of adding a touch of vinegar to any patriotic cup.

And three men listened to Dev that evening who were to find death in the Glen of Imaal, in the worst single tragedy in the story of the Irish Army, not yet healed from its Civil War wounds. Thirteen others who heard the call-to-arms wireless broadcast were to die in The Glen too.

Some were never to see again. And Corporal Dan Byrne, who grew up in Dalkey to a boyhood of mackerel fishing and climbing on the hills, was never again able to forget the sound of death in The Glen and the cold night sweats at the memory. Now in his seventies, he remembers it only too well.

Dan Byrne on home ground at Bulloch Harbour.

Before twelve months had passed, An Taoiseach de Valera was to prove that he was no alarmist. The country, at least Dublin, got its first look into the evil pit of war. Those were the days of the blackout; street lamps were cowled, friendly windows showed no light because black paper had been fitted against the panes. Gas for home cooking, through scarcity was a glimmer, Air Raid Precaution Wardens in round tin hats set off test airraid alarms and the men of the Local Defence Force and the Local Security Force, blue uniforms for the LSF and brown for the LDF, drilled in every large parish.

Then on a warm May evening in 1941, when even the Liffey seemed to have ceased to breathe, the heavy throbbing of large, burdened aircraft sounded over Dublin town and citizens looked fearfully at the sky.

The Ack Ack batteries opened up and pencils of white light from searchlights crisscrossed in the sky. Bombs thudded into the North Strand and in the rubble were soon to be found thirty-eight people dead and one hundred injured. And the Germans droned away into the night.

Two of the men who opened up with their anti-aircraft artillery that May evening were to die too in the Glen of Imaal.

Dan Byrne did not don a uniform to die for Ireland. His army number, which it is said a soldier never forgets, was 72952, and he joined in the hungry thirties because he could not get a job. His people, he says, knew a local colonel, a retired man, and it was he who suggested he could get him into the Artillery. That, you see, was quite a glamorous regiment. They had nice breeches and wore leather bandoliers, which gave the gallant appearance of men destined to climb to craggy heights and bearing across their broad chests, enough ammunition to beat off many enemies of the people.

Dan discovered that there was a bit more to it than that. He was paid thirteen shillings and two pence a week for his trouble and the cause and he had to keep the bandolier and the boots mirrored with brightness out of that fighting man's salary. It was "all found", he says but he never succeeded in finding it all.

He was all set to leave the Army and had packed his kit bag and walked across the square to report to somebody or other when he was told that he might as well bring the kit bag back, that war had been declared and that he was in the army again, after ten minutes of freedom.

He had been posted to the Artillery Barracks in Kildare and compared to the places where thousands of "Emergency Men" were to be housed, this was Toddy O'Sullivan's penthouse suite in the Gresham Hotel.

Many of these men who answered Dev's call had a reasonably high standard of education and some were even accustomed to picking out Mozart on the piano in the parlour. Now many of them found themselves picking out grass with a knife from between the cobbles on the barrack square in places like Collins's in Cork or shaving with cold water in the chilly military mansions of Dublin built to make sure there would never be another 1798.

And in these places the new croppies lay down to sleep on bed boards and trestles and woke to what they at first thought was a bugle wailing over a soldier's grave. For a pastime they tried to get the wet turf to light in the grates of the billets. And if they were musical, they were asked to move the piano into the officers' mess.

When they joined the army they were told by a burly, non-commissioned officer, whose voice would shatter corrugated beer bottles, that this was not Butlins, that the way to keep out of trouble was to keep your hair cut and call everything "sir", including the bloody barracks cat, and that the only right you retained was to crib – that meant complain. But that was an outlet more than a redress.

Dan Byrne remembers his part of soldiering in this army that never had to go to war. He remembers also that it had taken over from the British army of occupation words like jildi, meaning rigid about regulations, buckshee (straight from the soldiers' India), meaning free. And he remembers a seeming inheritance of keeping as many troops in the dark about everything in case they might get notions of grandeur and imagine they would succeed in scrambling eggs on brass hats. He had no illusions about having a field marshal's baton in his knap sack.

He remembers he did not know until almost the final hour that he was going to the Glen of Imaal and he did not know what he and the others were going to be asked to do. That was in September of 1941.

He remembers it well. The night before they were talking about what effect it would have on the war that the Shah had abdicated and that the Allies were to occupy Teheran and that the wireless had quoted the Assistant Secretary of the US Navy as saying that U Boats were operating close to the American coast and were a war peril to the U.S.

Orders came to go to the Glen of Imaal. They left from Kildare in their own open trucks. They were to meet, but did not know it because they were not told, another contingent from McKee Barracks, Dublin. It was a warm September evening and they stayed overnight in an old house over which towered Lugnaquilla, so often sheathed in mist, and a place where climbers were always warned by a red flag that the Army were firing or testing or blasting down in The Glen.

On this occasion, there were sixty troops in The Glen. After dinner, that is what the Army called lunch, Corporal Byrne heard that they were to witness a demonstration of an anti-tank mine. He had seen it all before because he had served longer than most of the people present and he knew that in these cases a dummy was usually demonstrated.

He had watched Lt. M. J. McLoughlin, a native of Rostrevor, do it before; been shown how to insert a charge primer into a mine that looked like a biscuit tin and be told how to cover it with grass, gravel or soil so that the driver of an oncoming enemy vehicle would not see it and the first pressure would depress the lid and cause a powerful explosion.

He recalled clearly a previous occasion when Lt. M. J. McLoughlin had said: "You are not allowed even one mistake with these things."

The group stood around the mine. The Officer, McLoughlin, knelt down to go into his routine. Dan Byrne, a few feet away and behind Acting Corporal John Cotton, watched the hands reach out to the mine, decided he had no interest in what he considered another boring dummy demonstration and moved away. It was Providence, he says, that move saved his life.

There was a deafening explosion, a red and yellow flash and the acid stink of explosives. The noise reverberated in the valley and came back from the cliffs and gullies of Lugnaquilla. He picked himself off the ground where he had been blown, thudded in the back as if by an anvil stroke of the Old Gods.

Then he saw the scattered bodies and where the mine had been was a bloody crater about seven feet deep and about twenty feet across. He noticed blood pumping from Cotton's head and moved across to him. It seemed ages before the moans of the dying and the cries for help registered.

Fifteen had met death in the afternoon, another was to die the next day and there were twenty injured. Medical resources were scant to say the least. They did what they could for their comrades.

Corporal Byrne and some of the others then lifted some bodies into one of the trucks and covered them with tarpaulin. The moans of the injured came from the other trucks as they moved off. And as they reached the Curragh, a priest came out to anoint the dead.

At the Curragh hospital, where he had helped to carry in his dead comrades, a nurse told him not to tell any of the injured that men had been killed. He declined to stay for treatment for shock. He wanted just to get away from the blood and the sight of death.

Some of those comrades whom he recalls with affection were deafened and others blinded. He remembers that the last time he saw one alive he choked with emotion when he said: "You know, Dan, yours was the last face I ever saw and that was the day in The Glen before my eyes were closed for ever."

Dan's only injury was the memory.

The survivors were given three days compassionate leave.

Liam Robinson
(Irish Press)
Dalkey United Yearbook 1982

The Dalkey School Project

I've no right to be here at all. I'm only a blow-in. I'm not from Dalkey, I'm from Donnybrook – and it's not the same thing at all. I remember the No. 8 tram well and could catch it from the bottom of Nutley Lane. I was in school in Dalkey for a while, swam off the back of Bulloch Harbour – until they discovered I couldn't really swim and I was sent off with the little ones to Sandycove Baths where the indomitable Miss Braddall taught the smaller ones to swim. She had a tough test for us to get through, across the width of Sandycove Baths, but I managed it with one foot subtly on the ground and earned my release back to Bulloch.

Later I came courting in Glenageary, a young girl who had grown up in Sandycove and in due course we found ourselves living in the house she had grown up in and sending our own children to school in Dalkey. This in time led to our involvement in the setting up of the Dalkey School Project and the movement towards the establishment of multi-denominational National Schools in Ireland. The first school was opened thirty years ago, but not before a long process which included our weekly markets in Dalkey Town Hall and all that went with those great occasions, the cooking, the baking, the waffles, the jungle crumble and much more. They were great social occasions, bonding occasions, for the troops involved in the campaign and in the early days we were happy if the profits made three figures.

And we tramped the street of Dalkey and its environs, conducting an enormous survey to try to establish if we were alone in what we were seeking, schools where all children could be educated together, schools which reflected the whole community, schools which welcomed diversity and learned from it. We found that very many people yearned for schools that united the community and did not want their children separated, segregated from their neighbour's children at school-time. Clearly it was an idea whose time was

coming. The first was Dalkey but now there are forty-four Educate Together schools all over Ireland - and more in the pipeline. It was not a compulsory change imposed on young parents but a new choice in a system which showed it had the flexibility to meet the new needs of a new time. At those weekly markets in the Town Hall we were in a building which harked back many centuries to when Dalkey was the main deep water port of Dublin. The castles in Dalkey, including the Town Hall, were fortified warehouses where goods could be stored before being carted along the hazardous route to Dublin through Monkstown and Blackrock. There was talk about a canal along the coast to carry the

Micheal Johnston, Fern Marnell, Luke Johnston and Aoife Jungman

commerce and then as time unfolded, a big new harbour, an asylum harbour, was built along the bare and inhospitable shore at

Dun Laoghaire. The granite came from the great quarry behind Dalkey and was trundled down on the truck railway to the shore. As technology changed, sail was giving way to steam and wood to iron, steamships and the railways were revolutionising transport at sea and on land.

The nineteenth century saw many changes, one of them was quite revolutionary – the growth of leisure and the invention and codification of games – football, in its various forms, hockey and hurling; the establishment of bodies like the GAA and the IRFU to control and administer these new organised sports. Many activities which had been work related were adapted for leisure. The hobblers who used to race their rowing boats out to meet the clipper ships coming into port were involved in a tough business: the crew that got there first won the unloading of the cargo - that really was work – but from it was developed the sport of rowing, another of the great sports of Dalkey and one which particularly interested me.

I was involved in a different branch of the sport, the upriver version in eights and fours, pairs and sculls. They were long elegant craft that would be swamped in the open seas for all their sophisticated technology of sliding seats and outrigged oars, built for more speed on calmer waters. But essentially the fixed seat skiffs of the east coast ports from Ringsend down to Wicklow – Ringsend, Dun Laoghaire, Dalkey, Bray, Greystones, Wicklow – are at the heart of the sport of rowing as much as any of the great clubs of the Irish Amateur Rowing Union, except perhaps that they had one great advantage: the men from the ports have for generations salt water in their veins, the sea and rowing have been part of their lives, their work and their traditions for centuries past. The town and city boat clubs of Ireland have the disadvantage of trying to teach landlubbers how to work on water!

Dalkey is a privileged community: it has facilities for many sports and it has had, perhaps even more vitally, the volunteers, the workers who have given countless hours of their own leisure time to make it all happen. Coaches, administrators and helpers, the unsung heroes of amateur sport. The young people of our community need that and deserve it and they in turn will reward us with their successes and their efforts.

Curiously, for me anyway, there was a journalist in the latter part of the 19th century, R M Peter, who lived in Clarinda Park West and was described as the Aquatic Correspondent of The Irish Times; I suppose a hundred years later I could have been described as the "Aquatic Correspondent" of the Evening Press and of RTE, and I was living in Burdett Avenue, just a few hundred yards from where he had lived. He wrote about rowing in his paper and he even wrote a book about the sport. I was doing the same a century later.

Things have changed enormously in the past fifty years. Sport at the top these days has developed into a big and bruising business, very much driven by money. But at community level the real amateur, corinthian spirit prevails; it's about playing the games, rather than the ritualised warfare of watching them. The needs are still there for facilities and the volunteers to continue to make it happen. Dalkey United, Cuala, the Rowing club and many other sports do it for us, for our children and our grandchildren. Long may this work continue – and long may our communities flourish.

Micheal Johnson

Growing Pains

Paul McGrath ... retraces a complex childhood and the friends who kept a his dream alive

The outside world can look a scary place when seen through the windows of an orphanage.

I never really thought of my upbringing as unusual until the day came for me to find a place of my own. Home, until then, had been a necklace of institutions. First, Mrs. Donnelly's, then the Bird's Nest, then the Glen Silva and – finally - Racefield.

For ten years of my life, my name had been Paul Noblo Now I was Paul McGrath, aged seventeen and – supposedly - ready to go it alone.

Paul McGrath with Ray Dolan,
Hon. Sec. Dalkey United F.C.

It's hard to explain just how sheltered, how protected I had felt behind the stone walls of an orphanage. It was a strange kind of feeling. I mean, until the time came to go it alone. I had never drank, never been to a disco, never really socialised in any of the conventional ways.

I felt safe there. It was as if the sixteen or seventeen lads with me were my family. And, being honest, I didn't want to leave them.

Football, until then, had been my only recreation. While playing five-a-sides in the yard at Sallynoggin Technical School, I was spotted by Tommy Heffernan who asked me to play with Pearse Rovers at weekends.

At first, that created a bit of a problem. The master at Glen Silva didn't exactly warm to the idea of me playing organised soccer. It took a while for Rovers to convince him that I would be brought straight back after games.

This was my first introduction to proper, eleven-a-side football and - being truthful - I was the original headless chicken. I remember Tommy having to get a blackboard out to explain to me that - as a right-back -I would actually be expected to stay in that position.

I was about twelve at the time and a Chelsea fanatic. Charlie Cooke was God. We had dug a field with our own hands at the back of the Glen Silva and now, rather than mimic Cooke and Osgood, I started imagining what I was going to do in those games with Pearse Rovers at the weekend. This was my introduction to leagues and divisions, to team-talks and game plans. Life, suddenly, was heaven.

But, at age 16, I had to leave the Glen Silva Home and Pearse Rovers, having – essentially – become too old for both. Racefield on the edge of Monkstown was my next port of call, a final link in the orphanage chain before being left to step out into the real world. In many ways, it was a crisis time for me.

Football was my only true interest and, unknown to me, Mr. Johnston – the master of Racefield – was on the look-out for a club that might offer me something more than Sunday football. He sought a club that could give me a sense of community, a home.

I will go to my grave thankful that he found Dalkey United. My first year with Dalkey was one of the most enjoyable of my life. The football was much tougher – physically – than it had been in the schoolboy leagues with Pearse Rovers. But that wasn't any harm. It helped harden me on the field.

Football-wise, I was in Seventh Heaven after the switch. Playing regularly in a decent team as a midfielder or striker, scoring goals, hearing talk of English scouts monitoring my progress.

But then, something went seriously wrong. It was a club trip to Germany. Everything was fine on the field but, off it, I took my first drink. And, somehow, it was as if I knew that something bad had just happened to me.

All of the other lads had brought duty-free and one of them opened a bottle of port. I decided I'd have a drink just to see what it was like and I remember just feeling wonderful with it. I thought "Jesus, I can do anything here!"

I was perfectly happy in myself until we came home. It was rumoured at the time that Spurs were interested in me. But I was more concerned with the fact that the time had come for me to move out of the orphanage and find a flat of my own. The thought of that intimidated me no end. Frank Mullen, a life-long friend at Dalkey, secured a roofing job for me with the well known Hammod Family who had a roofing business and have been closely connected with Dalkey United from its star. I lived with Jimmy and his wife Connie until I set-

tled into working.

Looking back, the prospect just got on top of me. My whole world collapsed. Being honest, I can't recall much of the next eighteen months. Suffice to say, I slumped into a serious depression, recovered briefly thanks to the great work of Dr. Pat Tubridy and Mr Don Lydon & Staff at St. John of Gods, where Frank got me into as a patient, then fell into an even more serious relapse. Football, the love of my life, no longer mattered to me.

On the contrary, I vowed I wouldn't play the game again. Why? I don't know. It's as if I was blaming it for my troubles. Blaming the trip to Germany. Blaming that first taste of drink. This was the period of my life where good friends saved me. Where fellas like Frank (Mullen), Tommy Cullen, John Young and Johnny Dunne would spend their lunch hours just sitting at my bedside or kicking a ball with me out on the green of St. Brendans Hospital encouraging me to get better. One of them would call back every evening, they seemed to have a rota system that went on for the months I was a patient there. They wanted me to get back to playing football but, for months, I never even spoke to them. If they had given up on me at that point, God only knows where I'd be today. Eventually, my mind cleared a little and they got me back playing with Dalkey. Billy Behan, the famous Manchester United scout, was vice-president of the club and – with his son Terry on the team – Billy was a regular spectator at our games. It gave everyone a great incentive to get noticed.

With English clubs beginning to take an interest in me again, Billy was determined I would go to Old Trafford. But he felt I needed a season in League of Ireland football to prepare me for the professional game. That's what I got with St. Patrick's

Athletic, although not before a number of other Dublin clubs had decided I wasn't worth the risk.

Pat's were actually the third or fourth club approached by Dalkey and, after a ropey introduction, I gradually started to make my mark in League of Ireland football. When I first signed for Charlie Walker, I played at either centre-forward or midfield. Now Charlie disputes what happened but, after scoring a few goals to begin with, I recall struggling a little and Charlie telling me that the Pat's directors were worried. So Charlie decided to play me at centre-half against Limerick alongside one of my very best mates, Joey Malone. The rest is history.

Suddenly, everything just clicked. I started playing well and began getting write-ups in the papers. One night, Charlie called to my flat to tell me that both Luton Town and Manchester City were ready to buy me. Manchester United were also offering me a one month trial. I didn't need to hear any more. It was Old Trafford for me. While Dalkey were on another tour of Germany I travelled over to Manchester.

I actually travelled over with Barry Kehoe who played with Dundalk. If Barry hadn't come, I think I'd have gone home on the next plane. He was just brilliant company, one of the funniest guys you could hope to meet. Barry's wit took my mind off the scale of the surroundings and the pressure of having a month to prove myself. We were put into digs with Norman Whiteside and another Irish guy called Phil Hughes.

Initially, there was a problem with my registration and I had to sit out the first couple of reserve games. My most vivid memory of those games is of Barry lording it in midfield, pushing Ray Wilkins out of the way to take free-kicks, telling people what their jobs were. He was absolutely brilliant but, unfortunately, they subsequently discovered he had a slight medical problem and he never did get a contract. After a long brave struggle with illness he died, he was a great loss and a great lad.

I eventually got a game against Newcastle reserves which we won and I'll always remember Ron Atkinson asking big Norman how I had done when we got back to Old Trafford. "Brilliant" chirped Norman.

It was a strange month because it ended without me having a clue about United's intentions. I was due to fly back to Dublin to collect the League of Ireland "Young Player of the Year" award and no-one had said anything.

Then, just as I was leaving the reserve team coach – Brian Whitehouse – shouted, "See you back here on Monday!" That was it. That was how I found out I was to become a Manchester United player. Just one throw-away line. Six words that lifted me into the clouds. And the outside world no longer seemed that scary.

The MASTER Paul McGrath in action against Italy in New York during the 1994 World Cup.

43

Know Your Neighbours?

(A Series of interviews by "F.M. O'Flanagan" of "the Dalkey Sound" with well known residents of Dalkey)

MILO O'SHEA

F.M: Well Milo, on behalf of the many readers of "The Dalkey Sound" may I welcome you to the pages of our Christmas 1963 Number and may I also thank you for so willingly agreeing to being our first "interviewee" in our new feature "Do you know your neighbours?" You are fortunate to be living on the beautiful Vico Road, with its ever changing views of Killiney Bay from Dalkey Island to Bray Head. When, and why, did you come to live in "Ventnor" on the Vico Road?

Milo: Some nine years ago, F.M., in 1954, my wife – better known to the theatrical world as "Maureen Toal" – and I came to live on "The Vico". While on tour in the United States we had received a colourful postcard of the Vico Road from my father in Rathgar. The more we studied the lovely view of Killiney Bay, the more we were determined to set up home there on our return to Ireland. This we succeeded in doing and we have never regretted our choice.

F.M: Apart from that fateful postcard, had you other ties already with Dalkey?

Milo: Oh yes, very much so. My paternal great-grandfather was a Captain O'Shea, a master mariner, who lived about 1850 in "Eagle Terrace", Sorrento Road, Dalkey.

F.M: Have you any other Christian names beside "Milo" and were you called "Milo" after Milo Burke of "Khyber Pass"?

Milo: My full names are "Milo Donal" O'Shea. No, I was not called "Milo" after Milo Burke – though Captain O'Shea would have known him in his day – But after my maternal great-uncle, Milo O'Flanagan of the North Circular Road, Dublin.

F.M: You have a sturdy young son, Milo, how old is he now and what does he aspire to become when he grows up?

Milo: "Colum" will be 4 years and 2 months of age this Christmas and he wants to be an Engine Driver on the "Bray Line Trains". If there are no trains left when he is a man then he says he will settle for acting, like Mammy and Daddy.

F.M: What do you like best about Dalkey – apart for its natural beauty?

Milo: I like the Dalkey people's outlook on life. They are not only extremely friendly and hospitable but being used to actors, celebrities and "characters" generally, they just accept you for what you are, welcome you to their midst but never intrude on your privacy.

F.M: The "Dalkey Sound" is produced in Dalkey by the Conference of St. Dominic Savio, which operates a Boys' Club for some 130 local boys, what do you think of Boys' Clubs?

Milo: I regard such Boys' Clubs as an invaluable asset to any local community. In my professional travels in England,

America and Canada, I have seen only too much of what can happen to originally decent boys whose energies are not channelled into useful and pleasurable activities.

F.M: Do you, yourself, take a great interest in the care of youth?

Milo: Yes, I do. Despite the irregular schedules of an actor's life I have always made time for such works as the Red Cross Entertainment Corps, which entertains young people in hospitals, orphanages, etc.

F.M: Finally, Milo, what is your eventual ambition in the acting profession – musical, comedy, burlesque, character parts, Shakespeare?

Milo: Well, I play a "straight part" in a Telefis Eireann play called "Kochak and His Children". The part I play is that of a Jewish Polish Doctor during the occupation of Poland by Germany. I took this part on because I do not wish to be associated in the public mind with only one type of character. In reply to your question, I would say that though I have always enjoyed making the public laugh, yet there is something more satisfying in portraying pathos or tragedy, so in the future I hope to continue to perform in both fields of drama.

First published December 1963.

Ardbrugh Road in 1950's

I was born and raised on Ard Brugh Road, next door to old Mrs. Mullen and three daughters who never married, Kathleen Alice and Nora.

Kathleen

She was an elegant lady, of her time; she baked, sewed and made elderberry wine for special occasions. Although all three sisters were lifelong pioneers excepting Nora who was known to take the odd drop of brandy for medicinal purposes, their elderberry wine was about 40 proof.

Alice, the middle sister

Was a very hard worker. She kept pigs, hens and had a horse and car, which was kept, in the front garden. She tended a vegetable and fruit garden in the back and shared the produce with her neighbours. The pigs were kept in a sty at the end of the garden and once a year they were herded up the lane to market. The terrified squealing of the pigs as they were loaded outside my house is with me to this day. They were not the only ones terrified.

Alice and Noeleen in 1953

A big treat for me was to be taken on the horse and cart to collect "slop" (unused food) from all the houses in the area for pig food and sometimes if I was lucky I got a slice of bread and jam from Julia the cook in Santa Maria. We collected firewood on the green road, windfalls, branches and cones, all had to be dragged back home and chopped for fire. Alice built a little grotto at the bottom of the lane at the entrance to their cottage and it was my job to keep it with wild flowers while she kept a night-light burning.

Alice also did the washing in the boiler house, she had three big galvanized baths, one for washing, one for rinsing and one for starch and blue dye to stiffen and whiten the clothes. When the clothes were dry she heated three big irons on the gas stove and ironed them. Knickers and vests were aired on the oven door, at dusk the lamps were lit, gas lamp in the sitting room, oil lamps for the bedrooms. If you needed to use the toilet you had to go down to a shed at the bottom of the garden and bring a torch. The toilet roll was made from neat squares of newspaper cut and hung with twine on a nail on the back of the door.

Nora, the oldest sister

Nora a moaner (my Dad said he could hear her moaning from our house). A childhood illness had allegedly left her delicate and unable to work and up to the time of her death - she outlived both her sisters by many years - she never left the hill. an exception to this was late in her life when Paddy Darcy and his sisters took Nora for a Sunday drive in his Morris Oxford to

Wicklow. The Darcys were kind people who took their civic duty seriously but Nora complained that they always went the one way.

I had occasion to benefit from the Darcys kindness when as a newborn baby I failed to thrive and the doctor prescribed the milk of a cow as a remedy. The only people with a cow in the locality were the Darcys who initially refused Dads request (it was illegal to sell unpastuerised milk) but later on learning the nature of our need, relented and kept me supplied with daily fresh milk for six months free of charge. The cow came to a sticky end some years later when it swallowed a hatpin.

Imagine in my lifetime and I am still in my fifties - dry toilets, no electricity, no running water, the water had to be carried in buckets from the top of the flags. Pigs and hens in the back garden, horse and cart in the front garden. The first of the aunts died circa. 1970 and the old cottage was buldozed to make way for the new but the lane still exists and sometimes when I look down the lane, I fancy I can still see Alice as she goes with her buckets to fetch the water. Alice was my favourite and I think I was her's and her family and ours have been lifelong friends, May they rest in peace.

Noeleen with her parents, Paddy and Kathleen.

Noeleen Dunne (Larkin)
1 Desmond Cottages
Ardbrugh Road

Dalkey Rowing Club - A Short History

It is generally agreed amongst those involved in sport in Dalkey that one of the most successful sports clubs in the town over the last seventy five years or so has been Dalkey Rowing Club.

The club, which was founded in 1932, continues to survive in a healthy state to this day. The sea has always been a great attraction to the people of the town and adjoining areas, whether it is rowing, sea scouting, sailing, swimming, fishing or just walking along the shore enjoying the wonderful sea air.

Dalkey Rowing Club 1934/35

Back Row L to R: Sean Cunningham, M. Byrne, J. Dunne, Peter Devitt, P. Dignam, I. Bull, E. Reilly, Dick Foran, Willie Brown, Joe Smith-Brown, John Reilly, Willie Haughton.
Third Row: J. Heskin, J. Brown-English, J. Mitchell-Brennan, Jim English, Pat Reilly, J. Hammond (Stork), Larry Hammond, Allo White, William Mullen, Jack Devitt, P. English.
Second Row: M. Devitt, Doyle, English, Willie Reilly, J. Kelly, P. Whiter, "Barber" Young.
Front Row: P. Kinsella, Bobby Wright, Child, J. Brown, Moore, J. Larkin, Gerry Kelly, Gutney Kill, P. Kelly.

Generations of families have earned their living in the beautiful little harbours of Bulloch and Coliemore. The names of Smyth, Lawless, Spencer, Hammond, Murray and Lambe immediately spring to mind. Many more have made their living sailing the oceans of the world for most of their working lives.

Some of them paid the supreme sacrifice in coping with the unpredictable moods of the seas and oceans. Derek (Derry) Smyth of Bulloch, a great footballer, oarsman, fami-ly man and true gentleman, was such a man. Derek took early retirement to enable him to continue the family fishing and boating business at Bulloch, which had been run by his family for generations. He was an experienced boatman, having helped his grandfather and father in his spare time, when he was not involved in his football career and in other family commit-ments. He went out to sea fishing for lob-ster on 10th December 1974, never to return. An angry wind blew up and he was drowned. The shock that reverberated through the area was profound. Following his great loss, his wife and his children continued in the business with the same determination of generations of the Smyth family.

Two other great oarsmen and members of the great crews of the 1930's, Mick (Hare) Lambe and Sonny Price were also eminent seafaring men. It was tragically ironic that, having sailed on a merchant ship across the seas and oceans of the world during the Second World War, when so many vessels were sunk with enormous loss of life, Mick and Sonny lost their lives in the Pacific Ocean in a storm only days after peace was declared.

These great oarsmen of Dalkey Rowing Club are only three in a long list who lost their lives at sea down through the mists of time.

The very imposing yet simple memorial erected at Bulloch Harbour by the boat owners association to the memory of gallant Dalkeymen who gave their lives in

By strange coincidence in the summer of 1932 when Dalkey Rowing Club was formed, the finance for the purchase of the club's first racing boat (skiff) was provided by the owner of a small aircraft which crash landed into the sea just south of Dalkey Island. The senior crew of the club was practising in an old racing boat called 'The Sarah', which had been borrowed from the Murray family - boatmen at Coliemore Harbour. They were rowing southeast through Dalkey Sound when they saw the plane landing in the sea. They raced to the scene and pulled out the pilot and the one passenger, both of whom were uninjured. They brought them to Coliemore Harbour.

The founding committee of the club in that summer of 1932, Patrick White, John Doyle who had the barber's shop in Castle Street (which was subsequently taken over by Don McClure), Fred Hill (father of Harry Hill and his brother 'Gutney' - both top class footballers) and Tom English of Patrick's Road.

Dalkey Rowing Club 1939
L to R: Cox M.L. Byrne, Jim Foran, Mick Lambe, Dicky Foran, "Taedy" Dowling and Joe Mitchell, Trainer.

The wonderful gesture by the owner of the plane in presenting a new boat to the club provided a solid platform for the future development of the club. The new boat was called 'Blath na Farraige or 'The Flower of the Sea'. Success in competitions was experienced in their first season when the senior crew won many races and concluded a great achievement by winning the East Coast Championship at the Wicklow Regatta on August Monday 1932.

saving others is ample proof of the long tradition of involvement in seafaring.

The Champion Crew comprised Jim Foran, Mick Lambe (referred to earlier), Dick Foran and Thady Dowling. The coxswain was another great seaman Mick Byrne of St Patrick's Road and the Racing Boat was put in dry dock for the winter months in the Boat House at the pier at Coliemore Harbour, with the help of a crane that stood for many years on the pier at Coliemore Harbour.

Success continued through the 1930s into the early years of the Second World War. The crews included the Foran brothers, Willie and Jim Brown from Dalkey Hill, the Hammonds, Holmes and Murrays. In the early years of this war the club had to vacate the boat house on the pier and the boat was kept on the slipway during the winter months.

The club established a ladies' crew and purchased a second boat called 'The St. Malachy', the name that has been continuously used for the club's boat to this day. The crew, which won a series of ladies races in the summers of 1940 and 1941, was Greta Reilly, Gracie Hill, Maggie and Anne Brown, all of whom were prominent members of Dalkey Rowing Club and Cuala Camogie Club.

As WW2 broke out like most sports, the club was decimated by emigration as thousands departed our shores to seek employment abroad. The situation was exacerbated by a severe storm that struck the East Coast in the autumn of 1942 when boats tied up on the slipway were washed into the harbour and damaged beyond repair.

When the war ended the regattas became popular during the summer months when it became easier to transport boats to the various venues.

In the 1950s, success again became the lot of an ever improving club, a new generation of oarsmen started to make their names, those of Tony Delaney, Andy Kavanagh, Dan Rafferty, Pat O'Brien, Wally Knowles, J J Banahan, Willie Reilly, Mick Williams, Mick Mullen (Snr.) and Sean Cunningham are well recorded in the annals of the club.

The most senior member was Jim Hammond and in 1951 the crew of Tony Delaney, J J Banahan and Andy Kavanagh, led by the experienced Jimmy Hammond and coxed by Andy Delaney, emulated the great crew of 1932 by remaining undefeated throughout the season and becoming East Coast Champions on August Monday 1951 at the Wicklow Regatta.

While many races were won in the various seasons through the 1930s and 60s, the 'Golden Era' was the 1970s. There was a great influx of young lads joining the underage crews in those years that led to further wonderful seasons. Several East

1951 East Cost Champions
L to R: Oates Nolan, J.J. Banahan, Andy Kavanagh, Tony Delaney,
Jem "Gunger" Hammond, Andy Delaney (Coxwain)

Coast Championships were won. The leading exponents of the sport then were Colm, Dermot and Michael Comerford, the Newbank brothers, Pat Dalton, the Keogh family, Terence, Seamus and Brian, the Ellards and Kellys, Colm and Eoin Condon, Michael and Declan Mullen, Ken, Johnny and Gerald Cunningham.

The girls' team was also outstandingly successful with Michelle Brady, Eimear Comerford, Christine Walsh, Geraldine Greene, Helen Seix, Ann Golden, Linda Cunningham, Elaine Farrell, Jacinta and Tina Kelly, Carol Condon, Liz Bailey, and Yvonne Rooney making a wonderful contribution.

However, not diminishing in any way the achievements of all, the most outstanding success was arguably when the schoolboys' club won the All Ireland Championship at Carnlough Regatta in Co Antrim in 1994.

The members of the winning crew on that historic weekend were David Cunningham (Jnr.), Colm Harper, Darren Hughes and Garrett Duffy, with Frank Duffy on cox.

Frank Duffy, along with the late George Ellard R.I.P., were probably two of the greatest administrators in the club's history. Frank was the longest serving Honorary Secretary in the history of the club, serving in that office for 23 years. Under his stewardship the Irish Coastal Rowing Association was formed and Irish crews are now competing successfully at Regattas in the UK and Europe.

He was also the inspiration behind the purchase of the club's HQ at Rockford Avenue, Dalkey.

While countless people have contributed and brought honour to the club through its history, its very existence, with all the other sports clubs and voluntary organisations, improve in a significant way the quality of life of all the people of Dalkey. Long may it remain so.

David Cunningham
Michael Mullen (Senior)

The 1966 Under 16 All Ireland Open Champions Dalkey Rowing Club. L to R: David Cunningham (Junior) Garrett Duffy, Darren Hughes and Colm Harper.

Long term secretary of Dalkey Rowing Club George Ellard

First record of a Rowing Regatta held in Dalkey

Monday, 17th August 1868
Dalkey Boat Races

These spiritedly got up races came off today near Dalkey Sound, opposite the handsome grounds of Mr. Leslie, who left his place at the disposal of the Committee for the occasion. The weather was fine in the extreme, and a number of gay-looking yachts came down from Kingstown, and added to the beauty of the scene. Towards evening, the grounds mentioned became crowded by a very fashionable assembly. A fine military band, that of the 17th Regiment arrived and performed in an excellent manner a brilliant and suitable programme of music.

The boat races were as follows:
First Race, for a prize of **£1.5s**, for four oared boats, pulled by fishermen's sons.
"Racer", Michael Flanagan owner, **Dalkey**
"Fanny", N. Flanagan, owner, **Dalkey**. This, the first race was a series of fouls from start to finish, but nevertheless showed some good pulling. Finally the **"Racer"**, passed the winning flag, the **"Fanny"** coming in contact with a boat as she was coming to the winning post.
Second Race, for a prize of **£6**, for four-oared boats belonging to, and pulled by, fishermen of **Dalkey** and **Bulloch** only:
"Commodore" Michael Flanagan, owner, blue flag, Dalkey
"Kate", Michael Murphy, owner, green flag, **Dalkey**

"Eliza", George Smith, owner, white flag, **Bulloch**
"Sarah", Patrick Smith, owner, red flag **Dalkey**
This was the chief fishermen's race, and was well and fairly contested. The course passed over was about a mile and a half in extent, and had been so laid out as to permit a view of the race throughout. The **"Kate"** and **"Sarah"** led out from the start, which took place at 3.30 p.m. and exhibited a strong and well-contested pull in a heavy current.
Coming up channel with the tide, the **"Eliza"** led for some time, but near the finish, the **"Sarah"** put on a spurt, and won the prize by about six both lengths. Other races prolonged the sports till a late hour, and they closed with a display of fireworks by Mr. Lawrence.

Dalkey – A Walk on the Wild Side

For most people, wildlife activity happens at the corner of one's eyes. Yet there is nothing nicer than when one is rewarded with a glimpse of a robin or a blackbird in one's own back garden. A pleasant stroll around Dalkey can offer us plenty to see and become a visual feast.

Bulloch Harbour on a raw, windy, spring morning. I stand, well wrapped up, looking out to sea, armed with binoculars. Gulls circle about. They seem to own the sky. Herring, great black-backed, common and black-headed gulls. A cormorant pops up from below the surface with a small fish in its bill. It quickly gobbles it down in case the pesky gulls try to steal it. Close to the shore, on a bollard, a prettier gull called a Kittiwake watches the activity of a small wader. It is flicking over pebbles looking for tiny sand hoppers. It lives up to its name, a turnstone. To the left, standing like a statue, is the ever-watchful grey heron, the tallest wild bird in Ireland, often referred to as a crane. It's after a bigger and better prize, a fish.

They all seem to become aware of two large black shadows that can be seen moving just below the surface. The cormorant gives them a wide berth. With playful wonder, two grey seals break the surface of the water, pop their heads up and then head closer to the wall of the harbour. They seem to know something that the gulls are also privy to. Then a kind old gentleman with a white beard appears with a black bucket full of fish heads and other tasty morsels and casts them to the sea like bread to ducks. There is a feeding frenzy as gulls swoop down to cash in on this bountiful breakfast. Another seal appears from nowhere. It's a male bull seal. It takes the lion's share of the fish heads, yet there seems to be plenty to go around. The grey heron has spotted some morsels that even the gulls have missed. It swoops down and with its dagger-like bill, stabs at a fish carcass, then flies away to a suitable perch to swallow it in peace. Soon the food is gone. The man returns to his house. The seals vanish like phantoms below the surface. The gulls flit away over the rocks. The water becomes calm again. Even the heron and cormorants have moved away.

I walk up to Dalkey village. A pied-wagtail flits about on the roadside flicking its tail, telling predators like sparrow hawks, "I'm too fast to catch". A hooded crow sits on a high branch cawing loudly. Two magpies swoop by, heading for a garden. A wood pigeon coos from a tree. After a pleasant cup of coffee and a warn scone I head off for Killiney Hill. As I move onto the hill a painted lady butterfly sits warming herself up after her long migratory journey. There is a beautiful smell of coconut in the air from the gorse flowers shimmering like gold. A stonechat sits high on a birch. It's happy to show itself off. It's got a beautiful red breast and black head. A bill full of insects indicates that his female partner must be nearby sitting tightly in the nest, on her clutch of newly laid eggs. A wren sings loudly, a big voice for a small bird. A pocket Caruso! It too has a female hidden in the gorse bushes.

Voices carry in the wind. Young men rock climbing in their brightly coloured helmets stand out against the grey granite. I walk up the steps to the top and take in the view. Two kestrels can be seen hovering in the wind, tails fanned out. They hang there motionless. One begins to unwind like a spider on a web string. Then it drops towards the ground in a swoop, breaking off at the last minute and returning to the sky. Gerard Manley Hopkins' 'The Windhover' right there, eye height.

Later I go over the far side of the hill and scan the sea. My patience is rewarded after a time. Two harbour porpoises, porpoising through the sunlit waters. As dusk approaches, I return home. Passing down through the woods, I disturb two badgers foraging below the trees. They scurry away. Signs indicate there's a sett nearby. Some muddy tracks and upturned sods where they have been digging for grubs and worms are the only hint that they have been there. A long-eared owl has been ghosting about. It leaves a tell-tale feather below a pine tree; it's very soft to the touch. The evening sky with its beautiful yellows and orange afterglow is like a Turner watercolour. My head is filled with beautiful images and thoughts. What's that ahead of me on the Metals? It stops, stares at me, then casually pads away into the darkness. A red fox. What a special day. Life is made up of good moments.

Don Conroy

Match of the Day – Forties and Fifties Style

It was the late forties and early fifties on a Saturday afternoon. Hyde Park, or Dr Wright's Field in Dalkey was where my older brother and I played football. Winter and summer, a loosely organised match took place. The players were mainly in their late teens, twenties and early thirties, the talents were disparate and the individual garb was varied.

The match was the fulfilment of a week's anticipation. We left my brother's Ford Prefect at the entrance to the park and proceeded to the nearest goalmouth, which was usually a congealed mass of mud. (There was no official football pitch until some years later.) We were always early. With a tingling expectation, we put on our boots and stuffed our trouser bottoms into our football socks.

Invariably, there was a slight fear as we waited. Would there be enough players to make up a match? Would someone bring a ball? Our fears were always allayed. Gradually the rest of the participants would materialize. Some would drop over the distant wall, others would emerge through gaps in a nearby hedge. In dribs and drabs the cast of performers congregated.

A general atmosphere of chaos preceded the process of team selection. The motley crew would ultimately be sorted into two groups of comparable strengths but not without argument.

Once the game started, a frenzied seriousness took hold. Instructions would be bellowed from one end of the rutted surface to the other. Emotions ran high. During our long, fantasy-driven afternoon, there would be shouts of desperation, frustration and anger. Deep feelings of injustice and warnings of retribution were common. However, on a positive note, the laughs, roars of approval and the occasional brush with ecstasy more than made up for what might have been a passing annoyance. At best, the euphoria felt from heading in a centre or drilling one past the despairing dive of Frank Mullen could last for some time.

Names spring to mind: John Keyes and John Maher. Jock Brown with his deadpan expression. Des Comerford, who was always cool and strong and tolerant of lesser mortals such as myself. Willie Reilly, forever a defender and stoically taking abuse when a nippy winger outpaced him. The Babe Smyth, who had a hard shot and took no prisoners. Derek 'Snowy' Smith, who was as solid a defender as the granite

Jim "Gus" Farrell.

which surrounded the house he was born in at Bulloch Harbour.

Probably the cleverest was Twig Fox, the little midfielder with a bald head and talent to spare. He could dance through tackles like a Dervish in a minefield. It should be noticed that the tackling would not be found in any coaching manual. There were wild lunges, flailing legs, body checks and all forms of physical violence that the lower extremities can inflict. Twig dismissed such attempts at hindering his schemes as mere trifles. Invariably, he would slip the ball through the turmoil around him to an unmarked accomplice.

Seamus Gannon was also a very nimble player, a tough Nobby Stiles type. Those of us who were less nimble had to content with the crunching challenges of Pat O'Brien. Their legacy might be apparent well into the following week.

The character who stood out, literally head and shoulders above everyone else, was Jim "Gus" Farrell. Well over six feet tall, he was in the affections of everyone.

In fairness, Gus did not have the silky skills of a Twig Fox or, indeed, the talents of his famous brother Peter, of Everton and Ireland.

Gus would crouch at the back of his defence issuing encouragement and instructions. He would point at players to be marked and spaces to be covered. Whilst his admonitions might have had tactical substance, nobody ever listened. Everyone did their own thing. Gus had huge boots, the biggest I had ever seen. Whilst he was always clean in his aggression, his tackles rarely achieved the objective. When he fell down, he occasionally took an age to reassemble himself for the next joust. Occasionally, he would venture upfield when his team won a corner-kick. Should the ball be cleared beyond an imaginary penalty area, Gus might connect with the toe of one of his size twelves. The ball would explode from his boot in a wavering, crazy trajectory that would cause heads to duck and bodies to flinch. As the ball

sailed high and wide towards a distant wall, the end result was a moan from the frustrated goalkeeper who had to run fifty yards to retrieve it. Gus would lumber back to his position, head down, his face a frown of disbelief. A cursory excuse would be directed towards his nearest critic without any sign of malice. Then, turning he would assume his mantle of authority and continue to clap his hands in offering encouragement.

There were others whose efforts, wit and comradeship always enriched the experience. Pat Lacy and John Myler. Frank Quirke and Paddy Darcy, Paddy Thorpe. There were the Kavanaghs, Pat and Bartle and Joe McDonald.

In hindsight, the qualities of the players may have left a lot to be desired. There were flunked tackles, appalling shots, clumsy interceptions and often a litany of errors, not to speak of lack of vision. But the weekly ritual was a rite of passage for us teenagers and a respite of sorts for the older ones. It was certainly a male preserve. The relationships formed were one-dimensional and some of us never knew each other in any meaningful way. For years we went there in those times of relative innocence.

In essence, the match was the epitome of our week's expression. We were welded together for two hours each Saturday by an eager desire to impress both ourselves and our peers. On a good day, we did both.

Nowadays, I sometimes see an odd survivor of those painful and pleasurable afternoons. It may be at a traffic light or in a corner of the Dart. A familiar face will grin or nod the head and I'll wonder if his thoughts are like mine.

Don Farrell

Father Willie Doyle S.J.

One of the bravest Dalkey sportsmen must surely have been Fr. William J. Doyle, who was born on 3rd March 1873 at Melrose, Dalkey Avenue, our family home for the last 19 years until we recently relocated to a smaller house which we built in the grounds. He was known by his contemporaries, many of whom survived and resided in Dalkey up to the 1950's and 1960's, as Willie.

Fr. Doyle was the embodiment of courage, whether it was by taking long swims to and back from Dalkey Island, swimming along the seashores of Dalkey Sound into Killiney Bay, or rendering comfort and spiritual assistance as Chaplain to his troops in the unimaginable horrors of the battlefields of Flanders and The Somme during the First World War.

He was reared in Dalkey and spent his childhood years playing tennis and swimming. He played his tennis in the fields of Dalkey Quarry and swam in the same locations as many of us nowadays: Coliemore Harbour, Bulloch, The Forty Foot, the Vico and White Rock. As a young lad he caused concern for his parents Hugh and Christina, and his older brother, Charlie, by his regular excursions to Dalkey Island unaccompanied.

In 1884, Willie followed his brother to Radcliffe College, Leicestershire, England, where he was a boarder for six years, during which he excelled in tennis, cricket and rugby.

The two brothers would spend their Christmas holidays with family members in England. Their sister married and settled in England. During some of those years, Willie would come home to Dalkey and spend Christmas in Melrose celebrating Mid-Night Mass on Christmas Eve..

In 1890, he returned to Ireland, where he continued his studies in Clongowes Wood College for a year. During his stay there he fell into bad health. He suffered with seri-

Fr. Willie Doyle SJ resplendent in his army uniform

ous stomach and digestive problems, which continued for a number of years. During that time he lived on Dalkey Avenue and was very involved in helping others who were ill or infirm. He always remained in good spirits and spent a lot of time helping the poor of the area. He was described as being good humoured and kind despite his almost continuous ill health.

During those years he decided to become a priest. He resumed his studies in Belgium, Clongowes and Belvedere and was ordained on 28th July 1907. He taught for several years in Belvedere and then went to teach in Belgium and France.

When the First World War was raging, Willie was appointed Chaplain to the 8th Royal Irish Fusiliers, 16th (Irish) Division on 15th November 1915. On 17th February 1916 he received his orders to join the forces in France. His first experience of battle was at Loos where he was caught in the German poison gas attack on 26th April. He ministered to the soldiers in the midst of battle displaying a total disregard for his own safety. He was mentioned in dispatches but his Colonel's recommendation for the Military Cross was not accepted because he had not been long enough at the front. He was presented with the parchment on merit of the 49th Brigade.

In May 1916 he had a lucky escape, which he described in a letter to his father thus: "I was standing in a trench, quite a long distance from the firing line, a spot almost as safe as Dalkey itself, talking to some of my men when we heard in the distance the scream of a shell. None of us had calculated that "this gentleman" had made up his mind to drop into our trench, a couple of paces from where I stood. What really took place in the next 10 seconds I cannot say. I was conscious of a terrific explosion and the thud of falling stones and debris. I thought the drums of my ears were split by the crash and I believe I was knocked down by the concussion but when I jumped to my feet I found that the two men who had been standing on my left hand, the side the shell fell, were stretched on the ground dead, though I think I had time to give them absolution and anoint them. The poor fellow on my right was lying badly wounded in the head but I myself, though a bit stunned and dazed by the suddeness of the whole thing, was absolutely untouched, though covered with dirt and blood."

"I found the dying lad, he was not much more than a lad, so tightly jammed into a corner of the trench that it was almost impossible to get him out. Both legs were smashed, one in two or three places, so his chances of life were small and there were other injuries as well. What a harrowing picture that scene would have made. A splendid young soldier, married only a month they told me, lying there, pale and motionless in the mud and water with the life crushed out of him by a cruel shell. The stretcher bearers hard at work binding up as well as they may, his broken limbs; round about a group of Tommies looking on and wondering when their turn will come. Peace for a moment seems to have taken possession of the battlefield, not a sound save the deep boom of some far off gun and the stifled moans of the dying boy, while as if anxious to hide the scene, nature droops her soft mantle of snow on the living and dead alike."

In August 1916 he took part in the fighting at Ginch and Guillemont. In December 1916 he was transferred to the 8th Battalion of The Royal Dublin Fusiliers. He met fellow Jesuit Father Frank Browne who was attached to the 2nd and 9th Dublin. His concern for his men shines through his letters and diaries.

He was awarded The Military Cross in January 1917, though many believed that he deserved the Victoria Cross for his bravery under fire. He took part in the attack on Wytschaete Ridge in June 1917. Fr. Browne was transferred to the Irish Guards at the start of August which left Fr. Willie to service four battalions by himself.

He had a number of close calls before being killed by a shell along with three officers on 17th August, on Frezenberg Ridge. He was recommended for a DSO at Wytschaete and the VC at Frezenberg.

He has no known grave but is commemorated on the Tyne Cot Memorial (panel 144 to 145).

Recently his memory and that of all his brave comrades has been revived by a song written and sung by one of Ireland's best known singers, Johnny McEvoy. If one walks into the museum in the picturesque little town of Perrone, on the banks of The Somme, one is immediately drawn to a large, framed tribute to Willie Doyle. It contains his photograph, a brief description of his life in Dalkey and a comprehensive account of his service in the battlefield, depicting his courage and bravery.

He was not one of the greatest sportsmen that Dalkey produced but a man with a passionate love of sport, he was one of Dalkey's bravest sportsmen.

It is a pity that the town of Dalkey that he loved so much and the country that sacrificed so many young men "in the defence of small nations" have totally forgotten him.

Frank Mullen, Chairman of Dalkey United AFC and myself had the honour of installing a plaque on the entrance to Melrose in August 2007 to mark the 90th anniversary of Fr. Willie's death on the battlefields of Flanders, hoping to ensure that this great Dalkey man is remembered in the future and his sacrifice will never be forgotten

Dermot J. Duffy
The Coach House, Dalkey Avenue

The Dublin Fusiliers

Johnny McEvoy

When I was young and in my prime, I thought I'd take a change
To join with my companions and fight the war in France.
John Redmond said, "When peace has come old Ireland will be free
And you'll return brave heroes from the war with Germany.

CHORUS
And in my dreams, I see them still come marching down the years
The boys who stood beside me in the Dublin Fusiliers.

There was Johnny Roche from Dolphin's Barn and Micko from Ringsend
And Willie Doyle from Dalkey Town, no better as a friend,
We marched together through the mud the like you've never seen
And as we marched we sang a song 'The wearing of the green'.

CHORUS
And in my dreams, I see them still come marching down the years
The boys who stood beside me in the Dublin Fusiliers.

Poor Micko fell at Messines Ridge while trying to take the hill
A German bullet brought him down, his body cold and still
And Johnny Roche and Willie Doyle though they were never found
Like thousands, they still lie today beneath the battle ground

CHORUS
And in my dreams, I see them still come marching down the years
The boys who stood beside me in the Dublin Fusiliers.

Now I am old not wanted here, a stranger in my home
I sit alone in my back yard and watch the sun go down,
But medals are no good to you when you are old and grey
And the taste of gas upon your lips will never go away

CHORUS
And in my dreams, I see them still come marching down the years
The boys who stood beside me in the Dublin Fusiliers.

They will always be remembered . . .

The following, as far as can be ascertained, are the names of the Men and Women of Dalkey, who gave their lives in the Two World Wars.

1914 - 1918 War

Alex Atkinson
Vivian Barton
Douglas Bethune
Thomas Bethune
Conrad Betts
Thomas Butler
Archiebald Cathie
Jim Curtain
Reg DeFerras
Fr. Willie Doyle, S.J.

Simon Enpey
Myles Fawcett
Fred Greene
Tom Greaves
Henry Hithchens
John Hollowey
Dorothy Jones
Arthur Kendall
Rev. John W.E. Powell
Paddy Redmond

1939 - 1945 War

Robert Boyle
William Boyle
Arthur Dowse
Herbert Dowse

Robert Lister
Eric O'Dea
John Oswald Sharp

They will never grow old . . .

Rosaleen Stanley, Hill Cottages Killiney with her fiance Tom Greaves prior to his departure to serve in the first World War, he was killed in action and Rosaleen subsequently married William Murdoch of Glenalua Road Killiney, whose daughter Mary Murdoch married Michael Byrne and they carried on a fish and poultry business in Castle St., Dalkey

Between the wild and the street

My father was born beside the sea in Sligo, but still I did not see the sea until I was nearly 20. Now I see the sea continuously from my back window and could not be without it. From my living room I look over Dun Laoghaire Harbour and across to Howth. On a clear day, you can see the Mountains of Mourne, head raised raised ghostily over Sutton, peering back at Dalkey.

At my front door I look onto Dalkey Quarry. Sometimes, especially on a Tuesday night in summertime, I stand at my front door listening to the voices of the rock-climbers in the quarry, invisibly calling to each other across the rock, and once again I cannot believe my luck.

Sometimes, as we come to the end of a rough winter, when the winds have pummelled us from the north and the east, and we have stayed indoors more than is natural in such a place, I find myself walking again across Dalkey Hill as though for the first time. I think, How could I have forgotten this, or suggested I had forgotten it by staying indoors? Why have I been neglecting to come out and look at such an extraordinary place? Walking home again, I am visited by the same thoughts every time, as I retrace the steps which brought me here from the flatlands of County Roscommon and to be able to call this place my home.

John Waters

What Dalkey represents for me is much more than mere aesthetic beauty. It is a place where I can encounter the wilderness, albeit in a distilled form, and yet live near to the street. Both aspects are, I think, vital to me. People who think they know where I come from always seem to regard me in a certain way because they imagine I come from what they call 'The Country'. But I come from no such place. When I was a child growing up in Castlerea, I lived on Main Street, which, when I think about it now, had about it the qualities of a short stretch of city. It had a roadway with near constant traffic which I could listen to as I fell asleep. It had those incessant sounds that make the city live in the imagination as much as in space, the sound of Guinness barrels being unloaded at dawn and the drone of a train in the distance, kind of thing. It had the regular lines of the steetscape, the sharp corners, the signposts that tell you where to go, all of which creates a kind of box for your humanity that contains it and explains it. It had the Fair Green, the church, a couple of small cafes, where the people congregated in various dispositions. It had shops where you could get food, ice cream, things to read or wear, and where you could get your shoes repaired or your radio retuned and where the tradesmen multi-tasked as they talked to their customers about the life they shared without questioning it much.

I have never recognised myself as coming from 'The Country'. When I walked out my front door, I was in the Universal City.

And when I walked out my back door, I was in the wilderness. The gardens behind our houses had long since run into one wide continuity, bordered at the end by the River Suck, which had an island in the middle which you could access by means of a tree felled on the town side in Roddys' Field. It only now occurs to me that, as a child, this wild place existing so close to the beat of the street was fundamental to my formation, to my very nature. The street sought to seduce me to a new reality, but the condensed wilderness of those gardens kept me in touch with what is infinite within myself. I used to walk around with my life's companion, Fumble, a skinny, ugly, but intensely loyal animal, a dog trapped in the body of a cat. For some reason I always carried an iron staff, perhaps to ward off wild animals, and we would go hunting together, seeming to have walked straight from the pages of Huckleberry Finn or Just William. And in an eternity of a summer's afternoon, I would lie in the hollow of the island with Fumble purring at my head, utterly alone in the human universe, connected to the sky and the core of the earth, part of the continuity of time and yet momentarily resting on some cosmic journey. Then I would return to the street and be seduced once more.

Dalkey, I have only gradually come to realise, recreates these conditions to perfection. This, precisely, is why I love it here. When I came to Dublin first I lived in more typical suburban locations in Ballinteer and Booterstown, and then for a couple of years in the centre of town. Each location had its own qualities, but it is only when I settled on Dalkey that I came home to a place where the conditions of my childhood seemed to pertain in the most intense form imaginable, with the sea sort of thrown in to seal the deal.

I remember the first day I came here, in 1990, when I began house-hunting after getting my first real job, with the Irish Times. The first thing I encountered was Castle Street, with its castelled walls and its mid-morning hum of life. There was a tiny cafe then just opposite the Ulster Bank, and I went in and had a cup of tea and a bun. I had come purely out of curiosity. My house-buying budget was dictating that I live somewhere else, in Stonybatter, perhaps, or Ringsend. I had come to look at the shell of a house on Barnhill Road, which a cunning auctioneer had placed enticingly, but also fraudulently, just beyond my means. Those four walls without a roof were beyond my reach then. But still, those twenty minutes looking out on the life of that Dalkey street was enough to convince me that this is where I should stay. I had no idea how I was going to do it, but I knew I could never live anywhere else.

Castlerea Main Street c. 1930

Eventually, putting my shirt on the line, I bought the cottage on Ardbrugh Road where I imagine I will stay for as long as this cosmic pause endures. The street is a little more distant than that of my childhood, but, although I cannot hear the

Guinness barrells clatter onto the concrete, I can see the distant and reassuring movements of Castle Street from my attic window.

In the night, I hear occasional cars passing by my bedroom, enough to half-wake me occasionally to the sense that I have regressed forty years. And then, the car having disappeared into the infinity of near silence, my ear shifts to the wilderness just across the road, to the pre-dawn chorus and the hum of the other reality, the whisper of trees and the distant grumbling of the sea. I stand at the door on a summer's evening listening to the rock-climbers and sometimes fancy I hear the purr of a cat who thinks he's a dog, and have to pinch myself awake. If I half close my eyes, I might be under Ben Bulben.

For 17 years Dalkey has been home to me, and for the past twelve a home to my daughter Roisin and me. We love it so much that sometimes we take it for granted, and then we walk out again into the spring sunshine and are reminded that we live in what is really the corner of Heaven. So far we have not been able to access the central area, but this is only a matter of time.

John Waters

Overlooking Dalkey Town from Dalkey Hill.

Great Sporting Traditions

Dalkey has a history of vibrant sports clubs dating back over one hundred years. The Dalkey tug-o-war team of the early part of last century was known throughout the country as one of the most powerful and successful in the game. In the 1920's they were All Ireland Champions and won many honours in the D.M.P., Tramway and Guinness Sports meetings. They were also successful in Provincial Championships.

It is worthy of note that sports meetings took place annually in Gibbs Fields off Barnhill Road in the area where St. Begnet's Villas now stands stretching in the fields at the rere of Eamonn Walshe Motors on Barnhill Road, which incidently was the site of the Parish School. This was the era prior to the building of the current national schools and following the times of "The Hedge Schools" which was also in the same field. They took place at this venue from the early years of the century up to the early 1930's. Like all outdoor events prior to the advent of TV and other distractions, they attracted very large crowds and were of great benefit to the social and business life of the community. Names that figured prominently in those great tug-o-war teams were Paddy Thomas, Willie (Wexford) Byrne, so called because of his violin and singing of "The Boys of Wexford", Mick Mullen, Paddy Keyes, Jim Byrne, Nick Keyes (Hugh Leonard's father) and Tom Byrne. They trained on a rope secured to a hook in the cliff face on the west wing of Dalkey Hill Quarry. Dalkey Hill and the fields of the quarry were the centre of a variety of sporting activities so it was probably natural that Dalkey United started "on the hill".

Tennis was also a very popular sport in Dalkey. The Torca Tennis Club had its clubrooms on Dalkey Hill in the grounds of the Darcy's family home.

If one stands on the Upper East Quarry of Dalkey Hill and looks down on what remains of Darcy's fields, one can see the ridges of two of the four tennis courts of the club, which prospered from c. 1890 into the early 1940's. The late Edith (Edi) Darcy, who was a prominent member of the tennis club, often spoke of the damage caused to the courts by the British Army, when digging for buried weapons during the War of Independence.

Her brother Paddy had been arrested for his activities and sent to jail in England, where he had also been detained following the 1916 Rebellion. Paddy, who was wanted by the authorities for some time, was identified from a photograph of the Dalkey Hurling Team, of which he was captain, which appeared with the players' names in

Dalkey Rifle Club at Dalkey Hill Quarry 1896

a daily newspaper. Jack Thomas and Jimmy Nicholson were also imprisoned during the War of Independence.

It was easy to understand why such searches for arms took place in the Quarry. The Dalkey Rifle Club had their firing range and clubrooms in the east wing of the quarry. The ruins of the clubrooms could be seen up to approximately twenty-five years ago. The building was, in fact, occupied by a family named Sullivan until 1947/1948. The Bull's Eye Target Frame was fixed to a cliff face and was used for practice during those troubled years by the local unit of the I.R.A.

The authorities of the day were not far wrong with their information of firearms being hidden on Dalkey Hill; they were, in fact, hidden over the rafters of the pigsties of Michael Mullen at 4 Ard Brugh Road. The British Army and the Black and Tans raided the house several times looking for his son, my father also named Michael, but always stopped short of entering the pigsties, which had rafters lined with wood to store the firearms and ammunition. They obviously did not realise that the pigsties could be converted for such use.

Cycling was one of the most popular sports of the latter years of the nineteenth century and the Reynolds brothers, Harry and Bob, were two of the best-known names of that period. They were born in North County Dublin but came to live in Dalkey. Bob, in his early years, was the stronger of the two but a heart condition ended his career. He bought a shop on the site where the bookmakers shop now stands on Convent Road. He continued in this business until the early 1950's. Harry won the World Sprint Title at the World Cycling Championships in 1896 and lived for many years in 2 Sandycove Avenue West. He went on to win many other sprint championships in Ireland and Britain. He retired and concentrated on building up the cycle shop business in Convent Road. His brother, Bob, lived and worked there well into his seventies and he sold the premises in 1952.

The late Tom Doherty established Vico Motors there a few years later. Tom was a

Torca Tennis Club
Back Row, L to R: Paddy Murphy, Eamonn Quirke, Larry Doyle, Michael O'Meara, Paddy Loughlin, Threadgold, Billy Davenport, Joe White.
3rd Row, L to R: Paddy McDonagh, Bessie Davenport, Paddy Delaney, Eileen O'Carroll, Tom McNamara, Lily robinson, Tom McCarthy.
2nd Row, L to R: McDonagh, Mrs. Wilson, Bessie O'Carroll, Ada Fitzhugh, Gordon.
Front Row, L to R: Dan O'Connell, Violet Robinson, David McDonagh, Mrs. Wilson, Eileen Fitzhugh, Mollie O'Carroll, Mr. Wilson.

great supporter of Dalkey United and generously sponsored one of our schoolboy teams of many years.

The cycling tradition continues in Dalkey to this day, with Sorrento Cycling Club under the direction of founder member Danny O'Shea and his enthusiastic assistants. It provides excellent facilities for young cyclists in the area to develop their talents. Founder member Jimmy Egglington and another of Dalkey's great cycling legends, Mick Byrne from Dalkey Hill, are always available to advise these young lads. A cycling legend Mick Byrne certainly was, as indeed was his father P.J., who was Irish National Sprint Champion in 1924, 1925 and 1926. P.J. won numerous Provincial Track Championships during a long and distinguished career. It is safe to say that Mick Byrne's career covered one of the most exciting periods of sporting achievement ever. It covered the grim war and post-war years.

Accompanied by Kit O'Rourke, also born on Dalkey Hill, and Shamie Thomas from St. Patrick's Avenue, they were making headlines on a weekly basis during the cycling season. The highlight had to be when the three of them were selected to represent Ireland together in the first ever Multi-Stage International Race held in Ireland in 1952. The event, which received widespread media attention throughout the country, with thousands lining the route in towns and villages, was won by Brian Haskell of Liverpool.

Three member of the Irish international team took the next three places. The great Shay Elliot was runner-up. Billy Long (currently living in Killiney) was third and our own Kit O'Rourke was fourth. The three lads acknowledge the brilliant support which they received from Mick Byrne and Shamie Thomas. It was a thrilling moment for the thousands who lined the streets of Dublin on that glorious Sunday afternoon to see three Irishmen, Shay Elliott, Billy Long and Kit O'Rourke, leading such a renowned international field across the finishing line at Wood Quay.

For the many people from Dalkey who were in Dublin to see three great Dalkey sportsmen being part of such a successful Irish team it was a very special experience. As that great all-round sportsman Jim (Gus) Farrell said on the bus back to Dalkey it was a "rare experience, a memory we will always cherish." How right he was, it is one of my great sproting memories. Great sportsmen they truly were and they went on to give many more great performances.

Sportsmanship of a unique kind was demonstrated in a very profound way during the Bray Cycling Grand Prix in 1954. Shay Elliott was competing in his last big amateur race in Ireland before leaving to start what was a very successful professional career in France. The large crowd lining the seafront in Bray were truly willing him to victory. On the third last lap passing along the seafront in Bray, Shay and Mick Byrne were leading the field by

Liam Horner pictured here holding the prestigious Manx International Perpetual Cycling Trophy won in 1967 in a thrilling race from a top class British and European field. A dominant national and international performer during the 1960/70 era. Liam remains to this day a highly respected figure in Irish cycling circles

approximately 100 yards, having broken away on the Putland Road Hill. Shay got a puncture, the field passed them by. Mick jumped off his bike and handed it to Shay, who chased the field, battled his way, passed them out and, amidst great excitement, won a thrilling sprint to the line. Shay insisted on having Mick on the winner's podium, a great tribute to a great sportsman and a true gentleman. In 1996

Cuala Team of 1920s

Mick helped to raise over €3,000 for our club. Shamie unfortunately died at a comparatively young age but his contribution to the excitement of those years will never be forgotten.

Kit O'Rourke was certainly one of the leading cyclists in Ireland in those years. Forty-six years after holding the Irish Fifty Miles Championship and establishing national records at thirty and fifty mile time trials, he was elected best all-round veteran in 1998. In 2003, at a sprightly seventy-five years, he broke the record for over seventy year olds at ten miles, twenty-five miles and fifty miles. An outstanding athlete by any standards.

Up to a couple of years ago if one drove up the Dublin or Wicklow mountains any fine Sunday morning and you were likely to meet these "veterans" on their bikes, up to a couple of years ago, accompanied amongst others by the late great Liam Horner from Bray. Liam was Ireland's leading cyclist in the 1960's, being the first Irish amateur to win the Isle of Man International Grand Prix and many other international races in the U.K. and Europe, not to mention numerous Irish titles. Truly remarkable athletes, Liam, his wife Geraldine and family lived on Killiney Road for many years.

The greatest Dalkey swimmer was Claire Small-O'Dwyer. Claire O'Dwyer, better known in Dalkey as Claire Small, was born and reared beside Coliemore Harbour, and is one of the most remarkable sports personalities that not just Dalkey but Ireland has ever produced, By any standards, her record of success in the very competitive swimming world is truly outstanding.

For Claire, it all began at the age of fifteen when she joined the Otter Swimming Club at Dun Laoghaire Baths in 1957. The same

Kit O'Rourke on left with the Great Shay Elliot, RIP, Tostal 4 Day Race 1953.

baths that have become a disgraceful monument to urban neglect for many years. She spent numerous hours every week training and building up her strength in the treacherous currents of Dalkey Sound (the stretch of water between Dalkey Island and the mainland). She became Irish 100 yards Butterfly Champion in 1960, Irish Freestyle Champion in 1954 and 1965. A member of the team that won ten relay Irish Championships, she won the 100 yards

Leinster Championship every year between 1957 and 1970. Between these years, Claire won thirty gold medals, twenty-three silver medals and eight bronze medals in the Leinster Championships.

She retired from competitive swimming in 1970, having married Hugh O'Dwyer in 1968. They have three children: Linda, Ken and Karen, and three grandchildren. In the early 1970's, the World Masters Swimmers Association was formed. This quickly became a worldwide swimming organization, similar to the Golf Senior Tournaments. While her career in her younger days was outstanding, her new career as a masters swimmer was amazing. The following are the details:

1991 European Masters Championship in England: three gold medals, two silver medals and broke two European records.

1992 World Masters in U.S.A.: one silver medal, three bronze medals and broke two European records.

1993 European Masters Championship in Germany: five gold medals, two gold medals with the Irish relay team and broke three European records.

1994 World Masters in Montreal, Canada: one gold medal, three silver medals and two bronze medals.

1995 European Masters in Riccione, Italy: three silver medals and two bronze medals.

1996 World Masters in Sheffield, England: six gold medals and broke two world records.

1997 European Masters Championship in Prague, Czechoslovakia: four gold medals, one silver medal and broke three European records.

1999 European Masters Championship in Innsbruck, Austria: five silver medals.

2000 World Masters in Munich, Germany: two silver medals and three bronze metals.

2001 European Masters in Palma, Majorca: six gold medals and broke two world records.

2002 World Masters Championship in Christ Church, New Zealand: two gold medals, two silver medals, two bronze medals and broke two world records.

Each year from 1996 to 2002, Claire competed in the British Open Masters Championships. She won thirty-two gold, thirteen silver and two bronze medals. She is the only Irish Masters Swimmer to hold World Records and the first ever to win gold for Ireland. She represented her country at various classes over seventy times. She was so busy winning championships in so many parts of the world that it was not

P.J. Byrne, I.R.C. & Harp CC. 1924 and Dalkey Hill All Ireland Sprint Champion 1924.

until 1995, thirty-eight years after her swimming career started in Dun Laoghaire, that she decided to try to add a victory in the Dun Laoghaire Irish Times Harbour Swim to her incredible record. She entered the race in 1995 and, at fifty-three years of age, duly won it.

She says that this was a very special occasion and, following her victory, her thoughts went back to her early days in Dun Laoghaire in Blackrock Baths and the hard training in Dalkey Sound, swimming over and back to Dalkey Island. While the training conditions were by no means ideal, she trained in the cold waters with her teenage pals, some of whom continue to swim in the cold sea in Dun Laoghaire, the Forty Foot and other local swimming spots, all year round. Friends like Jennifer Cassidy, Helen O'Connor, Molly Molloy and Jane Dillon-Byrne were constant companions during her teenage years.

Other enthusiastic swimmers during these years included Jack Smith, Larry Williamson, Carol Walsh, Fergus Barron and Nicky Burke; all of whom gave her great support.

Her late parents (despite all the frights she gave them), her family, her husband Hugh

East Coast Rowing Champions 1976.
L to R: Kevin Carroll, David Cunningham,
Terence Keogh, Pat Dalton & Michael Comerford.

and her children Linda, Ken and Karen, have been particularly supportive during the second part of her career as a Masters Swimmer.

A master swimmer she truly is, Dalkey's only World Champion. Yet despite all her success, all who have known her all her life agree that she remains the gentle, unassuming and truly kind person that she was when she first started swimming forty-five years ago.

One of the most colourful characters ever to grace the sporting scene in Dalkey was the late Tom Ross, who was a leading figure in the swimming club for many years.

He was instrumental in building the changing rooms on Bulloch Pier, which still stand there today. He succeeded in persuading the management of the Australian Swimming Team, which was in London for the 1948 Olympics, to come over the Blackrock Baths for a two day gala under the banner of Dalkey Swimming Club. The Manager/Coach was a friend of his. Needless to say, the gala was a great success, with a sell-out crowd. Tom became Chairman of Dalkey United in the 1960s. He was an enthusiastic chairman for several yeas and was a great loss to Dalkey when he passed away.

One of the best amateur snooker and billiard players ever to represent Ireland was Dick Brennan. This sport was popular in Dalkey over seventy years ago. The old snooker and billiard club had its pavilion at the rear of what became 'Ma Reilly's Paper Shop', brilliantly described in some of Hugh Leonard's stories on Dalkey, including his story in this publication. Hugh, or Jack as he is known to us, has always been supportive of our club and other organisations within the town. His famous 'Da' was a member of the great Tug-o-War team referred to in this article. Snooker faded away in the pre-World War Two years but came into prominence again in 1950, with the establishment of Joe Baker's Saloon and Snooker Club over Hick's Butcher's in Castle Street. The club became a great social centre and held many epic tournaments and several exhibition games. The great Fred Davis and Horace Lindrum, both World Champions in Billiards and Snooker, appeared in these exhibition games. When talking about those years, the names of Gerry Mooney, Michael Hayde, George Ellard, Pat and Peter Heneghan, Joe Sharkey, Paddy McDonald and Eddie Hick invariably are mentioned as being amongst the best players to figure during the years when the club was so popular.

George Ellard's name is also deeply engraved in the history of Dalkey's Rowing Club, which is the oldest established club in Dalkey. It has a long and proud tradition stretching back over seventy years.

Dalkey Table Tennis Club flourished for many years. The efforts of the late Betty Wilmott and her husband 'King Larry' were wonderful. They were great servants of the club, whose greatest player was Ann Marie Reilly. Ann Marie Reilly was born and reared in Dalkey. She had a remarkable record over many years, representing her country at table tennis. The Reilly family have contributed in a very significant way to Dalkey United since its foundation, her dad, Charlie, played for the club for many years and was an excellent full-back, her brother, Paul, also played for the club and was a very strong defender for many seasons.

In 1973, at the age of seven, Ann Marie started to play table tennis in Dalkey's Table Tennis Club, Hyde Road, Dalkey. The table tennis club was run by Larry and Betty Wilmott for the next twenty years. Over one hundred children attended the club and were coached every Saturday and Sunday by Larry and Betty.

Throughout those years, the club moved to Epworth Hall on Rockford Avenue and to the Town Hall in Castle Street, Eventually the club moved back to Hyde Road, which was then the Cuala Sports Hall.

Ann Marie won her first tournament at Wayside Open, aged nine years and was number one in Leinster and Ireland in three age groups: under 12, under 14 and under

Cuala Camogie Team 1942
Back Row, *L to R: Jimmy Brown, Mollie Butler, Marua O'Loughlin, Cissie Kealy, eileen butler, May McDonald, Lilian Phelan, Greta Reilly, Paddy Butler*
Middle, *L to R: Mick Mullen (Sen), Mary Reilly, Maggie Mullen, Maggie Brown, Annie Brown, Eileen O'Loughlin, Tom Byrne*
Front, *L to R: Kathleen Phelan, Alice Reilly, Katy Mullen, Paddie Wright.*
Boys: *Martin Doran and Billy Byrne.*

17. She played at county level and for Leinster in the Inter-Provincial Championships, which were held in a different province each year. She played at this level for under 14 and under 17.

Ann Marie's first trip away was at the age of ten to Rhyl in Wales, where the Leinster squad did very well. In 1978, at the age of eleven, she represented Ireland for the first time, in the under 14 team, in the European Championships, held in Barcelona, Spain. She went on to represent Ireland on nine occasions. Between 1978 and 1983, she represented Leinster and Ireland every year, at many venues throughout the U.K. and Europe.

At the age of eighteen/nineteen, she played in some under-21 tournaments and was successful in those. She continued to play at senior level, on and off, over the next twelve years, up to the age of thirty-one.

In 1995/1996, Ann Marie represented Ireland and played in the Senior Women's British League with three other girls, two from Leinster and one from Ulster. She won Senior Leinster and Irish Championships. In the doubles tournaments, she had great successes on a number of occasions with her partner Geraldine Leonard.

We would need several pages to list the history of gaelic football, hurling and camogie. Suffice to say, the G.A.A. has played a prominent role in providing facilities for boys and girls to participate in what is such a great sport. Dalkey United were happy a few years ago to present their neighbours, Cuala, with some old framed photographs of G.A.A. teams from the 1918 to 1922 period. Many of the players in those photographs are parents, grandparents and great-grandparents of people who have been or are currently involved in sports clubs in Dalkey at the present time. Once a family becomes involved in sporting activities, the interest usually continues down through generations.

The town is indeed fortunate that the names of so many of its sons and daughters are indelibly inscribed in the history of its sporting endeavours. Indeed, the names of many who gave their time and energy to ensure that the best support and facilities are available to them will be similarly inscribed.

Undoubtedly the greatest player that Cuala ever had was the late Mick Holden, who was one of the inspirational figures in the great Dublin team that won the All Ireland Final in 1983. He was also crowned 'King of Dalkey' by the beautiful Rose of Tralee, Brenda Hyland, in 1984.

Frank Mullen

Dalkey Rugby Club 1949
Back Row: Gaff Gregan, Colie Farrell, Tommy Hughes, Pat Hickey, Joe Dunne, Cathal O'Connell, Fred Kenny, Dermot Ryder, John Byrne.
Second Row: Eddie O'Hanrahan, Crydon Schormann, Bob Thomas, Joe Keegan.
Front Row: Willie Campbell, Joe Smyth.

A Great Player - Phil Kelly

Phil Kelly was born at 4 Leslie Avenue, Dalkey on 10th July 1939. He played all his football in England after the family emigrated to Sheldon in Warwickshire in 1947. He played schoolboy football and signed for Wolverhampton Wanderers in 1958. He played for them until 1962 when he was transferred to Norwich City where he played until injury ended his career in 1967. He made a total of 131 league appearances during his short career and he also played 5 times for the Republic of Ireland gaining his first Cap: a friendly game against Wales at Dalymount Park on Wednesday, 28th September 1960.

It was the first visit of the Welsh National Team to Dublin and Wales won by 3 goals to 2.

Cliff Jones of Spurs scored 2 goals for Wales and Phil Woosnan got the third and winning goal.

Fionan Fagan scored other goals for Ireland the second from the penalty spot when Johnny Giles was taken down in the area.

His last game for Ireland was against Czechoslovakia in a World Cup Qualifying match in Prague on Sunday, 29th October 1961. The Irish team were beaten by 7 goals to 1 our heaviest defeat in our history.

The Irish team that day was Noel Dwyer (Swansea) Phil Kelly (Wolverhampton) Noel Cantwell (Man Utd) Ronnie Nolan (Shamrock Rovers) Charlie Hurley (Sunderland) Mick McGrath (Blackburn Rovers) Frank O'Neill (Shamrock Rovers) Amby Fogerty (Sunderland) Peter Fitzgerald (Chester City) Johnny Giles (Man Utd) and Joe Hegarty (Blackburn Rovers). The Captain was Noel Cantwell. He transferred from Wolves to Norwich City and after fighting against a lot of serious injuries his career ended in 1967 when he was 28 years old.

Phil, who comes to Dalkey almost every year, loves to walk around the hills and roads is a cousin of the great Peter Farrell. Jim (Gus) Farrell both of whom have passed away and Shelia Farrell who thankfully is still with us and gave so much of her life organising the girl guides and other voluntary groups in the town.

He is a true gentleman and one of Dalkeys long list of great sportsman and women.

Phil Kelly, 3rd from right in back row between Ronnie Nolan on his left and Joe Whelan on his right. John Giles is in centre of front row.

Don McClure - Dalkey Saloon

When the Angelus rings at six in Dalkey, Don McClure turns the key in the door of his wonderful barbering saloon and wends his way slowly with his small hold-all up the hill to Killiney and home. Don never went out to collect speed records. He believes the one about God making a surplus of time. For forty years, man and youth, he has been turning the key in the same lock, although in the good old days when majors were majors and real Dalkey men knew their station in life, that door was often open until ten at night. So he is the oldest trader in Dalkey.

Although his shop front in Castle Street is unique, it would never win a heritage award. Long ago the barber's pole fell down and stayed down. When John Doyle painted that shop last it was a lovely shiny red and Don McClure's was in bold black capitals. But that was a long time ago and it rained a lot in the meantime. No stranger could now pick out the name of the artist who practices within and Don has a rooted dislike to shoving up the rateable valuation with fancy frills.

As he wisely remarks, "Why waste paint putting up a name when everybody knows where I am?" And at a pound [€1.27] a skull he must be the best value in the hair trade.

The interior of the saloon is in keeping with the façade. It does not have the clinical gloss of an operating theatre. But then Don is not doing heart transplants.

There is the oil heater, a cutting from a calendar in lieu of an old master, a waiting bench and the two great chairs designed a long time ago with practicality in mind for the shave, the haircut and the shampoo.

It was Horace Porter, Woodbine smoker, one time swine farmer, but most of all barrister, who can hitch a gown like Rumpole of the Bailey, being of the landlord classes, who asked Don to set up business here. Mr. John Doyle, the incumbent had died, after a satisfying lifetime of yielding a cut-throat razor and keeping local heads respectable.

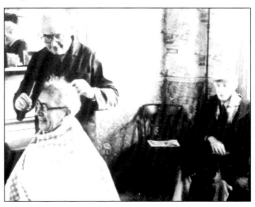

Don trims Dessie Swords hair while Ned Mullet waits patiently.

There was another barber in Dalkey then and his saloon graced the site now occupied by La Hiff Restaurant. His name was Jack FitzGerald and when he departed this life he bequeathed his barber's chair to Don. He too, like Don and John Doyle, was the best informed man in Dalkey and district; philosophers of the scissors and razors, who often prepared clients and friends for the final launching pad and mingled their own learning with that of their clients who would, from the throne in Castle Street, wrapped up to the chin in the protective toga, heavily dispense knowledge.

He is often asked how much Dalkey and his clientele have altered down forty years. He has no early recollections of BMWs tearing through windows in Castle Street. In the days when the clock over Findlaters told the time, people knocked before they came in.

In the forties he recalls times were lean. Dalkey was like Dead End Gulch. Shutters were as common as ditch water. You could have bought half the place for a song. But then nobody had a song. And none of Don's customers ever saw a bank manager at close quarters, although it was rumoured they got quietly stoned in the yacht clubs on the commission they got from flogging insurance policies. The salary they got, it was said in the barber's, wouldn't keep an arse in their trousers.

Ms Reilly's newspaper business was thriving in those years with her growing tonnage of unreturned newspapers forcing clients into a narrow channel in the shop. Don was one of the few privileged with a peep in the real back of the shop. There she showed him a perfectly equipped barber's shop all set up and ready to go. But she would not sell him a comb out of it and was tight lipped about its origins.

Those were the days of the Number 8 tram, which plunged and swayed its way to Dublin in forty minutes. Don McClure remembers it fondly. A great comforting ship of lights, particularly in winter, offering the same magic longings as the sight of a liner putting to sea.

No tits or magpies pecked the metal tops of the bottles then because milk was dispensed in a warm personal way by Jack Thomas or Bill Gibb or Purcell's from Sorrento Dairy. All hot from the cow and always a tilly for the cat. The trams ran to the door of O'Grady's tobacconists, now

The Arches. Dr Enwright had taken over the dispensary work from Dr Wright. And who knows that it was Dr Enwright from Listowel who attuned 'Our darlin' sons in the Valley of Knockanure'?

Nurse O'Connor was the midwife who lived across from where the Club stands. Then it was Murphy's and her husband Stephen, an ex-British Army man, was a good paying customer. The wife had a tongue nearly as sharp as Ma Reilly's and Don remembers she could screech the slates off a roof when yer man came home listing to port.

Yet the ladies, of the better classes that is, wore picture hats embellished with enough fruit to make a strawberry pie. Major Beatty, owner of one of the first motor boats, beckoned a finger to men on bollards in Bulloch as if he was summoning an unruly retriever. The gentry strolling on Vico Road after church on Sundays were escorted by men whose only other exercise in their later years was polishing the medals they got for polo in India or the retirement silver mug presented by the mess one sad evening after sun downers.

There was the naval lady – well, that's the way she was dressed, who strutted through the streets uttering commands in a strident voice. She is long since gone to God, and maybe remembering far off naval battles which proved the manhood of her class.

Don's clients frequented the Town Hall shows. Better than the Royal they said. You could see on the stage everybody from Mocky Duggan to Bamboozalem.

Some of the McClure customers were non-conformists. But his was a confessional, less hair-shirty than Father Creedon's. And they knew it. Even in those days it was common in Dalkey to have the resurrection before the burial and many a man came to be shaved for a wake and came out to see the corpse being wheeled into Manzor's pub, later Searson's.

Arthur Duffy of the Queen's had a red setter named 'Whiskey' and it never seemed to occur to his master, recovering from the night before in the sanctity of McClure's, why his wife was always dead on target in search of him. 'Whiskey' used to wait patiently stretched on the pavement under the barber's pole.

Pat Thunder before he sat down under the apron for his beauty treatment, requested a small service of Don, to slip out and bring him a bottle of Winter's Tale sherry. Old Con Hayes, a commercial traveller, came for a shave and a cure. Always during the Holy Hour. A Baby Power and half dozen stout. Then McClure, the comforter, would have to go up to Finlaters for a pair of duck eggs and a pound of fat cooked bacon. When this simple repast was consumed, he passed into the hands of Jimmy Byrne the hackney man who brought him home.

Spud Murphy, another Army pensions man, from The Square, insisted on hoisting the Red Flag during the Congress and a neighbour of his Joe Healy on pension day spent £8 on Baby Powers, all wrapped in pink paper. This was accomplished by trading in a food voucher. The pink paper was hung on a nail for you know what.

Not all Don's customers were so inelegant. John Joe Higginbottom, who lived at the back of the railway and was well heeled, summoned McClure to his red bricked residence when he required to be shorn. The job done, he would point to a decanter on the sideboard. His barber knew his duty and a glass of twenty years Irish Whiskey was rubbed into the back of Mr H's neck to keep away winter colds.

Shaving went out for the last time about four years ago. Only one client was left and then somebody gave him an electric razor for Christmas.

Don has met men with tough beards. The worst was Jem Delaney, an ex-tram driver, he broke an open razor on his left jaw.

Not all the men Don shaved were alive. Someone had to shave the dead. The fee always proffered was a pound and a glass of whiskey; although on one occasion a widow offered him two pounds to rescue a set of valuable false teeth from the loneliness of the grave.

In later years, Don became friendly with a lot of men who were uneasy with this unisex saloon cult. So men like Seamus Ennis, Monk Gibbon, Sean O Faolain, Flann O'Brien and Liam Redmond came to the chair for that real personal touch. And one of his oldest clients is one of the longest serving Dalkey men – Dessie Swords who tolls the bell.

Father Meagher never goes to the saloon to say the Angelus and so Don is much relieved.

He cringes at the memory of Father Creedon. This clerical gentleman used to choose just before twelve o'clock or just before six for his haircut or his chat. And then the bell would ring and in a mighty voice for a small shop he would intone the prayers: "And as sure as God, I would have Protestants or Jews or other persuasions who out of respect would have to stand up and keep the heads down".

Liam Robinson
Dalkey Festival Brochure 1985

It is in sameness that we can recognise our identity

In 1978, I wrote a note for the Dalkey United Silver Jubilee brochure. I probably used an old-fangled typewriter, which today would be as outmoded as a quill.

Then in 1982, I wrote another article in the club's yearbook and I was using an electric machine which – wonder of wonders – could store all of forty pages of text on a cassette, Technology – itself a new word – could go no further, we thought.

In 2003, another anniversary - a golden one – came and to my surprise I found myself not merely still in harness but working with a word processor – whatever next? But continuing to wish that every day had forty-eight hours in it. Looking at the front cover of the Silver Jubilee, I took note that the photograph was out of date, for there is a tram sailing down Castle Street and, what is more, it seems to be an open topped tram! Even now, however, the town has not changed much in its externals.

Look closer, the Town Hall appears to be its old self but is now our Heritage Centre: a museum and history lesson, both in one, and this could be called History without Tears. I say this immodestly, having written the text for the exhibits. And there are other changes under the old facades. Findlater's clock still ticks – or fails to tick, according to temperament – outside Super-Valu.

The newsagent's, Gemma's, which was itself the successor of Da Lundy's, where guiltily I bought my first ham sandwich (in those days you ate food, other than sweets, at home), is itself now no more. The bread shop still prospers and it too has its claim on the past, for it was once Mammy Reilly's shop, with tall, closely-packed towers of newspapers crowding almost ever inch of space, until there was room enough for only Mammy to stand in, with her customers out in the rain. And at the far end of the town, Jack Wickham, himself a Dalkey monument, has retired.

There are shops that sell paintings and another dealing in mere gewgaws. And, of course, there are restaurants of exotic kind: Chinese, Indian, Thai and Italian. The Club and Finnegan's merely look the same as they once did but inside they resemble the Tardis in Doctor Who, looking the same as ever on the outside and are vast once you enter.

Alas, not only is the No.8 tram no more but the No.8 bus has gone too – to the inexpressible grief of us all – and if the new Dalkey United yearbook had a photo on the front cover, it would show a Castle Street packed with cars, some not moving at all, others intent on mowing down imprudent walkers. "It is the bright day that brings forth the adder", Shakespeare says, "and craves wary walking." One could apply the same wag of the finger to the thousand or so motorists who infest roads designed for a score of horse-drawn carts.

If I seem to cling to the past, it is not because I am an old Josser who is on principle opposed to change. It is in sameness – a good sameness, mind – that we can recognise our identity, like meeting an old friend. Give us the good life by all means but with space enough to accommodate its trappings. Well it can be truly said of Dalkey United that it is the same, only different. It grows, it gets better, and yet it has its values as of old and continues to be its own self.

As before, I wish it well and if anyone ever makes a film about the club, I have a perfect name for it, and I pray that no one has already used it. I mean, what about Back to the Future?

Hugh Leonard
Dalkey United Golden Jubilee Book, 2003

The Dalkey Gold Rush

What inhabitant of historic Dalkey has not heard of Ettie Scott and her history, more strange than fiction.

The year 1834 is not so long gone by but this quaint burgh of the Middle Ages has a legend more fascinating than that with which, almost in our own days, this fair girl has invested 'The Town of the Seven Castles'.

In October of 1834 a piece of gossip began to be whispered about among the good people of Dalkey, which sent a thrill of excitement from one end to the other of the little community. Dalkey, I must remind the reader, was not then the stately and fashionable place that it is now.

If you would see the Dalkey of 1834, then level, in imagination, the present handsome villas and edifices, restore to it the quarry pits, and pile up all over the place the granite boulders with which the piers of Kingstown (Dunleary) now break the sweep of the Irish Sea – sprinkle the bleak and inhospitable mountains with poor quarrymen's huts, and – there, reader – that is the Dalkey which, at the date alluded to, was startled by the report that a vast quantity of gold lay hidden away under the 'Long Rock', beneath the very feet of the inhabitants, and waiting only for toiling and trustful hands to rend away its covering and seize it.

The author of the report was a young girl, familiar to everyone in the village by the name of Ettie Scott, of Honey Moor. Her father was an intelligent Scotsman, holding a subordinate command under Mr Smith, one of the contractors for Kingstown Harbour. Yet, though of so humble a station, Ettie was known as being what the Dalkey folk described as 'off the common'. She was singularly beautiful, noted for a certain romantic eccentricity of speech and action.

She was fond of reading romances and of wandering alone over the hills towards Rochestown or Shanganagh. Her disposition, though occasionally moody and always shy, was, under ordinary circumstance, affectionate and loveable.

Where it all started.

The thrilling report of gold lying concealed under Long Rock was not allowed to remain a vague 'rumour of a doubt'. The authoress of it made it ring from one end of the village to the other. Her creed had but one apostle – herself; but then, what may not be affected by one whole-hearted apostle, especially a beautiful girl?

Ettie had dreamt, or rather had 'seen in dreams', again and again, vast hoards of gold stowed away under Long Rock – a point far enough away from the quarry works actually in operation. She had not lent herself easily to the fancy. But the vision had recurred again and again. Then she had become possessed by the conviction and had spoken out, at first to her family and intimate friends and then, as these proved incredulous, to anyone that would hear.

She had a plausible theory too, by which she accounted for the presence of the treasure in such a place. The Danes, it was noted, had had Dalkey as one of their strongholds in old times. Equally well-known was their habit of hiding in the earth treasures stripped from the then munificent shrines, till there was a cargo sufficient to carry away in their ships.

Long Rock, then, had been made a hoarding-place and the battle of Clontarf had prevented the depositors from recovering their treasure.

In two days after the public and formal announcement of her mission by Ettie Scott, all Dalkey was in a craze about the hidden gold. A crowd of honest quarrymen at once pinned their faith on the girl's word and placed their brawny arms at her command.

Pat Byrne, a dairyman of the place – a most enthusiastic believer in her dreams – acted as her vicegerent. A gang of gold-seekers was formed, with a secretary and directorate, and with Ettie as supreme controller. Money was subscribed 'galore'; picks, blasting powder, crowbars and all the paraphernalia of quarry work were purchased – torches, too, which lighted up a scene worthy of the pencil of Rembrandt or the pen of Ettie Scott's illustrious namesake – an inaugural ceremony in which formal possession was taken of Long Rock by the diggers and Ettie, with dishevelled hair, repeated to them and to a vast crowd standing round in the outer darkness, her vision and her assurances.

Here was the mot d'ordre given by her, and still preserved in popular tradition: 'Work – watch - believe and be silent as the grave while working. Wait with patience – for the hidden treasure of the Dane will be surely found'.

Twelve hours, between sunset and sunrise, was the working time to which at first all were limited by the girl's mystic ordinance and never was such work done in that space by human hands. The rocks were rooted out, bored and blasted in hundred weights and tons. Many abandoned their former work and quarried altogether for the fascinating prospects of Long Rock. Those who retained their usual day labour after some time, however, added to it several hours of night work, under Ettie's direction; and the wild sea-washed rock, starred with torches and studded by the uncouth midnight toilers, was a sight to see!

It was remarked that during the whole course of the work, the Dreamer never once relaxed the solemn and impressive mien which she had assumed from the first. She usually sat upon a rock, watching the progress of the miners and holding in her hand a game-cock, the sacrifice of which was to quell a certain gnome or fairy who was to make his presence felt, if not seen, on the first exposure of the Dane's treasure. For more than a month these scenes were witnessed by the people of Dalkey and by the crowds of visitors whom curiosity attracted from Dublin; yet no gleam of the precious gold met the glance of the sweating quarrymen or the fixed gaze of the maiden seer.

The denouement of the episode, although not without great interest of its own kind, is such as we should gladly alter it, were our narrative other than a recital of facts.

By a small expenditure of ingenuity and of their medical lore, these young 'Jackeens' calculated on producing an effective substitute for the gnome who was delaying so wearily in putting in an appearance at Long Rock. For this purpose a number of black cats collected from the streets of Dublin were conveyed in a boat under cover of night to a recess at the base of Long Rock. A long line of sponges soaked with spirits of wine and turpentine was then attached to each cat's tail and the animals were rubbed all over with dry phosphorus, producing around them a ghastly halo like that which children make on their palms in bed with a damp match.

The cats were then marshalled with their heads directed up the ascent and were set off with the sponges in full blaze.

The joke had been carefully planned and executed and it was a complete success. As the gang of thirty-five miners were picking away might and main, suddenly there was an eruption of hideous spectral forms, as if from the very bowels of the mine. The horrified workers, dropping their tools, reeled back with exclamations of terror and, after a moment's petrified stare at these eerie figures, rushed away pell-mell from the spot.

Nor did they ever return to work.

The enterprise, already failing in popularity, was from that moment utterly discredited: and even when, some days after, the joke was discovered, no one was found to raise a pick again in search of the Dane's treasure.

Poor Ettie Scott died soon after, partly from the worry of this event, but, strange to say, not before she saw her prophecy in great part fulfilled. The Dublin gentle folk who had flocked to Dalkey out of curiosity were struck with the beauty of the place.

Gold did flow from the rock indeed, for, within a few months, thousands of pounds were paid to the 'aborigines' of Dalkey to purchase sites for the stately edifices and charming villas which at this day render Dalkey one of the gems of our eastern coast.

Pat Byrne's share of Long Rock was sold by him for a round sum and on it stands the present beautiful dwellings of 'Lota', 'Inniscorrig' and 'Elsinore'.

First Published J.J. Gaskin 1869
in Irish Varieties

The Way We Were

Once upon a time, when Dalkey was a much smaller community and people knew of no other way of achieving their goal other than making it happen for themselves, they did just that. Those Dalkey people who are old enough will nod nostalgically as they remember the Dalkey Pipe Band being formed and the sight of it marching through the town, resplendent in swirling kilts and sporrans, not to mention the excitement whipped up the steady beat of the drums. They will remember too the birth of the Dalkey Musical Society whose wonderful shows coaxed them from their warm firesides on dark winter evenings to the glamour and spectacle of, say, a Gilbert & Sullivan opera in the Town Hall.

The beneficiaries of all this effort might have taken it all for granted or, on the other hand, they might have marvelled at these achievements when they realised that, in the case of the Pipe Band, a premises had to be available and uniforms and instruments had to be bought. Also, in the case of the Musical Society, stage sets created and made, musicians paid, not to mention the cost of either making or hiring the theatrical costumes. How did they do it, these people of little means? Nothing drives like need, they say, but there was another ingredient, of course, and that was an indomitable community spirit and a firm belief in self-help.

So it happened that the next generation, influenced by such great people, continued to provide for the social needs of the community, old and young, and these needs inevitably included sport. Football, hurling and swimming clubs were formed, around which fundraising events were organised, bringing families together to inspire yet another generation. It is my memories of this generation that have prompted a stream of consciousness causing me to put pen to paper as a tribute to them.

At the outset, I have to hold up my hands and confess that I only married into the Dalkey community and, by old Dalkey-ite standards, would be considered a "blow-in". However, when my son joined Dalkey United AFC, I got the opportunity to prove that I was made of the "right stuff". My husband, Pat, had played for Dalkey United in his time, so between us we did what we could to support the Club and naturally, our son. Thus we found ourselves involved with other highly motivated people comprising the management and officials of the

Dalkey Pipe Band 1930
Front (l to r): Jack Nolan (Pipe Major), R. Nickolson, K.
Thomas, A. O'Rourke, K. Reilly.
Middle: James Nickolson, P. Carroll, T. Reilly, Jimmy
Byrne, Paddy Butler, Jim Byrne, J. Newbanks, K. O'Sullivan
Back: Danny Friel, Jack Wallace, Dennis O'Toole.

Club and, of course, the parents. I write this piece as a tribute to all of them.

Like the Pipe Band and the Musical Society of old, sports clubs have costs which have to be met and Dalkey United was no exception. Public/players liability

insurance, lighting and general mainte-
nance of the grounds, the building of a
clubhouse all incurred great expense and so
parents and, indeed other members of the
community, rowed in behind the
Committee with a view to raising money.
The level of support for fundraising was
very impressive, but the highlight of the
year was the annual Christmas Fair in the
Town Hall, organised with military preci-
sion by a Committee led by Frank Mullen
fundraiser extraordinaire, whose efforts on
behalf of Dalkey United continue to this
day.

*L to r: Pat O'Brien, Thea Feeney, R.I.P.,
Eamonn Feeney, R.I.P., Noreen O'Brien at the
Silver Jubilee Dinner in 1978.*

The campaign started early in November of
each year when a door-to-door leaflet drop
informed householders of the intended
date, time and venue for the sale but, more
importantly, asking for contributions of
saleable items which would be collected
throughout a week nearer to the date of the
sale. As most helpers worked during the
day, the collection had to be carried out,
door-to-door, between the hours of 7-9
p.m. on cold dark winter nights. (Yes,
there was a time when people felt safe in
their homes and still had enough trust to
open their doors to strangers after dark.)
The collectors worked in pairs, one with a
car to carry all the booty. The wives and
mothers were invaluable on this exercise,

using their shopping experience to assess
the value, shelf life and storage needs of the
items donated. These stalwarts were bred
from the progenitors of recycling, long
before the word was ever used. They were
a resourceful lot – "wilful waste made woe-
ful want" having been taught to them from
an early age. So, at the end of a busy day,
they would turn up at people's doors mask-
ing their tiredness in gleeful banter, learning the art of diplomacy as they declined
invitations to "come in for a cup of tea"
while accepting a most unsaleable item
with feigned gratitude. Promises to bake
for the Bread & Cake Stall would be elicit-
ed from contributors before they knew
what was happening.

The car would soon resemble a Jumble
Sale on wheels filled for the most part with
tinned imperishable foods, toys, books,
plants, clothing, electrical goods and general bric-a-brac which would have to be sorted at the end of each night and stored. Also
at the end of each night the collectors,
tiredness forgotten, would arrive home
with uplifting tales about "the generosity of
people".

When the big day for the Christmas Fair
dawned all the same hands would be on
deck, having worked the night before setting up and arranging stalls, the men erecting the enormous "Wheel of Fortune" centre stage, where prizes donated by local
shopkeepers and businessmen would be
raffled off to squeals of delight and disappointed groans. The Cake Stall was always
the first to be sold out, while bookworms
lingered at the Book Stall swapping stories
of "great finds" amongst the dusty and well
thumbed pages. At the Crafts Stall mothers
stood proudly over the fruits of their labour
and cast a wistful eye as the product of
many hours work was carried off by an
appreciative grateful purchaser. Children,

who would have been given a few "bob" to spend on the day, ran excitedly from stall to stall hardly believing their new found freedom of choice, while at the same time learning the hard lesson that money has a way of vanishing very quickly. But their involvement on the day taught them a second lesson – that their pleasure on the field came at a cost and that cost was met through the hard work and commitment of their families and a group of people who had the imagination and tenacity to set their Club up in the first place and, more importantly, continue to keep the ball rolling to this day.

To try and name all the people involved in the founding, funding and ongoing success of Dalkey United would be folly, as it is so easy to inadvertently omit a name thereby causing offence. However, I must make an exception in the case of Betty Doran who sadly, recently passed away. Betty not only gave enormous time to the Club's fundraising right up to last Christmas despite her serious illness but also put great effort into work on the Christmas Party of Dalkey's Old Folk, Cuala GAA Club and other voluntary groups. She will be greatly missed. May she rest in peace.

My part was small compared to the continued, ongoing efforts of others but I offer this piece as a memoir of the early days as a tribute to all those who have made Dalkey United A.F.C. the success it is today.

Betty Doran R.I.P.

Noreen O'Brien

Dalkey Church Choir 1951 with members of Dalkey Musical Society
Front: Hynes, Walsh, P. Curran, J. Byrne, D. Byrne, Fr. Maloney, M. Quinn, P. Lamb, T. Conlon, J. O'Sullivan, S. Davis.
2nd Row: L. Donlon, D. O'Sullivan, S. Hayden, J. Friel, J. Dunne, P. Lacy, N. Mahoney, V. Dunphy, J. Maher, R.I.P.
3rd Row: Cunningham, J. McGuirk, L. Doran, F. Quinn, R. Byrne, J. Hammond, M. Carroll, D. Friel, M. Kavanagh, P.
Lambe, P. Dunne,
4th Row: D. McGuirk, P. Brown, P. Magee, C. Byrne, D. McWilliams, D. Kenny, H. Magee, R.I.P., W. Murphy, R.I.P., J. Kelly.
Back Row: L. Dowd, R.I.P., J. Morris. R.I.P., F. Quirke, T. Byrne, G. McDonald, J. Kenna, B. Byrne.

Dalkey Swimming Club

Dalkey Swimming Club was founded in 1941 by Tom Ross (who worked for many years in Albright and Wilson, Dun Laoghaire). Tom was a man with a social conscience and his aim was to make swimming available to children (initially boys) from every part of the community in Dalkey. The annual subscription was very low and could be paid by instalments. After a few years Tom Ross famously remarked at a Committee meeting that the Club should also embrace ladies and a ladies and girls section was formed.

In the early days, Tom was assisted by J.J. Kennedy, about whom it was said (by himself) that the only time he passed by the Scotch House on Dublin quays, was when he swam past in the Liffey swim. Other founder-members were Jim Byrne of Castlepark Lodge (Hon. Handicapper) and Jimmy McGlone (Hon. Starter).

The Club got under way at Bulloch Harbour, where points races were held weekly in the summer, on Sunday mornings or Tuesday

Johnny Nieland, Jed Byrne, A. O'Rourke, Tom Kelly, M. Fanning, T. Duggan, T. Kelly, Marty Mooney, V. Smyth, Jimmy Burns, T. Duggan, Phil Hickey, J. Seaver, Pat O'Rourke, Tex Reilly, Gus Smyth, P. Cullen, Joe Smyth

evenings, depending on the tide. Races were over 25, 33 and 50 yards, but swimmers had to be able to cover twice the distance in order to return to the "platform".

The Club's best years were in the 40s, 50s and 60s. An annual swimming and diving gala was held at Bulloch and the Club sent teams to the other clubs which were active in the area – among them Sandycove, Otter, Bray and Bray Cove. Longer swims were organised – Sandycove Harbour to Bulloch; White Rock to the Ramparts and Dalkey Island to Coliemore Harbour. A

shelter was built on the pier at Bulloch, after considerable fund-raising efforts. Many children were taught how to swim, Michael Fanning teaching the boys and Maurish Duggan the girls.

Michael Fanning was also the champion swimmer of the Club for many years. His name appears as winner on the Ross Perpetual Challenge Cup for the years 1941, 1942, 1943. That was a handicapped race (other winners – Joe Quirke in 1948 and Dermot O'Sullivan in 1959) but Michael also regularly won the scratch races at various distances. Other notable performers were Morty Mooney, Mick Stopford and Tom Healy in the early years and later on Peter Murray, Gus and Vincent Smyth and Paddy Cullen. Jimmy Duggan regularly won the Pringle Cup presented by the Headmaster of Castlepark School "for graceful diving". For the ladies, Valerie Murray and Nuala McColl were regular winners at swimming, and Maurish Duggan and Marie McGilton at diving.

The Club's water-polo team was very successful in the 1950s. Starting in 1951 in the Youths under 18 league, the team under Fergus Smyth's captaincy quickly progressed, successively winning the Novices, 3rd and 2nd Divisions, to get into the Leinster Senior League. They did very well in that league, until in 1957 half of the small squad emigrated (most, happily, later returned). Apart from Fergus and his brother Vincent, the members of this successful squad were Pat and Frank O'Rourke, Pat Byrne, John (Tony) Duggan, Tony Kelly, Paddy Cullen and Michael Fanning.

The Club was financed through modest subscriptions and continuous fund raising – dances in the Town Hall and Cliff Castle Hotel, jumble sales, raffles, whist drives in the council chamber of the Town Hall – even a midnight matinée (!) in the old Astoria. An active committee was key – and included Tom Ross, Jimmy McGilton, Paddy and Maurish Duggan, Phil Hickey, Gus Farrell, Michael Fanning and many others. They were greatly assisted by an older generation who provided venues for meetings and other support – like Mr and Mrs. Murray of Epworth.

During the winter, the Club transformed itself into a Dramatic Society and in the 1950s put on a number of plays (O'Casey, Lennox Robinson and others) in the Town Hall. Most of them were very funny, whatever the intentions of the authors

After the 60s, the Club declined, perhaps because more indoor swimming facilities were becoming available but also because of increased pollution at Bulloch. It was formally wound up in 1999 when some of the old committee members called a special meeting to dispose of some unexpected assets – a prize bond in the Club's name and long forgotten won £ 100. What to do? The Club was dissolved and the money given to the Parish Council.

A final word. This writer recently gave what could be found of surviving records of the Club (some minute books and miscellaneous papers) to the National Archives, where future generations will be able to learn something of the social activities of this community in the mid-20th Century. If anybody out there has other club records, they could be associated with the material now in the archives. And, by the way, does anybody have the minute books of the Dalkey Literary, Historical and Debating Society, which was very successful in the 1940s and 1950s?

Andy O'Rourke
a former Hon. Sec.

It Should Be Nurtured & Valued By All of Us

The little boy with the flaming red hair, short pants and freckles looked up at the kind barber. The boy had a dilemma and the barber was the only person in the whole world who could solve it.

Of course your hair will go black.

Really Don?

Of course son, it'll be black . . . like the Virginian's. I've seen it all before. Happened to your Grandad. And your Dad before he lost it all!

Just rub a bit of this hair oil in and you'll be jet black.

When? How long will it take?

What age are you now son?

Six, Don.

By the time you're ten.

Gift!

Now pop up here on the bench.

What will it be Dessie - A Terry McDermot perm?

No way and I'm not Dessie, I'm David, my Dad's Dessie.

Just the usual, short back and sides Don. Just tidy the young fella up laughed my Dad as he glanced up from the sports pages before returning to the Irish Independent.

My earliest memories of Castle Street were Saturday mornings in Don McClure's barber shop with my father. Don cut my Grandad's hair, my Dad's hair and now he was shearing mine.

Most importantly, everyone knew that Don McClure understood hair and his magic hair oil could turn hair black so that no one would ever call me rusty, redser or jaffa-head again. I'd be free to play marbles like everyone else without being slagged. Don was not just a barber, he was my saviour; through Don I would be redeemed.

As usual, when I peeked into the shop, Don put on his best Scottish accent, which he called Scothed, gently mocking my Grandfather who came from Scotland to Dalkey just after The Rising. According to Don, both my Grandparents - Suzie and Bobby - had "shocking Scotch accents".

Robert McWilliams didn't come to Dalkey alone; he came with aunties Bella, Sadie and Ruby, a demobbed Uncle Jim joined them after the war and countless others whose grainy faces peered out of an old photo on our mantelpiece. I was afraid of these faces from the past. They had that slightly grotesque, antique look of the 1920's.

Don McClure

Our tribe - the McWilliams, Nicholsons and Friels - moved en masse from Glasgow - leaving reasonably prosperous Scotland for Dalkey which was so far removed from the commerce of Dublin City that the first Dalkey United played, not in the Dublin but in the Wicklow League. My grandad had a sign writing shop on Castle Street where the Chinese restaurant is now but apparently Grandad had one fatal flaw as a businessman - he didn't like asking people for money! Over the years we must have figured out a way to survive because the McWilliams, Nicholsons and Friels are all still here.

Back then, Don had a plank that he'd carefully placed across the arms of the barber's chair so the young fella could sit up and see himself in the yellowed mirror. I loved the barber, the smell of hair oil, the wireless in the corner, the copies of the Daily Express and the football talk. I felt like this was my entry into the world of men. And Don conferred status on me by giving me the brush to sweep up the hair.

Saturday morning was always the same; sweeping up men's hair, pushing it into piles and getting twenty Sweet Afton for Dad, while himself and Don gossiped and laughed, talking about exotic creatures like Hard Chaws and Teddy Boys and go-boys interspersed with names like Cosgrave and Richie Ryan. These were men's things, things that I'd grown to understand. but at the time, this little freckly redhead just dreamed of black hair as names like Ned Mullet, the "Blue" Byrne, the "Wha" Byrne, "Harboy" Hill and Coco Brown were thrown about. Peter Farrell - the local hero and captain of Ireland - was always mentioned, as were Shamrock Rovers who at that stage were still packing out Milltown. As far as I was concerned, these names were the mysterious hieroglyphics of my father's past, people Dad grew up with - his gang.

I later found out that they were far older than him but at that young age, all the men seemed the same age, they were old, big, wore suits and smoked.

In the summer of 1953, Dad and a few friends decided that they'd had enough of kicking ball up on the quarry. It was time to put Dalkey on the football map. Dalkey United was born. They played for two seasons in Sallynoggin and then Dad wrote to the then Taoiseach, WT Cosgrave, secured Hyde Road for the club, and then with a loan of fifty quid from my great Aunt Bella for the gear, Dalkey United took to the park in the famed black and white strip.

According to Don, the first Dalkey United eleven played like Ajax, total football, free flowing and unbeatable. As Ajax with Cruyff and Neeskins and Jonny Rep were dominating Europe in the mid 1970s, nothing in the world would be more glamorous. Over the years, Dalkey United has become part of my family. Amidst legitimate charges of nepotism, I captained the under 12s, manfully assisted by my cousin Peter O'Brien, whose father Pat was one of my father's first eleven. In our five subsequent glorious seasons, we won nothing, but travelling in hope all over Dublin. Unlike today, back then parents didn't go to see games, so transport was always a hassle. One summer's evening against the mighty Everett Celtic in Bray, we set the world record for twelve kids squashed into my father's Hillman Hunter, faces shoved up against the back window, fellas screaming in agony at the bottom of the human pile that was the back seat. But we made it back to Hyde Road, victorious and defiant.

We were a deceptively slow outfit of kick and rush merchants but thanks to huge selfless efforts by the whole town we got to besmirch the name of Irish football far beyond the Borough when Dalkey United toured Germany in 1979 and again in 1981. Back then when Germany was rich, Ireland was poor, be-mulleted and displayed a frightening weakness for pixie boots. We might have been destitute but we had Paul McGrath, who was playing for the "big lads". The men whispered respectfully

David McWilliams with David Hennessey and Barry Mullen, Three former team mates.

when they talked about Paul's gifts. Paul went on to Old Trafford and the rest of us got as far as the 'Noggin and a trial with Joey's if we were really special.

Despite our evident shortcomings on the pitch, my Dad persisted as manager, talking tactics and strategy at half time, scouring the Evening Herald for results and fixtures and spending hours on the phone with officious league secretaries. My mother too suffered for United. She was driven demented washing filthy kit for "other people's children". but this is what volunteerism is all about. It is about sacrifice. Volunteers give their time freely so that other people can enjoy life a little bit better. Dalkey United was all about these people who turn up selflessly in all weathers to give something back. Volunteers create community and sustain communities. I am very proud of my Dad for founding the club. When he and his friends secured Hyde Road from the Corporation and - in a

move of unusual generosity between the codes - gave the top half of the field to Cuala, they created something of real value. Communities are sensitive ecosystems: they can be built and they can also be destroyed. Thousands of local lads have played for Dalkey and will continue to do so in the future. But clubs are like gardens: they need constant attention and care, which in turn, means time and money.

At a time when many complain of the atrophy of society, where we don't have time for each other, when our quality of life is being eroded, clubs like Dalkey United build bonds between people. We have shared experiences. A sports club is the gelling agent of community and Dalkey United is as much part of the town's personality as the Island or Coliemore. The unpaid volunteers who work behind the scenes make the place tick, they are the ultimate model citizens.

In a world that increasingly values the individual over the group, clubs like Dalkey United are beacons of sanity. It should be nurtured and valued by all of us. It binds us, roots us and generates a common, local experience that will never be forgotten.

In November of last year, I spoke at an economics conference in New York aimed at strengthening ties between Ireland and Irish America. The hall was packed with politicians, journalists and business people. After my talk all the chat was about exchange rates, budget deficits, venture capitalists and credit crunch.

"How's Dessie?" enquired a tall gentleman, whom I had never set eyes on before. "I'm your cousin", said Jim Friel, my father's cousin who had left Dalkey for Long Island in 1958. Within minutes we were chatting away and Jim was back in Dalkey in the 1950s, taking the bus to watch Dalkey United, telling me of the excitement in the town on a Friday night as the team selectors met in the Town Hall to announce the first eleven for the weekend's game.

He captured the tension and expectation of young lads who were dying for the honour of togging out in the black and white as they waited for their name to be called.

His face lit up as he told me of the sheer elation he felt when, that evening the Town Hall, he heard my Dad announcing the final vacancy, "Right half: Jimmy Friel".

Here was a man who served as a US marine during the Cuban crisis gushing about Dalkey United in a bar on 8th Avenue.

"I was so thrilled, I could have kissed Des McWilliams that night in 1955. I was recognised, I was going to play for Dalkey. It was our team."

David McWilliams

"The Bomber"

On the night of June 22nd 1937 Joe Louis took the World Heavyweight Boxing Championship title from James J. Bradock at Comiskey Park in Chicago and became known throughout the world as the Brown Bomber.

On the same night, or thereabouts given the time differential, my brother Jack Robinson took a black eye and a bloody nose from a callow youth at a pub called Hynes's on Lower Mount Street in Dublin City and became known throughout that same city as The Bomber. Joe Louis, in the fullness of time, may have lost his title but The Bomber Robinson carried his for life.

A Title Deed

It is fair to assume that General Hideki Tojo, and the Japanese Military High Command didn't calculate the odds concerning The Bomber's contribution to the Axis war effort, when they attacked Pearl Harbour, on December 7th 1941.

The effect of this historical shot in the back on The Bomber, at the time, was minimal, and only caused offence to my brother Paddy when, while walking back to the office from lunch, on the following day they bumped into Kashio Ishihashi. This urbane, amiable man, first secretary of the Japanese Embassy in Dublin had become friendly with the family in the previous summer when we were holidaying, and playing golf at Rosslare in County Wexford.

The Bomber offered him a cigarette while Paddy mumbled something about it being a pity that Japan was now at war with the U.S.A.

Producing a pack of Lucky Strike, a popular American brand Ishihashi laughed, 'Thank you no, but perhaps you would like to smoke one of mine.'

'And grinning like the damned ape he was.' Paddy put it later, then added, 'It is not on, you know: Bloody poor show.'

Feelings ran high, in neutral Ireland during the war years.

A year or so later there came a call from the decidedly, un-neutral North of Ireland. If there was going to be a second front in Europe; that is to say if the Allies were going to land armies on the German occupied continent, they would have to start thinking about billeting American personnel up there.

Jack Robinson

Pop saw this as an ideal opportunity to broaden the horizons of his eldest son, and suggested that he apply for the job of clerk of works on a scheme, facilitating this endeavour, in Omagh, County Tyrone.

The Bomber applied, got the job, and was off, lickety-split. He soon found himself working on the construction of an airfield under the supervision of the Royal Engineers, commanded by a man called

Colonel Andrews, who took a great liking to him. He worked there for about six months before he got a weekend off, and an opportunity to come home to see us.

To Mazie, for the first, and, maybe the only time, he was the welcomed, prodigal son returning, festooned, as he was, with unheard of luxuries, in a time of severe rationing; Hershey bars, chewing gum, spam, frankfurters, bourbon, rye, nylons. He gave me a G.I. forage cap with a brass U.S. badge, that I kept for years.

With all these free goodies, especially the nylons, she almost forgave him the Billy-goat incident.

'Marvellous up there in the North,' he told us. 'The Yanks will give you anythin' you want. They're all flyin' boys at the moment, comin' across the Atlantic in flyin' fortresses, and liberators, packed with stuff. Great leather jackets, fur lined flyin'-boots; I thought I had, meself, a pair after one of the big yokes crashed on landin', but one of them had a foot in it. Disgustin'!

In the meantime Colonel Andrews had written to Pop claiming it was his opinion that the Bomber was officer material, and if Pop approved he would recommend him for a commission in the Royal Engineers.

Mazie, while for it in theory, went a bit emotional, because, of three of her brothers who held commissions in the British Forces in World War One, only one returned and, he had been so severely damaged by mustard gas he was no longer any use to them.

Andrews, in fact, took the trouble to come to Dublin to see Pop, The Bomber was duly packed off to Preston, Lancashire as a trainee officer-cadet in the Royal Engineers.

The Colonel had done his job well. He had recruited another soldier for the war effort.

Little did he know what he was foisting on the Empire.

Nine months later, at home, in the early morning, the telephone rang. It was the Harbour Master at Dun Laoghaire.

'We have your son down here Mr. Robinson. Sending him home in an ambulance is out of the question. Can you come down and collect him?'

For someone imparting tragic news of an injured warrior returning from the wars, the man's tone left much to be desired'.

'We hadn't heard, is he badly injured?' Pop, taken unawares asked anxiously'.

'He will be if you don't get down here quickly,' The Harbour Master said rudely. 'He's drunk.'

Adrian O'Connor-Glynn wrote to Mazie from Leeds. Adrian was the brother whose health had been destroyed by mustard gas. After the war he married his nurse, who was now running her own nursing home in Leeds.

Dear Kathleen

Jack turned up here a month ago to visit us. Naturally we invited him to stay when he told us he was on leave. When I realised he had no intention of returning to his barracks he admitted he was AWOL and there was no way I could persuade him to return to his unit. I am sure you realise that in wartime there are harsh penalties imposed on people who shelter deserters.

After much argument he agreed to go home to Ireland so I gave him money for his fare, and a few quid spending money.

> *I hope he has arrived safely.*
> *Look after him.*
> *Your brother,*
> *Adrian.*

In reply to a letter Pop sent to Colonel Andrews, the Colonel explained, that on an exercise a few months back, The Bomber had been instructed to blow up a bridge, which carried vital supplies between two important military establishments.

The name of the game was to set the charges at night, undetected, place a red flag on the bridge indicating that the charges had been detonated, and that the bridge was therefore kaput.

It would seem The Bomber went the whole hog.

The bridge was kaput.

Which is why The Bomber fled.

'Well he's justified his title by the deed,' my brother Peter laughed. 'What else would a bomber do but blow things up.'

Regis Robinson
Brother of "The Bomber"

The Blue Flash

At four o'clock in the morning precisely on March 12th 1946, all the windows but one in Inniscorrig imploded, partition walls became concave, the Waterford glass chandelier in the drawing room crashed to the floor and the glass in the conservatory transferred itself, in sharp shards, on to the front lawn in a vicious sward two feet deep.

At precisely one minute past the hour Mazie exploded from her bedroom, her lightly slippered feet secure from the shattered glass like the bare feet of a Hindu Fakir walking on hot coals; also by the intense inward conviction that she alone knew the cause of the catastrophe.

'What has that drunken bugger done now?' she bellowed into the darkness, for no lights worked. Standing on the upstairs landing overlooking the inner hall, oblivious of the frigid East wind that now screamed through the house, she was experiencing tortured thoughts of The Bomber entertaining drunken louts in the basement kitchen, helping themselves to her food and keeping themselves snug by burning her fuel. It filled her mind to the exclusion of anything else; but she was afraid to go downstairs in the dark to see.'

Pop arrived at her at her side with Anne, then Peter, Paddy and Auntie Glad, finally The Bomber with a torch.

'What have you done this time, you fool,' she yelled.

But he had done nothing. A floating mine from some unswept minefield in the Irish Sea had detached itself from its mooring cable and, helped by an East wind, brought a belated hint of Hitler's late war to the citizens of Dalkey Rock just thirty yards to the North West of the Inniscorrig Harbour. The damage done locally was considerable and in the village, half a mile away, every shop front window was shattered. Even Ma Reilly, a wizened crone, who was thought to keep her money in her enormous, unwashed bouffant hair-do and slept on a mountain of old newspapers at night, was blown out of her repose onto the tramlines. Unhurt, apart from understandable upset, the incident is not as dreadful as it might seem, for she lived her life on four square feet of floor space just inside the door of her shop, the rest of which was packed, from around the four walls to the ceiling, with newspapers dating back to the turn of the century.

The miraculous qualities that had protected the Mazie's feet had by now disappeared and in an exceptional moment of tranquillity she quietly announced that there was glass everywhere and it was bloody cold and everybody should put on stout shoes and their warmest clothes.

The Bomber carried her back to her bedroom and found her shoes and warm clothes.

'What are we going to do, Johnny?' she asked Pop who had produced Aladdin Paraffin lamps.

'I'll make a cup of tea?' Auntie Glad suggested.

'We'll have a ball of malt,' Pop said, sensibly.

'It's terrible,' said The Bomber to Paddy. 'We'd better go out and see if there are any casualties.'

'Good show! I'll get my flashlight and I had better put on my uniform.'

Paddy had joined Maritime Inscription, a naval reserve, in 1941 when he had come home after five years of study at the Architectural Association at Bedford Square in London. He was full of expressions like, 'Wizard', 'Bang on', 'Chuck it', 'Good Show', and such like, which to me had been the very stuff of adventure during the time of the Battle of Britain when that was the much used slang of The Royal Air Force.

'Get your shaggin' things then and I'll go ahead over to see how Jerry is.'

Jerry Killeen, who lived across the road, was a very Christian man who worked for the Electricity Supply Board and was given to performing good works. He was married to a charming wife and had two delightful children, who later in life became a priest and a nurse respectively. Jerry had earned The Bomber's eternal respect and gratitude when, in 1938 he had suffered a particularly nasty succession of carbuncles and Jerry, with the hands of the healer he was and a little help from boiling water, cotton wool and a lancing needle, had driven out the causative malignity.

In the beam of The Bomber's torchlight, Jerry' his wife and two children stood in the roadway in their night attire frozen with shock and with the East wind.

'I think the roof is gone. Shine up your torch, and let's take a look.'

The beam showed rafters bereft of slates.

'Glory be to God,' Jerry whispered. 'Was it a bomb?'

'There was a hell of an explosion. I think it was a mine.'

Old Reynolds, who had a filling station and a car supply shop in Dalkey lived nearby in a house on the corner of a lane that ran up to join the road at the top of Victoria Hill, appeared carrying a flashlight. He was a plump man of few words with a florid face and red hair and just stood by them emitting a continuous whistle of astonishment.

'How is your place?' asked The Bomber.

'A1,' he replied, not prepared for a lengthy discourse.

'But you were right in line of the blast through the entrance arch to Cliff?'

Cliff was Cliff Castle Hotel that stood on the same granite outcrop as Inniscorrig. It had been, in medieval times, one of the seven castles of Dalkey; armed late-Norman keeps, used as warehouses when Dalkey Sound was the only, reasonable deepwater anchorage convenient to Dublin City.

All of a sudden there were torches and headlights all over the location. Sirens sounding, fire engine bells clanging, uniformed Local Defence boys shouting. They hadn't trained for five years in what was called in neutral Ireland during the late war, 'The Emergency'(The war years were cllled "The Emergency" in Ireland, 1939-1945), to be done out of enjoying the only emergency that had occurred in Dalkey in that five years.

'Feckin' eejits,' The Bomber muttered and headed through the arch in the high wall that fronted the hotel.

Mrs. Murphy from Wicklow, who had three pretty daughters and a sinewy husband with hooded eyes that clicked when he blinked, owned the hotel. Flo Rodgers, a chunky, good-looking North of England woman managed it. Albert, a silver haired jowled man with a potbelly and sallow skin was the headwaiter. He, for reasons nobody could figure out, had come to Ireland from Argentina. To find a head-waiter from Argentina working in a hotel in Dalkey at that time would have had the same shock value, then as discovering an Extra-Terrestrial in your bathtub, might today.

They stood there in the hallway in their nightwear, all in various stages of shock, some of the old hand, residents complaining about the inconvenience of it all.

There was Whelan the solicitor, who frequently lodged strenuous objections to our

Pop swimming bare in the sea at seven o'clock in the morning all year round. It must have taken an effort of great determination on the part of this protector of public morals to get out of his bed early enough to find an eyrie in one of the towers: the only places from which it was possible to witness this disgraceful exhibition. There was Mrs. Macardle, a Spanish lady separated from her husband, a famous Dublin surgeon, and her daughter Margarite. There was Dick Pugh, a jovial Welshman and boozing pal of The Bomber, whom most took for granted was a British spy, and a scattering of casual residents.

Flo Rodgers, efficient as ever, had produced Aladdin lamps and checked out the place for damage. It seemed the medieval structure built to withstand siege engines had stood up well to a twentieth century blast. There were no signs of destruction to be found.

The Bomber looked around. 'Inniscorrig is a feckin' shambles. Fascinatin', all the same, how this place didn't get a scratch.'

They all stared at him with varying degrees of comprehension.

'Are you all right, bach?' Dick Pugh asked.

'I'm grand, nobody was hurt in there, but I think there are going to be a lot of casualties brought in and I reckon you should open the bar. After all there'll be a need for brandy and stuff like that. The local defence boys are outside and the Red Cross will be here soon, not to mention the regular army. We should set up some sort of thing in the bar.'

Nobody thought to ask him why the dining room or the ballroom might have been better.

'To tell the truth, I wouldn't mind somethin' meself to settle the nerves.'

'Good idea,' Dick Pugh said.

'Open the bar.' Mrs. Murphy said.

Much later and after a huge crush of officials, newspapermen, army officers had taken to settling their nerves too; The Bomber serenaded a temporarily absent Miss. Rodgers in a way that had become his custom.

> Flo, Flo, I love you so,
> Specially in your nightie.
> When the moonlight flits
> Across your tits,
> Oh Jesus Christ Almighty.

Later still when brother Paddy arrived, his naval uniform soiled with effort, he met The Bomber being carried out on a stretcher by two Red Cross orderlies.

'We thought we'd take him home, poor man,' they told him.

As a fact of confirmable veracity, nobody suffered injury in the blast …. The Bomber had become its only casualty.

Later that day The Evening Herald reported that a Mr. Jack Robinson, when asked about his experiences in the explosion said: 'I saw a blue flash.'

* There was one incident in 1941 when a German Bomber, at dusk, mistaking a steam locomotive, stopped at Sandycove railway station, for the Holyhead/Dun Laoghaire Mail Boat that was docking in the harbour half a mile away. It dropped two small bombs and flew on over Dalkey where the regular army had a searchlight unit on top of a hill in Sorrento Park. Our heroes there turned on the searchlight and got a quick burst of Spandau for their trouble.

Everybody survived, including the Heinkel, which was impervious to lights.

Regis Robinson
Brother of "The Bomber"

The Bomber's Christmas Turkey

He loved the booze, did The Bomber. Pop said that there was never a circumstance, be it sad or glad, that The Bomber could not find an excuse to go into a pub.

'The Bomber is celebrating,' he'd say.

All his adult life The Bomber celebrated about ten hours in twenty-four but then , none of the family were exactly slouches when it came to enjoying refreshments. Even Pop who was, for the most part, an abstemious man.

At Christmas time, during the Second World War, when everything was scarce, rationed or hard to find, The Bomber was celebrating in the Queen's Pub in Dalkey. In those days it was a shambolic dive of a place owned by an alcoholic who'd only allow in boozers whom he considered to be professional drinkers, especially at Christmas time when there was an awful lot of amateurs about. It would appear that at some waning stage of the bonhomie,' a fella, as the Bomber used always call people he couldn't remember after a good night, lumbered him with a live turkey in a sack. The idea of bringing home a live turkey struck him as bang on, disregarding the fact that Pop was in partnership in a business with a man called Matt McCabe who controlled both the fish and poultry supply business in the whole of the city. So if there was a shortage of anything at home, most certainly it was not one of turkeys.

He said afterwards that he found himself sitting in the basement kitchen with a placid turkey, possibly asleep, in the sack and he didn't know what to do. He knew that he would have to kill it, but the idea of cutting off its head or wringing its neck didn't appeal to him. He said he dozed off a bit but soon awakened with a start.......
He'd had a brainwave. Quietly, so as not to arouse the sleeping house, he climbed the stairs up to the bathroom found the medicine chest, took it back down to the kitchen and found what he wanted, a bottle of chloroform.

'It was easy. I soaked an old cloth in the stuff, carefully untied chord around the neck of the sack without disturbing the bird and, like a flash, tied the cloth around the head and poured more of the stuff on to make sure of killin' it. After about ten minutes when I reckoned it was dead I took it out of the sack, plucked it, had a couple of bottles of stout and then for some reason fell asleep at the table.'

At about five o'clock in the morning all of us asleep in the bedrooms on the first floor were wrenched out of our dreams by the sound of Mazie's, hysterical anguish.

'That bugger, is drunk again and he has a crowd of bowsies down in the kitchen. Don't tell your father, it'll ruin Christmas.' When ruining Christmas had been a speciality for years, this was unfair, but Pop, up there in his bedroom in the tower would remain remote and uninformed as long as somebody could persuade her to stop screeching like a banshee.

Somebody did and in our crumpled night attire we all trooped down to see the fun.

'That's a good imitation of a turkey gobble,' I said.

Crashing around the kitchen, The Bomber, all sixteen stone of him in a miasma of feathers, unable to maintain a perfect balance, pursued a stark naked turkey, gobbling too, in hysterical anguish.

'Interestin' all the same, I'd of thought the

shaggin' stuff woulda killed it.' Was how he explained his carry on afterwards.

Later in the day, it was Christmas Eve, The Mazie cautioned us all again not to tell Pop for fear of ruining Christmas. Then at Christmas dinner the following afternoon she told him, herself and there was a row as big as a fight.

It was usually like that at Christmas. In fact it was like that all the time.

Regis Robinson

The Bombers house "Inniscorrig" in Dalkey.

Sea Mine Exploded - a more serious account

The Second World War lasted from 1939 to 1945. Ireland was officially neutral and this period was referred to as "The Emergency".

However, we did not totally escape unscathed – Bombs were dropped on Dublin North Strand Area, by German bombers, causing many deaths and serious injuries. Allegedly, these were intended for Liverpool on the other side of the Irish Sea. Another bomb was dropped near Sandycove railway station which was possibly intended for the Dun Laoghaire/Holyhead Mailboat Pier.

A number of floating sea mines were placed in the Irish Sea by German U-Boats and some came ashore on the beaches and rocks along the coast – many exploded harmlessly or were defused by the Irish Army.

The war had finished, when on Tuesday March 12th 1945 at 3.30 a.m., a sea mine exploded on the rocks on Coliemore Road near the Cliff Castle Hotel causing extensive damage to over 200 houses and shops in the Dalkey/Killiney area. The sound of the blast was heard in Clontarf on the other side of Dublin Bay.

Fortunately, the explosion happened in the middle of the night when most people were in bed, so there were no really serious injuries. The streets of Dalkey were strewn with flying glass from shop windows, etc., which would have certainly caused many physical injuries to shoppers and other pedestrians.

A massive clean-up operation was eventually put in place and hopefully most of the glass was recycled . . .

Dail Eireann discussed the matter and decided to allot the magnificent sum of 15,000 Irish Pounds, which they felt, should be sufficient to compensate people adequately for their losses!

In those post war days clear glass was difficult to obtain, so most windows were fitted with frosted glass, so one could not properly see out, so for a period it was like living in a large bathroom. Eventually, we got back to normal living . . .

Tommy Kelly

The Wright Stuff

On Saturday night last a relatively unknown group of retired footballers held their 35th annual reunion in Woodbrook Golf Club. Dalkey based, "Dr. Wrights' Ould Boys" first came together in December 1953 to recall memories of their playing days which were brought to an end when their pitch was acquired by builders.

Their first dinner was held in the old Beechwood Golf Club and was used to celebrate the return of Everton F.C. to the English First Division under the captaincy of "Dr. Wright's" most famous son, Peter Farrell. Signed by Everton in the summer of 1946 Peter broke his ankle while playing for his old club – the culprit being none other than his first cousin,

Paddy Glynn. Peter was well aware that his new employers would not take kindly to such an incident and so a cover-up was hastily put together.

The most important person in the scheme was the only genuine doctor in the group, Eamonn Kenny. He carried out the treatment and informed Everton that their new signing from Ireland had unfortunately broken his ankle while playing a genteel game of tennis.

national, Tommy Eglinton. The friendship continues to the present day and 'Eggo' is the only outsider to have infiltrated the ranks of the 'ould boys.' Others who made the grade include 'Harry Harboy' Hill who turned out for Huddersfield Town, Paddy 'Twig' Fox who played with Bohemians and Joe Smith of Bray Unknowns.

But at that first reunion the group had no name and it was to be two or three years before a suitable one was found. The credit goes to Kay Glynn, wife of secretary for life, Paddy. She quite sensibly interrupted one of the many informal meetings in her house to suggest that as they had played on "Dr. Wright's field," she could see no reason for not using the name "Dr. Wright's Ould Boys."

L to R, Seated: Pat Kavanagh, Peter Farrell, Paddy Glynn, Dr. Eamonn Kenny, President, Jim (Gus) Farrell, Tony Fox.
Standing: John Byrne, Jimmy Duggan, Des McWilliams, Mick Fanning, Frank Mullen, Mick Keogh, Jimmy Seavers, Jim Dunne, John (Champ) Phelan, Jack Kelly, Kevin McDermott, Paddy Fox, George Stirling, Viv Agar, Des Blair

Up until the mid-seventies the 'doctors' had no permanent venue but for the past twelve years Woodbrook Golf Club have played host and are well aware of their lack of any real medical prowess.

The cover story held up, despite a few close shaves, and Peter went on to enjoy a very successful career in England. Peter's great friend in those days was another Irish inter-

This has not always been the case; however, and on one occasion the guests were referred to as doctors by the staff all evening.

In the early days the 'doctors' provided their own party pieces for entertainment. Now, says Paddy Glynn, "we are most sophisticated and employ the services of a pianist but to keep with tradition the party pieces are still an important part of the evening."

If someone misses the re-union the offender is 'dropped' for the following year. Paddy points out though that ' this threat has yet to be carried out as the culprit normally gate-crashes the reunion, ignoring the suspension."

Sadly, this year, there will be a number of faces missing – Joe Quirke,
Des Comerford and Paddy 'Mocy' Duggan have gone to their eternal reward.

The 'ould boys' were the forerunners of Dalkey United F.C. and there is a link between them with regard to two of the most famous moments in Irish soccer history.

In 1949 when Ireland became the first foreign side to beat England on their own soil, Peter Farrell was a prominent member of that team.

Last June, 33 years later, another Dalkey footballer, Paul McGrath, played on the Irish team which recorded an equally historic 1-0 victory over England in Stuttgart. It is a fact that goes largely unnoticed due to the claims by ex-St. Patrick Athletic manager, Charlie Walker, that Paul was his prodigy. The correct version is that Paul was earmarked by Manchester United for a career in English football long before he went to the League of Ireland for a year's experience at a higher standard.

Editors Note: *Dr. Wrights Field was the area between Carysfort and Church Road where the Bungalows are now built.*

Barry Mullen
Southside, 16th November, 1998

Dalkey Man Remembered in Antarctica

Down through history, people consistently have been attracted to the challenge of exploring distant lands and, indeed, in more recent times, distant planets. Journeys to the Arctic and Antarctic have been undertaken for close on three hundred years. Many books have been written outlining the courage and determination of these men and their expeditions which often brought tragic results when they died in these vast, snow-covered wastelands. Some have been very interesting; others have been lacking in detail and not very extensively researched. No such criticism could be made in relation to two publications written in recent years by Michael Smith and Frank Nugent, and published by The Collins Press, Cork. For those remotely interested in the subject, both books make very compelling reading. Smith, in his book 'An Unsung Hero', gives the most comprehensive account about the incredible courage of Tom Crean, who was born and reared in Annascaul, Tralee, Co. Kerry. He made three trips to the Antarctic, returned to Ireland, and worked in his pub in Annascaul until he died in 1939. Tom's descendants run the premises to this day as a bar and restaurant, with lots of artefacts and souvenirs of his historic journeys on displays.

Statue of Tom Crean with "South Pole Inn" in background in Annascaul, Co. Kerry.

Frank Nugent is a very experienced explorer and mountaineer. He has journeyed along the paths of famous men such as Shackleton, Crean, and others. In his book, 'Seek the Frozen Lands', he has written an excellent account of the exploits of many Irishmen who went on those dangerous journeys since the early years of the 19th century. Among such men is one Hartley T Ferrar, who was born at 3 Grosvenor Place (off Sorrento Road), Dalkey on 28th January 1879. He graduated as a geologist at Cambridge University. Having been reared in Dalkey, he was a great oarsman, and he joined the expedition to the South Pole on the ship 'Discovery', which sailed from England on 6th August 1901. Captain Scott was the leader, determined to be the first to reach the Pole.

The late Michael Byrne with Stephen Roche

Ferrar was accompanied on the journey by two other remarkable explorers, Ernest Shackleton, who led another expedition in 1914, and Tom Crean. His geological findings establish that, at one time, parts of the Antarctic had been warm enough to grow trees and plants. For his success, there is now a glacier in Antarctica named the Ferrar Glacier. He became a renowned geologist and he married and settled in New Zealand, where he received an honorary doctorate, one of several honours paid to him by a number of different countries. He died in 1932 in New Zealand, where he is buried. A Dalkey man whose courage and achievements have been almost lost in the mists of time.

Michael Byrne
formerly of Sorrento Cycling Club

Gunger Jem Hammond
– The Last Of The Dalkey Hobblers

James Hammond, if you can find somebody to call him by that name, is the last of the Dalkey hobblers. For generations, his people have been seafarers and those who returned to coastal waters became hobblers or inherited the skills of this hazardous pilotage trade, which was practised before radar and echo sounding apparatus made navigation easier than it was for St Brendan and his crew, who lit fires on whales' backs. Irish country people use the term hobble to describe a rope on a horse's fetlocks to restrict its movements.

To men of the Hammond family, hobbling meant standing up in an open boat to row by pushing rather than pulling the oars. On the east coast, hobblers operated from Ringsend, Dun Laoghaire and Dalkey. The hobblers of Arklow dealt mainly with sailing ships. Their job was to pick up ocean going ships on their way to the port of destination and lead them to moorings - and they had no radios in those days. Crews could set out from three or four ports in all weathers and row, sometimes with the help of a lug sail, to "capture" a vessel. Only one crew would get paid and that was the first one to get a hook over the side of the vessel. The other crews got nothing.

The living depended on local knowledge of tides, wind variations, rocks, sandbanks and currents. A mistake cost many a man his life.

Captain Alan Bestic lived in Dalkey. He survived the sinking of the Leinster and the bombing of the Isolde and he is on record as saying that the most skilful and dangerous occupation he witnessed at sea was that of the hobbler.

To Gunger Hammond, otherwise known as Jem, and described as James only by tax gatherers, hobbling was a job he was designed to do since he fell out of the cradle. The name Gunger came about a long, long time ago because there were two Jacks

in the family and one of them went to sea in a German ship called "Gunger" and to prevent confusion one of the Jacks was inflicted with the nickname. The present holders, senior and junior, are very proud of the inheritance and would never want to waste a postage stamp to change it by deed poll.

Willie Murray with Gunger Hammond Senior and "Oats" Nolan

Gunger Senior's father had another nickname. He was called the Man With The Funny Hat. When there was a crane at the harbour for the use of the coastguards, who lived in the granite cottages up the hill, the Da wore a uniform cap to demonstrate his office as minder of the crane. He lived to be a great age and passed on the lore of the coast. He was around when Captain Hutchinson was an old man and although he was a nipper, he remembered the tales of Hutchinson's heroism. The Captain, who was virtually founder of the lifeboat service on the coast, lived in the house that is attached to Bulloch Castle. He was also Master of the Quarries at Bulloch and later harbour master at Dun Laoghaire. In his time, there were still a few artillery men in charge of the battery on Dalkey Island, as if Napoleon was still beating on the brazen doors of the Empire. Hutchinson had saved a ship's crew from the rocks at Sandycove in an easterly gale and lost an eye when a hawser whip-lashed when he was rescuing a vessel going down against a breakwater at Kingstown.

The Hammond family were aware that the Irish Sea and the coast around Dalkey suffered more gales annually than the Bay of Biscay - in term of frequency, not in terms of ferocity. Down the centuries, Dublin Bay was recognised as a hazard for sailing ships in easterly gales when, in nautical terms, its shoreline became a dangerous lee shore.

In Jem Hammond's grandfather's time, fifteen vessels were wrecked in a single night in Dublin Bay and it was another easterly gale, in 1807, that wrecked the troop transports, Rochdale and Prince of Wales, near Seapoint with a loss of 380 lives, filled the graveyard at Booterstown and led to the outcry which resulted in the East Pier being built.

No hobblers were ever lost out of Dalkey but in the early Twenties, three men were lost out of Tom Millar's Dun Laoghaire boat. An easterly wind was blowing and the boat was cut in two by a steamer. In the Forties, three of the Shortalls, also from Dun Laoghaire, were lost when they were returning from the Port of Dublin, having tied up a vessel at her moorings.

There were four hobblers' boats at Dun Laoghaire: Pudgy May's Dun Leary, Matt Shortall's Jealous Of Me. The Hughes' big blue skiff and the smaller boat of Tom Millar. The Hammond's boat was the Lizzie. She was a stoutly built skiff, twenty-two feet long, with a shifting lug sail which could be used on the stern, the bow or amidships. There was seventeen square yards of canvas and at most she carried a crew of four.

When a ship was sighted, the hobblers took off to intercept her in a grim race when the losers got nothing. Not only had the hobblers to be expert oarsmen but they had to have a man who was skilful with the hook. The hook was at the end of about thirty fathoms of rope attached to a scaffolding pole. When the hobblers drew alongside the vessel they hooked her in the scubbards and were carried along like a parasite fish to the Port of Dublin and there was always the danger of being sucked into the propellers.

Depending on the size of the ship, the fee for getting the ropes ashore and mooring it varied from £5 to thirty shillings for a small vessel. Even in those days when the money was shared, it was not an inducement to early retirement and Gunger Hammond remembers times when they were two or three nights at sea waiting for a ship that had been delayed. On such occasions, lighthouse keepers would give them pots of tea.

Then, as now, who you knew was as important as what you knew and the Dalkey hobblers had friends – locals of course, who worked in the Port of Dublin and kept them informed of the movement of shipping. The Hammond family had a less dangerous way of supplementing their income than avoiding propellers and the antics of threshing sharks chasing herring shoals.

They exported goats from Dalkey Island. In the Twenties, there were forty or fifty goats on the Island. Mrs. Emily Hammond owned about twenty of these and they bred away to their heart's content and needed no herder to mind them. The puck goat had a wicked manner and looked after all his ladies.

After the breeding season, a Belgian steamer would call to Dalkey, the City of Ghent or the City of Antwerp. They would blow in the Sound and the Hammonds would round up the goats and row them to the steamers. The Belgians, the locals said, would eat any bloody thing. They paid ten shillings an animal.

Gunger Hammond often had to shy away from the ferocity of the puck goat but only once as a hobbler did he fear the ferocity of a ship's captain. That was the night they got their hook into a strange ship whose skipper was not familiar with the ways of Dublin Bay, so he leaned over the side waving a cutlass and threatened to split any damned pirate who clambered aboard.

Liam Robinson
King of Dalkey Festival Brochure,
July 1988

The Fishermen of Coliemore

Witten by Mr. Michael Fanning (circa 1927).
Mr. Fanning was the grandfather of the famous
Dalkey swimmer, Michael Fanning.

I sat on a seat
with composure complete,
while the sea bird around me
did soar
dressed downy in white,
flying on with delight
by the harbour of old
Coliemore.

I looked towards the South
where the Sound has its mouth
and the Island displays a green
shore
'tis a picture most sweet
to view from this seat
by the harbour of old
Coliemore.

The Muglins so grand
where the Cormorants stand
to rest when their diving
strength's wore
to the left as you be
looking out to the sea
by the harbour of old
Coliemore.

Howth's lovely to view
'yond the waves rippling blue
and the steamers whose loud
whistle's roar
with ships in full sail
scudding on in the gale
by the harbour of old
Coliemore.

The fishermen there,
none can compare,
from young men to men, that are
hoar.
They are always found kind,
with a good natured mind,
by the harbour of old
Coliemore.

Billy Smith with love full,
and Jack called the gull,
Mike Hammond as brave as
a boar
Dick Archibold so free
and the good Murrays three
all lived round the old
Coliemore

May blessings come down
on these men of renown
who live by the line, net,
and oar
and may they rear up
a breed
who will ever succeed
in my wish by the old
Coliemore.

Getting Lost in Dalkey

The day long ago, I was in the only pub in Ventry (this was before the advent of Paudie O'Shea) when the door opened and, not surprisingly, somebody came in.

The somebody was a certain John Kavanagh, better known as Sean a'Chota, brother of Kruger and famous in his own right.

He had been caught in a blizzard on his way from Dunquin to Dingle and when he had finished shaking the snow off himself, he said in mellifluent Gaelic: "'Twas the worst journey since Scott went to the South pole."

On the Tuesday evening of last week, I too experienced an odyssey that left me a sadder if not wiser man. Listen my children and you shall hear.

It all began so smoothly that what eventually happened made the story seem like a romantic novel in reverse.

You know what I mean: in such a novel the hero battles through awesome trials and tribulations but comes into safe harbour in the last chapter – my experience was just the opposite.

The purpose of the journey could hardly have been more innocent: I was on the way to the Soccer Writers' Annual Banquet.

And I was looking forward to having a drink with Alfie Hale and swapping Cork jokes with Paul O'Donovan and exchanging snarls with Jack Charlton.

And so, in high humour, I set out for my first rendezvous: Dublin too has commuters.

I suppose I had always known it but not until that evening did I realise it.

There they were with their leather briefcases and their laundered suits – I could hardly believe that I was in Dublin. This strange feeling grew when I got on board the green train. It was so clean. Surely I wasn't in Ireland? And when it moved smoothly away, the sense of strangeness was rather accentuated.

Dublin 2, seen from the train, seemed part of a foreign city. Could those two corner pubs really be O'Neill's and The Trinity Inn? Of course they were – but suddenly in T.S. Eliot's words they seemed strange.

And my first-ever train journey came back

Castle St. 1946, hard to get lost then!

to me. I was about twelve and we were going to a football game in Tralee. I had often gone there on my rusty bicycle and knew every bush and tree on the road – but now this was a journey into the unknown. We passed through land so unfamiliar that it was a relief to see the outskirts of Tralee – I had feared the train was on the wrong line.

There was no such fear on my first voyage on the DART: every station had a clear signboard. And I got a childish thrill as the train roared under the west stand and drew up at Landsdowne Road. And now I believed that I had an inkling of how people felt as they came by train to the International games. Surely the train journey heightens the excitement. Usually I travel to Lansdowne Road on foot – to see how the ducks are doing in the canal and to sample the atmosphere in Andy Ryan's and Searson's. Now I make a mental note that some day I will come to a big game on the DART. And then the train glides off to Sydney Parade, a station which to me seems the essence of Victorian Dublin. And it brings back echoes of James Joyce and 'A Painful Case'. And not far away is the lovely ground where Monkstown Rugby Club runs their godly race. Soon we are in the suburbs and you can see houses from the back marina. And on we go past Scotsman's Bay – by now the train has shed most of its passengers. And soon I see Bray Head and the Two Sugar Loaves and I experience another dart – but this time in the stomach: journey's end is near.

And I disembark at Killiney, feeling rather proud of my adventure. Across the road is The Killiney Court Hotel. And I wonder why the Soccer Writers' Association haven't arranged their banquet for so convenient a place. And I ask the friendly young man in the ticket office to tell me the way to the Killiney Castle. He looks at me in amazement but his brain is in top gear: a city bound train is about to depart; he shouts at the driver to wait – and almost lifts me on board.

Not Worried

And all the while he is explaining to me that I should have got out at Dalkey – the hotel is only a few minutes' walk from there.

I am not unduly worried: time is very much on my side. And so I journey to Dalkey and on the way I envy two lads fishing below on the shore. And soon I disembark again. I can see nobody from whom I might seek directions – but am not perturbed: after all, the hotel is only a few minutes away. And so I set out on the last leg of the journey – or so I thought: before the journey's end I was almost on my last legs. I assumed too that from its name it would be easy to see: I assumed wrongly. And there followed a peregrination that probably took a few years off my life. The banquet was to start at eight; it was now about half past six – and so I had time playing for me. That was about the only ally I had. Should you ever get lost in Dalkey, you'll be very lost. I walked for miles; when I found myself almost back at Dalkey Railway station, I turned around. Why didn't I ask someone the way? There was nobody to ask. This is not the kind of territory where you'll see a man sitting on a wall, smoking his pipe, and hoping that somebody will seek directions. In Dalkey you can walk for mile after mile and not see a public house or a public phone or a public lavatory – believe me, it is alarming country. Until that evening I had never understood the implication of a house 'standing on its own ground'. Almost every house seemed to be a fortress: it would take a wild leap of the imagination to visualise someone knocking on a door and asking for the loan of a cup of sugar. Do not misunderstand me: Dalkey is probably a marvellous place to live – but it presents a hard face to the world. And I must confess that I found the names of some of the houses exceedingly sweet. I will refrain from giving examples. I struggled on and on, hoping that on some turn of the road The Castle might appear – and the only evidence I saw of human life were some exceedingly unfriendly dogs. At last

I came on a decent man collecting letters from a post box – and before he drove away in his little green van, he gave me general instructions. I walked for about two miles and met another decent man out strolling with his dog. The dog was decent too. And so armed with particular instructions I took a short cut through a quarry and to – the kind that I could never be. And there was an aroma rather different from that associated with Mulligan's of Poolbeg Street. Here was a symphony compounded of brandy and cigars and after-shave lotion and the kind of perfume that thinking men purchase for their lady-friends – those thinking men who happen to be very wealthy. I could overhear snatches of the talk – and, believe me, it wasn't about the prospects of Laois or even of Monaghan in the National League.

And as I cowered in my corner and gazed in awe at these sons and daughters of the brave new Ireland, I felt like a second-class mouse peeping through a hole at a purr of fat cats. I took my beating – but there was more to come. Where were the soccer writers? Where were Charlie and Brendan and Tom and Noel and Peter and their beloved brethren? Slowly the truth dawned – I had come to the wrong hotel. The beano was in Killiney Court. I was too ashamed to go there – it was now almost nine. And as I journeyed back to the city, I knew how Napoleon felt on the retreat from Moscow. And that is the unadorned story of why I didn't have a drink with Alfie Hale or swap Cork jokes with Paul O'Donovan or exchange snarls with Jack Charlton.

Con Houlihan (Evening Press)
Festival Brochure 1990

The Great Survivor

One of Dalkey's best known and most loved characters is Paddy Carroll, who lives on Hyde Road. On 6th May 2008, he celebrated his 91st birthday and at the time of writing he remains very active. One of the foremost authorities on flowers and gardens, he owned Saval Park Nurseries in Dalkey for many years.

Paddy's life story is unique by any standards. He was a formidable footballer, a member of the great Workman's Club team in Dun Laoghaire, which won so many honours in the 1930s, including the treble in the 1937/38 season. That year, they won the Leinster Junior Cup, the Athletic Union League cup and the League Championship.

That great team included Michael McDonald and Christy Kelly. Michael's nephew, Jimmy McDonald, played for Dalkey United for many years during the 1950s and 1960s. He was a leading scorer and won many honours with the club. Christy's son, Joe, gave many years of great service to our club. Joe won representative honours with the Republic of Ireland and was picked in our greatest ever squad in our Golden Jubilee Year.

Paddy Carroll

Paddy's life nearly ended prematurely in two successive incidents, one courtesy of Adolf Hitler and the other at the hands of a bus. On 21st December 1941, at 4:45pm, he was cycling home to his residence at Summerhill, near Sandycove Railway Station. The Second World War was raging across Europe. Hitler and his feared air force were bombing practically at will.

Paddy takes up the story: "I was within a short distance of my home. The blackout was in force. I heard the unmistakable sound of German bombers. We were so used to hearing them. On their nightly bombing raids over Britain and Northern Ireland, they would fly up from the English Channel and cross over the Irish Sea, up over the coast, to bomb the cities of Liverpool, Birmingham, Manchester, Glasgow and others. Some nights they would hit Belfast. After a time we could hear them flying back overhead. The sound would be different after they unloaded their bombs."

He goes on: "Somehow, I realised that a plane was flying lower than usual. I thought it was the start of what everyone called 'The Invasion'. I distinctly heard the whistling sound of a bomb falling. I jumped off the bike and ran along the footpath. Suddenly, there was a terrible explosion. I was blown up in the air and I landed on soft ground, which was a garden. I was then showered with clay, muck and stones from the large crater on the road.

I lay for a few moments to collect my nerves and then I shook off the rubble that was covering me. I stood up, discovered that I could walk, and decided to make my way on foot to St. Michael's Hospital. There was nobody around. Everyone stayed in the shops and houses, where they thought they were safe.

I was passing HCR Chemist in Upper George's Street when a woman pulled me into the shop. They cleaned me and I was amazed to find I was not injured and had no cuts.

When people started moving around again, I decided to walk home. As I got near the crater, I saw a large number of LDF (Local Defence Forces) and ARP (Air Raid Patrol) men digging with shovels. I asked a woman what they were digging for. Father John O'Shea from Glasthule was saying prayers.

The woman said they had found a bicycle belonging to a young lad called Carroll in the crater and they were digging for him. I told the woman that I was the fellow they were looking for. She started to feel ill and they brought me inside to my house. I was in a bit of shock for a few days but I was okay. I was very lucky. The story was all over the papers. I was playing football a week after Christmas."

He was not so lucky later. On "Little Christmas", 6th January 1942, Paddy was cycling over to Deansgrange to visit relatives' graves with his girlfriend Cissy McDonnell, from Corrig Road, Dalkey, later his wife for nearly sixty years, who has sadly passed away.

"Cissy and I were cycling over near Kill Avenue, going towards Baker's Corner. It was a holiday and there were patches of ice on the roadways.

There was a bus coming against us and it started skidding around the road. It crashed into me and, once again, I went into flight. This time, however, I landed on the roadway.

I was taken to Monkstown Hospital. I don't remember much about it until I arrived in the ambulance in the hospital. I was a few weeks in the hospital and was attending it for several months because of the injuries I received. Cissy was very upset. I thought a few weeks later how funny it was that Hitler's bomb did little harm to me but the bus kept me out of football for the rest of the season and out of work for months.

The one great thing was I had no lasting injuries and I had nearly sixty years of happy married life with Cissy. I have lovely children, grandchildren and friends. I enjoyed a swim in Sandycove or in the Forty Foot up to last year and if I don't feel like walking down and back, one of my family, who give me so much love and attention, drive me. I have the sport on TV and I walk up the town. I hope to continue to enjoy life for some years yet.

I am lucky that Hitler or the bus did not bring an end to it for me all those years ago. Thank God!"

Frank Mullen

Crowning of the King of Dalkey – A Long Tradition

It is eight years since most of the subjects of the kingdom of Dalkey met their King. On a wet November day, John O'Donovan, journalist and presenter of the RTÉ radio programme 'Dear Sir or Madam' was crowned 'King John the Good'. That was on the Feast of St. Begnet, 12th November 1975. Afterwards selected guests who had the price of the banquet sat down to a feed of roast lamb and sherry trifle in the Coliemore Hotel: all except King John because he was a tee-total vegetarian, not one of the usual marks of roy-

alty. His Royal Cellarer and Vintner, Jack Carvill, is still thriving and has a busy off-licence premises in Camden Street, Dublin. Frank M. Flanagan, the self-styled Recorder of Dalkey and the man who led the fight to prevent the closure of the Dalkey railway line, revived the Coronation Ceremony in modern times.

Norman Judd from Killiney was King before John and took it upon himself, as they say, to adopt a boar's head on a white background as his Royal pennant. On a cruise in the South Pacific, he had let it be known to the chief purser that he was the King of Dalkey and his pennant was flown for a day in honour of his presence until someone on the bridge copped himself on.

Noel Purcell was King before that again and right regal he looked with that beard which made him a tiny fortune in movies. In his Coronation speech, King Noel decreed that the publicans of Dalkey would reduce the price of the pint by a penny. But then, as now, the Dalkey publican had the poor mouth and things rested so.

Down the years, twenty knee-breeched courtiers in 18th century costume attended the King of Dalkey on Coronation Day. In latter times, the costumes were hired from a theatrical costumiers in Dublin and few of the attendants knew of the origin of the ceremony. It was a bit of gas and a day's

license to get locked without feeling any guilt.

One of Dalkeys most famous Kings Noel Purcell crowned in 1945

The full title is impressive:
'King of Dalkey, Emperor of the Muglins, Prince of the Holy Island of Magee, Baron of Bulloch, Seigneur of Sandycove, Defender of the Faith and Respector of All Others, Elector of Lambay and Ireland's Eye, and Sovereign of the Most Illustrious Order of the Lobster and Periwinkle'.

The Freemen of Dalkey inherited the right to elect this King through the boredom of young bloods back in the Dublin of 1787. They formed a club into which they roped wits, writers, poets and thinkers.

The summoned Pimlico Parliament – named after a district in the Liberties area – and from an Assembly Room there they hurled broadsides at the country's humbug and the pomposity of Dublin Castle and its hacks.

Thomas Moore wrote verses for them and John Phillpot Curran, the lawyer who defended many United Irishmen and was father of Sarah Curran, was one of their most pungent journalists.

In the meshes of their rebellious net, these wags had caught one Stephen Armitage, pawnbroker and printer, who was probably bored with pledges and typefaces. It was certainly well known that he did not love the establishment.

So in 1791, they sounded the most daring note of all. They proclaimed Armitage … "King Stephen the First, King of Dalkey, Emperor of the Muglins …" … for no particular reason at all except to take a poke at accepted standards and the fawning over royalty.

There can be pitfalls in this Kingship business as Stephen the First discovered. He unwittingly incurred the wrath of the Royal (British) Navy. When his barge on a starboard tack to Dalkey passed a man o'war, he ordered that a cannon be fired in friendly salute. The naval captain, who knew his Dublin and may have pawned a thing or two with Stephen, dipped his colours and shot off a twenty-one gun salute. But that was far from being the end of it. Questions were asked in the House of Commons in London.

"Why did a captain of the Royal Navy salute and pay homage on the high seas to enemies and disrespectors of the King?" The Captain was relieved of his command. Stephen himself fell foul of an authority greater than his own.

When he permitted one of his nobles to publish a proclamation claiming himself legally entitled to import 10,000 hogsheads duty free, the noble was summoned before the Lord Chancellor. This is the recorded dialogue.

Chancellor: "Pray what title is this you insist on carrying?"

"I am the Duke of Muglins."

"And what post do you claim to hold under the Government?"

"Chief Commissioner of the Revenue, Sir."

"What are your emoluments in right of that office?"

"I am allowed to import 10,000 hogsheads duty free."

"Hogsheads of what, pray?"

"Of salt water, my lord."

So the case was thrown out. But the downfall of Stephen the First came when he allowed the United Irishmen to infiltrate his Court. They popularised the ideas of the French Revolution and many of the broadsheets were printed at the royal (Liberty Style) press. So the officers of the law (Dublin Castle style) proscribed Pimlico Parliament and Stephen's crown was put into permanent hock.

Liam Robinson
Festival Brochure 1983

A New Dawn

The Dawning of a New Millenium by Eric Luke of the Irish Times showing the sunrise over Dalkey Island on 1st January 2000. By kind permission Eric Luke and Irish Times.

Ged and Paule Pierse.
Ged is Life President of Dalkey United Football Club

A Groud of Managers of Dalkey United Football Teams
Back l to r: Rupert Westrup, Tim Galvin, John Thorne, Tim Rafferty, Niall Coleman,
Colin Beecham, Jim Kerr
Front: Joe McKendry, Donal Norton, Wesley Curran, Michael O'Hara

Future Stars of Irish Football Dalkey Utd and Tongai of Springmakealy Colts, Celbridge, 2008.
Back: Evan Lossov, Keanu Shogbamimu, Mana Singh, Shawndale Shogbamimu, Abolaji Adefabi,
Gradi L. Dodo Conor Thorne, Mattie Rafferty, Declan Thorne, Harry Swords, Luke Bennett, Saul Wyse,
Eoin Cooney, Conor Doherty
Front: Dylan Colgan Killian McMahon, Ademoa Adefabi, David Ibrahim, Ciara McFarland,
Roisin Glasheen, Finn Howley, Mark Byrnes, James Wogan, David Flood, Tim Ibrahim

Under 8E 2007-08
Back l to r:Colin Beecham, Barry Mullen
Middle Row: Oisín O'Hanlon, Luis Faria, Donal McMahon, Cian Mullen, Harry Clarke, Amy Mullen and Jennifer Sheeran
Front Row: Eoin Beecham, Tito Henry, Timmy Holland, Adam Sheeran and Luke O'Hara

Under 8B 2007-08
Charlie Proctor-Quigley, Hugh Black, Matthew Simons, Conor O'Donnell, Patrick Whelan, Peter Collis, Max Airey, Rua McGlone, Celt Stephenson, Conor O'Sullivan, Harry
Manager: Anthony Quigley

Under 10D 2007-08
Back l to r: Karl Lawless, Paul Kirwan
Middle Row: Tarik Carrigy, Mark Synott, Ben McDonald, Declan O'Sullivan, Ben Cassidy
Front Row: Luc Healy, Joel McEvoy, Peter Lyons, Oliver Noonan, Brian Kirwan

Under 9D 2007-08
Back l to r: Peter Wyse, John Thorne, Tim Rafferty, Colin Byrnes
Middle Row: Conor Doherty, Mattie Rafferty, Calum Ramsey, Dougie Burns, Luke Bennett, Saul Wyse, David Flood
Front Row: Eoin O'Reilly, Mark Byrnes, Declan Thorne, James Dugan, Conor Thorne, James Cronin

Under 9A 2007-08
Back Row: Donal Norton, Neil O'Donoghue
Standing l to r: Liam Keaney Ian O'Kelly, Chris Dorsey, Jonas Serry, Ted O'Donoghue, Jonah Byrne
Kneeling: Joe McIntyre, Zola Henry, Declan Norton, Conor Curley, Sean Ballance
Missing: Nathan Johns, Cian Ryan

Under 9B 2007-08
Back l to r: Philip Bayfield, Julian Connolly, Michael O'Hara, Ref. Willie Davenport
Middle Row: Ross Meaney, Rory Murphy, Cian Caffrey, Jack Bayfield, Cian Reilly, Andrew Bodley
Front Row: Eoghan Clarke, Daniel O'Hara, Simon Rochford, Alex Connolly, Claire O'Reilly
Missing: John Bodley (Coach), Charlie Fitzgerald

Dalkey United U12 2003/04, the team went on to win the Sth. Dublin League and Cup in 2005
Back Row: Dave Hennessy, Sean Reynolds, Jack Danaher, Eoin Black, Michael Healy,
Robert Thorne, Conor Galvin.
Front: Rory McIntyre, Asile Algripy, Daniel Edwards, Andreas Olsson, Conor Healy,
Rob Heffernan, Tim Galvin

Big Mick McDonnell helping to deliver the late
Faye Redmond to inspect a guard of honour at
Tug-o-War Championship.

Steve Dalton loyal servant of St. Laurences Club
Castle Street, Dalkey which was founded in 1886 and
still continues to prosper today.

Dalkey Flowers which is managed by Vivienne Lush (Totterdell)
The Totterdell family have been trading in Dalkey for over 60 years.

Dalkey Island Swim 2008

Conor Galvin, winner of the Dalkey Island Swim 2008 in a record time pictured with Fred Espey on left
who finished fourth and Frank Mullen, Conor's grandad, who finished the swim in twelfth place.

Leabharlanna Poibli Chathair Bhaile Átha Cliath
Dublin City Public Libraries

*Vinny McMahon with his late mam and dad
Phil and Hugh.*

King Jim, 1983 with Johnny McEvoy

Members of the Royal Court in 1983, Tim Ryan and Larry Wilmott.

Dalkey United Academy 2007

Helmut Sundermann, Peter MacNulty, Chris Boyle, Cedric Wampach, Martin McGannon, Roberto Costanza

Adam Russell	Ciaran Crozier	Georgie McCarthy	Niamh O'Hara
Adam Wilson	Conor Murphy-Rogers	Jack Flynn	Oliver McGannon
Alex Cameron	Cormac Moore	Jack Skakie	Ross O'Neill
Aran Moore	David Austin	Jessica Austin	Ross McCabe
Benjamin More O'Ferrall	Dylan Jameson	Josh Filgas	Sam Elliott
Billy Soden-Murphy	Eve Harvey-Graham	Kai Jordan	Sam O'Neill
Caetano Considine Esquiual Faria	Finn Sundermann	Luca Costanza	Sam Roberts
Cal McWilliams	Finn Vella-Murphy	Luke Hamond	Sean Gul
Charlie Cullen	Fionn McArdle	Matthew Jungmann	Sean Comiskey
Charlie McCarthy	Geoffrey Fenelon	Matthew Garvey	Tom MacNulty
			Will Boyle

Captains of Four League Chapionships 2006/07
L to R: Pablo Schofield U.16, Charlie Connolly U9, Cian Caffrey U8, Chris Farrell Senior Team.
The first time Dalkey United ever won four League Championships in the same season.

The late Frank O'Rourke and his wife Gisela.
Frank was Vice-President of Dalkey United in 1979 when he organised the sponsorship of the
clubs first trip to Wattenscheid, Germany. He was well known in rugby circles having
played for Bective Rangers R.F.C. and was manager of the Wolfhounds rugby team.
He died on 13th November 2007 R.I.P.

Ellen Mullen and Cathy Tucker on the way back from boating trip off the Cork coast, 2007.

Where are they now!
Dalkey Harold Boys School 1989-90.

Happy grandchildren, Christmas morning 2007.
L to R: Caoimhe, Amy, Conor, Cian, baby Niamh sitting on Katie's knee and Ellie

Joint Manager Ken Nugent   *Joint Manager Niall Coleman*

Dalkey United U16 Premier League Champions 2007

Mary Coyle who has taken great care of St. Patrick's Square Garden, Dalkey.
Mary continues on the tradition of tending the garden started initially by the late Jimmy McClure, a pictur-esque oassis in the middle of Dalkey.

King Finbar with Santa Claus while Fergie Brien peacefully awaits his little Christmas Gift from Santa.

Two of Dalkeys well known stalwarts Dymphna Redmond with husband Willie.
Dymphna has given many years of her life in voluntary work serving on Dalkey Community Council, and
helping in organising the Ladies Club, Girl Guides and Church Choir.

Dublin County Champions 1991

Back Row: Colm O'Leary, John Sullivan, Paul Nolan, Mick O'Shea, Mick Morrissey, John Treacy (Capt.), Mick Holden R.I.P., Marting Dempsey.
Front: Colman O'Driscoil, Karl Shutte, Martin Walace, Damian Byren, Colm O'Giolláin, Brendan Ryan R.I.P., Vinny Holden. Mascot: Dan Holden

Discussing old sporting memories.
L to R: Liam Cooke, Tony Walsh, Kevin Smith, Paddy Egan

Leinster Senior League Division 1A
Champions 2006/07

Back: Tim Galvin, Ray Dolan, Vinny McMahon, Paddy Egan, Patrick Montgomery, Graham Lawlor, Thomas Gough, Fergus Martin, James Dixon, Craig Britton, Chris Farrell, Ian Britton, Stephen Martin, Lee Archibald, David Jordan, William Dunne, Barry Mullen.
Front: Jonaton Kavanage, Brian Burgess, Frank Mullen (Chairman), Matt Britton (Manager), Ged Pierse (President) Graham O'Hanlon, Jason Egan, Ross Britton, Peter Borza (Vice_Chairman).

King Frank off on Cruise of Kingdom 1985 with Dun Laoghaire RNLI
L to R: Joe Lawless 2nd Cox, Damian Offer, Queen of the Sea, King Frank, Miss Dalkey Island, Billy Scully, Tony Molloy, Eric Offer (Cox), Tony Drumond and Joe Wildes.

The Big Wheel on Dalkey Hill

Throughout the years that Dun Laoghaire Harbour was being built there was a large wheel on top of "The Flags" on Dalkey Hill. It was used to lower the bogeys, each carrying three ton of granite to the metals and onto Dun Laoghaire. This painting of the wheel, showing Dublin Bay and Howth Head in the background is the work of Anne Porter, the great great grandmother of Eileen Porter, whose son Michael Goode is seen below holding the historic piece.
Photographs taken by Stephen Crozier.

Some Interesting Details About Dalkey

1171 A.D.
Murtough when co-operating with one Rory O'Connor to besiege Dublin encamped with his forces in Dalkey.

1358 A.D.
Dalkey had its own dignitaries as can be gathered by an order issued by Edward III that, 'The Provost and Bailiffs of the Town of Dalkey are commanded to allow the Master of a Spanish Ship arrested by them to depart'. There is no record of what response, if any, was made.

1386 A.D.
Philip De Courtney, First Lord Deputy of Ireland, landed in Dalkey.

1610 A.D.
With the Liffey practically uncharted and its waters often nearly lapping the walls of Trinity College, the 'Sound of Dalkey' was recognised as the port of Dublin.

1787 A.D.
Stephen Armitage 'Respectable Bookseller and Pawnbroker' was proclaimed King of Dalkey and the 'Royal Fleet' travelled by sea to Dalkey Island surrounded 'by His Court'. He issued proclamations, and orations were delivered on the Island. 'The Court' returned to the mainland after becoming 'dry' and having quenched their thirst, preceeded by merrymaking and festivities.

1796 A.D.
Stephen I reigned on and on 16th August 1796 he set sail from Sir John Rogerson's Quay and journeyed to Dalkey 'on board a fleet of light brigantines, under the command of Lord Neptune, Lord High Admiral of Dalkey'.

1798 A.D.
On the nights of 24th and 25th May approx 1,000 insurgents from Wicklow and Carlow camped on Dalkey Hill in preparation for the imminent Rebellion of 1798.

1841 A.D.
The Church of the Assumption was opened in Castle Street, to cater for the growing number of parishioners in the town, and also for the people of Dalkey Village (Dalkey Hill).

1843 A.D.
St. Patrick's Church opened to cater for the parishioners of Dalkey, which was expanding rapidly because of the opening of Ireland's first railway from Westland Row to Kingstown.

1852 A.D.
The Church of the Assumption was extended and the Tower built. The altar was moved to its present position from what is now the back of the chapel.

1870 A.D.
The Gate Lodge and School House were built at St. Patrick's Church, at a cost of £1,000, which was donated by Charles Leslie Esq. The gas fittings for the building were supplied by Messrs. Curtis & Co.

1891 A.D.
In August of that year, Mr. Charles P Cotton C.E.L.G.B. Engineer Inspector

presided at a meeting in Dalkey Town Hall for the purpose of enquiring into the necessity of granting a loan of £1,300 for the purpose of erecting a concert hall in the township. Mr R W Walshe Sec and Surveyor of the Township said that the new hall would be 72 ft in length and 36 ft in width. It would accommodate 208 for dancing, 250 for dining and standing room for 750. The cost would be £1,150, including £92.10.0 for furniture.

1893 A.D.

The following were Commissioners of the Township of Dalkey – W K Clay Chairman, R W Walshe Secretary, A J Callow JP, J Milo Burke, Peter McDonnell, Christopher Higginbottom, John Leahy, W E Porter and Hugh O'Neill.

1901 A.D.

On Sunday, June 1st, 1901, the local branch of the Gaelic League organised the coronation of the organisation's president, Douglas Hyde, as King of Dalkey Island. But Dublin Castle reacted in their usual heavy handed way by issuing a Royal Proclamation banning the ceremony.

This did not deter the local Gaelic Leaguers, who organised a highly successful outing attended by hundreds of day trippers from Dublin, facilitated by a special 8d excursion fare on the Dublin and South-East Railway. Local boats then ferried them across the sound for 5d return. A procession of pipers and 'Druids' was organised and at four o'clock in the afternoon a public meeting was addressed by several Gaelic League members, including the president of the Dalkey Branch, E A Fournier. A resolution was passed 'That the work of the Gaelic League is worthy of the support of all Irish people'.

1913 A.D.

During the 1913 Lockout trams driven by strike breakers were blocked by local workers who had lost their jobs because they refused to leave the Irish Transport Workers Union. The incidents led a local priest, Father Healy to write to Dr Walsh, the Archbishop of Dublin, who was holidaying in France, to inform him that Dublin was enduring 'a veritable reign of terror ... our only hope of salvation lies in a policeman's baton'.

Dalkey also boasted the only businessman who was a recorded victim of the violence that occurred during the Lockout. John Hollwey was a leading ship broker in Dublin and vice-chairman of the Port and Docks Board. He was shot outside Mulligan's public house in Poolbeg Street, when a scab fired at a group of strikers and missed. Fortunately Hollwey survived with nothing worse than a bloody crease across his forehead.

1916 A.D.

The 1916 Rising largely passed Dalkey by although the 'King' of Dalkey played an unexpected role in its aftermath. Among those arrested was Count Plunkett, the father of Joseph Plunkett, one of the signatories of the Proclamation of the Republic. Other prisoners, concerned for the health of the old man in Richmond Barracks, managed to keep news of his son's execution from him for a considerable time. One gambit they used to distract his attention was to arrange a drama, 'The Pretender to the King of Dalkey', which had Eamon de Valera in the lead role of the Pretender and the count as the Judge in the case. The labour leader William O'Brien and future president of Ireland, Sean T O'Ceallaigh, also had leading roles. Paddy Darcy of the 5th Co. Dublin Company IRA and James

Nicholson were the only volunteers from Dalkey arrested after Easter week and they may have been involved in this production. Dev was a regular visitor to Paddy Darcy over the years and attended a function to mark the 50th Anniversary in 1966 in the Town Hall Dalkey and met some of the people who had been involved in crowning of the King at various times and also survivors of the War of Independence. (See Page 13).

The later troubles impinged more directly on Dalkey and G Company of the 6th Battalion of the IRA was based there. The OC was Charles Somers. The other officers were First Lieuteuant Joseph O'Rourke, Joseph Heaslip, First Lieutenant, Daniel Byrne, Second Lieutenant, John Thomas, Quartermaster, Thomas Haughton, Adjutant, Thomas Greene, No 1 Section Commander and Michael Byrne, No Section Commander.

Most of the Volunteers, came from Dalkey and still lived there many years later when the following list was compiled of survivors and their wherabouts. They included:

James Devlin - Tram Terrace, Dalkey.
Joseph Ryan - Carysfort Road, Dalkey.
Peter Devitt – Convent Road, Dalkey.
Michael Kearns – Tram Terrace, Dalkey.
James Byrne – Corrig Road, Dalkey.
Patrick Staunton – 21 Dominick Street, Dublin.
Michael Mullen – St Patrick's Avenue, Dalkey.
Charles Mooney – Convent Road, Dalkey.
Michael Keyes – 3 Anastasia Cottage, Dalkey.
Patrick Keyes – Dalkey Hill.
William Byrne – 57 Rollins Villas, Sallynoggin.
Thomas Byrne – Shamrock Cottage, Dalkey Hill.
Michael Byrne – Shamrock Cottage, Dalkey Hill.
Thomas Mullen – St Patrick's Square, Dalkey.
Patrick Reilly – St Patrick's Square, Dalkey.
Thomas Reilly – O'Donnell Gardens, Glasthule.
Jack Kelly – Monkstown Farm, Monkstown.
William Mooney – Rockfort Avenue, Dalkey.
Patrick Mooney – Grangegorman Hospital
Leo Rowe – 1 Eagle Terrace, Dalkey.
Patrick Rowe – 1 Eagle Terrace, Dalkey.
Joseph Robinson, Mount Salus, Dalkey.
George Byrne – 21 White's Villas, Dalkey.
Leo Treston – Imall, Dalkey Hill.
James Carr – St Patrick's Road, Dalkey.
Patrick Byrne – St Patrick's Road, Dalkey.
Martin McDonald – 22 Tubbermore Avenue, Dalkey.
Michael Mullen – 3 Leslie Avenue, Dalkey.
Jack Ledwidge – Royal Terrace, Dun Laoghaire.
James Nicholson – White's Villas, Dalkey.
Patrick Murdoch – Carysfort Road, Dalkey.
Michael Byrne – Glyn Cottage, Dalkey Hill.
Martin Hughes – Dalkey Hill.
James Byrne – Shamrock Cottage, Dalkey Hill.
Jack Lynch – The Bakery, Dalkey.
John Keane – Church Road, Dalkey.
Myles O'Neill – 1 Patrick's Road, Dalkey.
Jack Furlong – Deans Grange.
Michael Martin – address unknown.
Patrick Thomas – Australia.
William Meagher – Deceased.
Thomas Hogan – Deceased.
Thomas Dunne – Deceased.
Charlie Williams – Dundalk.
William Mooney – Rockford Avenue, Dalkey.

Mr O'Kelly – Pine Hill, Dalkey.
Mr O'Kelly – Darley Villas, Coliemore Road, Dalkey.

Some members of the Company were among 30 suspected rebels arrested in a raid by Crown forces on Sunday, April 17th, 1921. They also included John Kavanagh, a member of the Urban District Council and Dr King, who was the Medical Officer at Stillorgan Dispensary and a visiting surgeon at St Michael's Hospital in Dun Laoghaire. Most of the men were arrested in their homes at breakfast. It cannot be be established how long they were held in custody.

1925 A.D.

A fragile peace was established when the Civil War ended at the end of 1924.

Many republicans were disgusted with the terms and quite a large number emigrated. During 1925 mainly because of a drop off in funding from U.S.A., there was a cutback in Republican activities. Some of the executive of the I.R.A. including deValera, Frank Aiken and Sean Lemass, had been going down the path of a political future. Others including Tom Barry, Peadar O'Donnell, Sean McBride and Maurice Twomey were against the concept.

On Saturday 14th November a general I.RA. convention took place in Dalkey (while details of the event are available from O'Donnells Papers in U.C.D.

archives, they do not contain the name of the exact location in Dalkey. Committing such details to paper would have been a dangerous practice in those times).

A new constitution and a new direction was drawn up and presented to the convention by Frank Aiken.

O'Donnell said that the proposal by Aiken should be rejected and he put forward a counter proposal: *"the army of the Republic sever its connection with the Dáil and act under an Independent Executive, such Executive be given the power to declare war when in its opinion, a suitable opportunity arises to rid the Republic of its enemies and maintain it in accordance with the Proclamanation of 1916".*

Mick Murphy, C.O. Cork No. 1 Brigade seconded O'Donnells proposal *"to save the I.R.A. from the jaws of Leinster House to the field of battle".* The counter proposal was carried and a new army council was elected with Andy Cooney as Chief of Staff getting an implicit mandate *"to lead the I.R.A. back from the steps of Leinster House to the field of battle."*

Some days later many who had attended the convention were arrested and imprisoned in Mountjoy Jail. Late in November a very well planned operation was drawn up by George Gilmore from Dun Laoghaire and he along with other local members under the direction of the new executive carried out a dramatic rescue and freed 19 of the prisoners.

Dalkey Olympic Wrestling Club

At a meeting of the Olympic Council of Ireland sitting beside the late Felix Jones then President of the IABA he suggested to me the possibility of forming a wrestling club in the recently completed Sports Centre in Dalkey. Wrestling complimented Boxing which was the major sport in the Sports Centre, the two sports having had a close relationship over a number of years.

At that time I was serving as assistant National Coach to the IAWA and had recently returned from completing my International Coaching certification . I was also delegate to the Olympic Council of Ireland representing the IAWA.

The proposal on the formation of a wrestling club in Dalkey was put before the Executive Council of the IAWA and was duly passed

Initially a few local boys between the ages of 7yrs and 16yrs joined and as the numbers grew the club was able to compete firstly at Mini level ie 7/10yrs with a little success. Gradually with growing numbers we were able to compete at schoolboys,10/14yrs Espoirs 15/18yrs and Cadets to U21yrs There are two types of Olympic wrestling practiced, Greco Roman and Freestyle. In Dalkey we practiced Freestyle.. Progress was slow at first as all of the boys were unfamiliar with Olympic Wrestling, most of them thinking wrestling was what they saw on TV, some being somewhat disappointed they could not punch or kick an opponent as they did on TV. Olympic Wrestling is a highly disciplined sport and any sort of foul play is severely dealt with, even to the participants behaviour outside of club activities,

Progress became rapid , the club was very lucky when two young American boys joined, the Carey brothers, they were very experienced competitors having wrestled through the US High School programme over a number of years and were not only competitors but also lent a welcome hand at coaching the Minis the basic skills of the sport. At about the same time the late

Michael Fanning, whose son Michael Jnr was in the club came along to help.

Ken Cunningham, All Ireland Senior Champion at 19 years of age.

Training took place on Tues and Thurs 7-9 30pm and most competitions took place on Sunday afternoons in Dublin, Belfast, Sligo, Derry and Dalkey

In competition in the early years there was some success, particularly at mini level as they learned the skills much quicker than the older boys. Fairly rapidly over the space of 2/3yrs results began to improve dramatically at all levels,even up to Seniors. Several local boys were very successful, winning Irish Championships at various weights and levels, some that come to mind were Ken Cunningham, Joe Cole, Mark Healy, Gerry Hutton, Niall and Kieron McGowan, David and Peter Byrne, Michael Fanning Jnr,

Joe Cole with his mum Bernie was Irish Juvenile Wrestling Champion in 1971,72, 73 and 1974 and British Champion 1976.

Phillip Feddis, Paul Ryan, Ciaran Irwin, Mickey Byrne, Maurice Keegan, Barry Dunne,John Eble, Rory and Ciaran O'Connor and of course the Carey boys Funds were raised by a small weekly subscription and through the generosity of Dan Finnegan of Finnegans famous pub, hosting the then fashionable Cheese and Wine parties which were hugely successful . Parents contributed finger food and various items for the raffle which contributed handsomely to the club finances

In the short life of the club, Dalkey reigned supreme, winning as I have said earlier Irish Championships at.all levels up to Seniors, Ken Cunningham being the only winner at Senior level when he was just 19. Dalkey also remained unbeaten in Inter Club League competitions in the last 3years of the club

Unfortuately when the Sports Centre changed hands there was no room for other sports other than GAA and even though we relocated to Newpark School in Blackrock where we could only have 2 hours on Sunday mornings it was not enough to sustain the interest and keep the club going and sadly after a few months the club ceased to function, folded its tent and passed into history

Harry Byrne

The Last Tram to Dalkey

The month of July in the Summer of 1949 did not provide any world-wide incident of note which people would be able to recall instantly in the years ahead. The economies and inhabitants of most nations were still recovering from the traumas of World War II or "The Emergency" as it was known here. The port of London experienced a three week long strike by dockers, Ireland's Harry Bradshaw lost the British Open Golf Championship following a play off and Pope Pius XII warned that any catholic found to be aiding Communists would be excommunicated.

The people of Dalkey of that time who are still with us remember that particular month for an entirely different reason. An event took place in the town which brought an era to a close. The happening in question commenced with the departure of the No.8 tram from Nelson's Pillar for its last journey to the terminus in Castle Street, Dalkey, On board the tram that fine Saturday evening apart from those there for

Ma Reillys Old Shop now the very popular Country Bake shop run by Margaret O'Toole and her friendly staff.

purely nostalgic reasons were driver, the late Wally Hayes from Glasthule and conductor, Michael Roche from Dalkey. Michael who worked with the Dublin United Tram Company for 45 years remembers the occasion well. He can still recall the festive atmosphere generated by the large crowds in the main street of Dalkey, many of whom were souvenir hunters. They were determined to get their

hands on some part of the tram to take home and keep as a memento of their old means of transport. The trams were viewed favourably by most as they ran on a regular and efficient basis.

A No.8 tram left the City Centre for Dalkey on average every eight minutes. The No.7 tram from town to Marine Road in Dun Laoghaire ran at intervals of four minutes.

Michael Roche,
Conductor of the last Tram to Dalkey

Nowadays the general public more or less accept the fact that buses don't run to schedule at times or they don't care because they have cars but in the era of the tram it was different. People demanded service and they got it too.

Although large crowds stood on the main street that evening there was no campaign to keep the trams in service and the following day the buses ran. Everything returned

Tim Kerins Pharmacy on the site of the old Dalkey Tramway office in Castle St.

to normality within a short space of time. It also brought to an end Michael Roche's days of working on a transport system that he and plenty of others regarded as one of the finest in Europe. Michael went on to work on various bus routes serving Blackrock, Kilmacud and of course Dalkey. He was not fully in favour of the decision to do away with the trams as he held the view that they could still provide a more than adequate service for the people

Ma Reillys paper shop in right c. 1918, Kellys Butcher shop next door, Tobins Vegetable shop and Dalkey Tramway office where Tim Kerins Pharmacy is today. The No. 8 tram in background at the end of the line preparing to return to Nelson's Pillar in O'Connell Street.

of Dublin. Michael was not alone in his belief. Not long after the No.8 tram ceased to operate he met a priest from Brisbane, Australia. When the priest was told by Michael about the trams being phased out he was astonished. In Brisbane the success of the trams had been so great that they were undergoing a major extension of the network. Forty years down the road there is little left in Dalkey to remind people of what was once taken for granted as part of everyday life.

The tramyard and its few tracks are all that is left on the main street. Those who walked along Barnhill Road up to a cocuple of years ago were able to see one of the old trams. It was used not for passengers but to transport directors of the company along the lines and to the various garages. There are some people who managed to get souvenirs such as cushions or nuts and bolts off the trams before they were sold to a Spanish Company in Bilbao. It was not deemed necessary, however, to advertise false times for the running of the last trams to prevent extensive damage as took place in London when their era of trams came to an end. Michael however does not need any such souvenirs as he is quite contented with the memories he has of his many years working on the trams.

Barry Mullen
King of Dalkey Festival Brochure 1989.

P.S. With the development of the Luas Line Michael who has now sadly passed on was 100% correct with his views re the departure of the trams.

Barry Mullen
June 2008

Tom Ross - A truly great character

One of the most remarkable Dalkey men during the 1940's ad 1950's was Thomas H. Ross who lived in "Pacelli", Hyde Road, Dalkey with his wife Sarah, his daughters Jacqueline and Joan.

He died suddenly on Castle Street, Dalkey on February 17, 1966. He was 54 years old. He was a great swimmer and cyclist in his youth. In 1943 he founded Dalkey Swimming Club and he devoted a great deal of his spare time building up the swimming club. It beame a very important part of their lives for many in Dalkey and the galas that were held in Bulloch Harbour for many years were the highlights of the summer seasons. (See Andy O'Rourke's brief history of Dalkey Swimming Club on Page 84.)

He was involved in so many voluntary organisations that it would be very difficult to give details of them all and the important role that he played in each of them.

Savio Youth Club in Dalkey. He was also Chairman of Dalkey United and was the driving force behind the erection of the first floodlights at Hyde Park in 1959. He served on the management committee for many years and on the night he died so suddenly he had just left the St. Laurences Club where he was also a member, having listened to the draw for the Quarter Finals of the F.A.I. Senior Cup where the "giantkillers' of that season Dalkey United had been drawn against Waterford who were one of the leading teams in the League of Ireland at the time. It is probably fair

Dalkey Swimming Club 1943
Back Row l to r: Tom Ross, Paddy Duggan, John Murray, Michael Fanning, Bobby Neiland.
Front Row: Maura Piggott, J.J. Kennedy, Marie McGilton

During the war years he served in the L.D.F. and was a member of the Dalkey Development Association. However it is for his energetic energies that he expended in helping the growth of sporting activities within the town that he is remembered for by many to the present day.

He was on the committee of St. Dominic

to say that his favourite sport was swimming but to this day he is remembered by many in the town because he was held in such high regard by everyone who was remotely interested in the wellbeing of the town he himself had such affection for.

Frank Mullen

Dalkey's Trains

In the early 19th century it was decided to transfer the Mail Boat from Howth to Kingstown because of a silting problem in Howth.

In order to service the Mail Boat, it was decided to build a railway from Dublin to Dunleary, which was renamed Kingstown in 1821 after the departure of King George IV. On 28th February 1831, an Act of Parliament was passed in the House of Commons clearing the way for the setting up of the Dublin to Kingstown Railway. In 1834 the railway arrived at Kingstown, the first train left Westland Row with the steam locomotive Hibernia in charge. It was the first steam locomotive to be built outside England. Building the railway cost in the region of £130,000. A census of traffic in Dublin city was taken on each day from 1st February to 31st October 1830. The passing traffic was counted as follows: 29,256 private carriages, 5,999 hackney carriages, 113,000 private jaunting cars, 149,000 public cars, 20100 gigs, 40,485 saddle horses and 28,297 carts.

The Board of Public Works granted a loan of £37,200.

Steam locomotive from Dalkey arriving at Killiney Station.

The method of propulsion for the line was to be the atmospheric system, this comprised of a leather tube with a piston inside connected to a carriage and pulled along by vacuum.

Trains were to run every hour on the hour between 9.00am and 4.00pm. The fares were First Class 1 shilling, Second Class 8 pence and Third Class 6 pence.

On 4th April 1833, a meeting was held in Seneschal's Court House of Kingstown, to discuss the extension of the railway to Dalkey. Hackney men and traders fearing loss of business objected strongly but were outnumbered and it was agreed to extend the railway to the fishing village of Dalkey. In 1835 work began on the extension, which was to be of a single track to Dalkey.

Unfortunately the local rats took a liking to the grease covering the pipe and was subject to frequent breakdowns.

On Monday 28th September 1842, The extension to Dalkey was opened, after a period of testing. The line was offically opened to passengers on 29th March 1844. Trains ran from Kingstown at thirty-minute intervals. The fares were 3 pence for 2nd class and 2 pence for 3rd class, there were no 1st class carriages.

The pumping house in Dalkey was burning a ton of coal every four hours and only supplying steam for ten minutes each hour. This was deemed not to be economical and after a major breakdown the last atmospheric train ran on 12th April 1854 and the line was thereafter run with steam locomotives.

In August 1844, I.K. Brunell, of the Great Western Railway in England came over to survey a route from Dalkey to Bray around Killiney Hill and hence from Bray to Rosslare around Bray Head.

Steam services continued up until the 1960s. diesel trains took over in 1963 and 21 years later in 1984 we got our present day DART system and modern electric trains with a frequent service to the capital. Sadly the coming of the DART system spelt the end of the extension to Carlisle Pier, which gave the line its reason for being built in the first place.

Bill Garrioch

Dermot (Snowy) Smyth 1920 -1974

Dermot, or Snowy, as he was more commonly known due to his snow white hair was born in No. 8 Pilot Cottages situated on Bulloch Harbour. He had 3 brothers, John, Paddy and Brendan. He also had 3 sisters, Fanny, Annie and Eileen. He started his playing career with St. Josephs as many still do. He also kitted out for The Workman's Club, Guinness's Brewery, both Dalkey Utd. and Dalkey Celtic.

During Dalkey United's inaugural year 1953/54, whilst they were training for their very first Cup final they had nowhere to change so Snowys father-in-law, my Grandfather, PJ O'Loughlin let the club kit out in his garage at the back of his house on Ardbrugh Road.

He played in his usual position of fullback for Dr. Wrights Old Boys. His love of sport didn't just lie on the football pitch. He was an accomplished oarsman, representing Dalkey Rowing Club for many years. He added further to his trophy cabinet by throwing darts for The Four Feathers, who played out of McDonaghs Public House in Dalkey.

Dad started his working life on a torpedo boat in The Irish Marines in 1938. In 1940 he left and went into Guinness Brewery in Dublin. It was from here that he retired in 1972. From the age of 14 he fished lobster pots with Shiner Smyth out of Bulloch Harbour. In those days fishing pots were a lot harder than today. Engines of any description were a rarity, so in order for him to get as much as he could he would go long distances from the harbour. One of his fishing grounds was over at the Pigeon House and the Bull Wall near Dolymount.

To achieve this he rowed over and back, sometimes fully loaded and in all weather. It was doing this that Snowy was tragically and cruelly taken from us. He was drowned whilst fishing alone on the 10th of December 1974, the day before his 54th birthday.

Donal Smyth

Snowy Smith with Dalkey Celtic the Cup winning team.
Back Row: John Myler, Billy Byrne, Pat Lacy, Frank Quirke, Vincent Dunphy,
Mick Dunne, Derek (Snowy) Smyth, Ned Mullet, Jim (Gus) Farrell.
Front Row: Jimmy Mitchell, Leo Brown, Langan, Robbie Carter, Jimmy Lawlor,
Mick Brien, Des McWilliams, Benny Lynch. 1959

My Dalkey United Experience

I joined Dalkey United at the age of 12 years in 1978 after a chance meeting with the Club Chairman Frank Mullen who suggested to me that I join the football club. My very first memory of Dalkey United was of me lying on my stomach doing press ups with the now deceased Mick Dalton coaching us. In hindsight I can now see how football and Dalkey United in particular was to play such an important part of my life. To be honest it had never crossed my mind to play soccer until that meeting with Frank, but I played Gaelic Football and Hurling for the Harold Boys' National School in Dalkey under the guidance of the Headmaster Frank Mullen (a cousin of our Chairman of the same name) and Sean

O Gormain. I was to go on and also play Gaelic Football and Hurling for Cuala for a few years on Saturdays as well as soccer on Sundays. When I was sixteen I made the decision to stick with Dalkey United in the soccer because I felt it was too much to play the different sports.

I have a lot of great memories from my time with Dalkey United such as the trips to Germany in 1979 and 1981 and the Solar Cup in Liverpool in 2004. One of my favourite memories was meeting Pele who shared the same flight to West Germany on our trip in 1979. Furthermore we had the great ooh aah Paul McGrath with us at the time, who unknown to us was going to go on and have such a distinguished career for both club and country. The highlight of the trip in "79" was staying with a wonderful family who really made us feel welcome and on our departure gave me a very fitting black and white, club colours knitted jumper and scarf. I was the only one of the three that stayed in his home to benefit with this present, I must have left an impression. My highlight of the trip in 1981, though there were many to choose from had to be the visit to Berlin. We got to visit such places as the Olympic Stadium even getting the chance of a quick swim in the pool. But the best was the visit through Checkpoint Charlie and the trip into East Berlin. When we were going through

Checkpoint Charlie we were only permitted to take 25 German Marks which had to be exchanged for the East Berlin currency which was like monopoly money. This visit was to leave a lasting impression on me and I was a bit shocked to see a mural on the Berlin Wall, if I remember correctly the words "Bobby Sands RIP" were sprayed onto it.

The last trip I was on was to the Solar Cup in 2004 where I went as Team Manager for the under 12's. To be honest I found this to be very difficult taking sole responsibility for the team due to the fact the Manager Tim Galvin could not make it due to work commitments and I was not good at asking for assistance. But in hindsight it went very well regardless, losing only in a very tight semi final. Again the highlight of the trip was going to Anfield to watch Liverpool play Charlton Athletic. Furthermore we got to see Bolton draw 2-2 with Aston Villa in a very entertaining game at the Reebok Stadium.

On the football side of things with Dalkey I really loved to play. I suppose you could say I lived for the game because it gave me such a passion that I found myself in a sport that as far as winning was concerned I did not get to win a single league or cup as a player but still kept turning up. When there was no game to play at the weekends due to bad weather or any other reason I found myself feeling a loss. It would have me praying for good weather the following week.

Pele, one of the greatest footballers of all time.

I have fond memories of us competing against the German clubs that we visited or when they came to visit us. A couple spring to mind, the first being the wonderful free kick I scored against the German keeper Thorston Kromer whom I was to stay with while on the trip in 1981, the second being when we got to the football club (shattered) after a day and half journey over sea and land. When we were being allocated the Family with whom we were going to stay for our duration, Thorston let out a roar, "I want Sex Pistol", which referred to me, due to the fact that when they were over the previous year I was wearing a Sex Pistols t-shirt. A few years later Thorston wrote me a letter with a photo attached to it confirming that he was the drummer of a punk band that himself and some of his mates formed.

I really enjoyed my football with Dalkey and was very proud of playing for my hometown club. So you can imagine that when I had been playing all my football for the club when I got dropped for a while that I felt I had to go elsewhere to get a game. I went to Corporation Celtic in Sallynoggin who were in the same League and who were beaten at home earlier in the season by Dalkey by a score line of 4-1. I played ten games for Corporation Celtic scoring six goals but the goal that stands out most is the winning goal against Dalkey. To make it harder for the Dalkey lads, was the fact that, they had been asking me how I was getting on with the Corpo team, I would tell them I scored, they would suggest that the other team was crap, therefore you can imaging their faces when I was to score the decisive goal.

I went back to Dalkey United for a few more years to play second and third team football with the Digger Dalton, Billy Haskins and Joe Dowling. When I was with the club I would spend a lot of time travelling around Leinster doing Linesman for both the first and second teams. Somehow I managed to lose contact with the club and was to have an absence of some years.

I am very grateful to have had the opportunities that have come my way since being part of Dalkey United Football Club. Even through the horrendous years of my battle with alcoholism and drug misuse, I still clung to the wonderful game of football, if just about. Somewhere in my twenties I drifted away from Dalkey United and into a world of addiction and self-hatred and looking back I am amazed that I am still alive today and even more amazed at how well my life has turned around. All my life I worked in the building game, while hating it, but never had any confidence or self-esteem to learn a trade or to change career. It was just over eight years ago when my live was to change for the better, I got sick and tired of being sick and tired, of alcohol taking every bit of dignity and peace of mind from me.

Strangely enough it was another chance meeting with Frank Mullen, this time in the Dun Laoghaire Shipping Centre that was to get me back to the club as the Assistant Manager of the under twelve's with Tim Glavin. I was to find it extremely difficult in the beginning because I really believed that I had nothing to offer, but worse still, I felt that I wasn't good enough. The first two years as assistant to Tim were a living nightmare as all types of horrible feelings were to emerge from the intensive counselling that I had been doing as part of my recovery. As I said previously I had never experienced the winning feeling as a player, but that was to change while assisting Tim at the under 14 stage. After being relegated from division one and been beaten in cruel fashion in two semi finals by premier division teams we came back all the better for our experiences. The next season we won the Division Two Championship losing only one game, but the really amazing thing about this team was they went on and won the Premier League Cup defeating all the top sides in that age category. First they had to win their way out of a group that contained two division one and the top premier league Liffey Valley F.C. who were unbeaten in about four years. We had to beat Liffey Valley, which we did 3-2 to get a play off with St. Francis which we won 4-2 to play Blessington in the quarter final. We played Blessington who had just clinched runners up in division one and beat them by a score line of 6-1, which could have been more but for some desperate defending. So on to the semi final

where we were paired against Ashwood who had been crowned first division champions and this was to be an amazing performance when the Dalkey lads won by a scoreline of 9-0. The final was played up in Tallaght against Liffey Valley who were out to avenge their only defeat in the previous four years. But God was looking down and smiling on the Dalkey lads who were to inflict a second defeat on Liffey Valley by a scoreline of 3-1. This was to be the first double by any Dalkey Utd. team in 20/30 years. The most amazing thing about that was the fact these boys only trained for one hour a week if you were lucky enough for them to attend. After such a great season and proudly looking forward to the promotion to the Premier Division it was no doubt a shock to hear that our two top players who scored 93 goals between them signed for St. Joseph's and worse still our excellent centre half we still stayed up regardless. But the team was again to progress to the Semi Final of the Premier League Cup where they held their own, but eventually lost 3-1 with the Home Referee giving two dubious penalties, the only penalties conceded all season, bar the penalty shootout in another cup against Leixlip United.

On to the next season and after struggling to field a team in the under 16 section and work commitments I found myself needing a break because I was feeling burned out from my job as a youth worker and Assistant with Dalkey. Therefore I had to make the very hard decision to quit, because my work involved me working unsocial hours.

I am very proud to say that since those early days of my recovery, that my life is now thriving and I am definitely not the person I was. It is from doing the work on myself that I am six years out of building work and am now working as an Outreach Youth Worker for the past four and a half years. I am in a job that I love doing and I get great satisfaction from knowing that my life experiences which were mostly unsavoury, can now help others. In my job I work with kids from nine to nineteen in all types of settings from football to alcohol, drugs, street work, and on programmes which allows me to bring the young people into different prisons so it may act as a deterrent. I have been able to bring in the two wonderful fellowships of Narcotics and Alcoholics Anonymous into the young people in my work therefore hoping that they someday will find a place of sanctuary from the pains of addiction. When I started doing youth work it was through a C E scheme which I did for two years before being employed by Catholic Youth Council/Dun Laoghaire Youth Service. When I was on the C E scheme I was an assistant to Suzanne Cox who was the Outreach worker and doing the job that I am now doing at present. I have done some courses so that I could get some qualifications for youth work. The course that sticks out most in my mind is the one year Addiction Studies Certificate from Maynooth College, which is held in Stillorgan. When doing the course I found it extremely difficult due to the fact that I was in the Dublin RCC receiving counselling on Mondays and also a Men's Group on Wednesdays, while then going to my Addiction Course on Thursdays. Needless to say I found that extremely hard, but was glad that I had my support systems in place. I am delighted to say that after all the hard work that I was to gain a second class honour, not bad for a lad who couldn't sit in a class in school.

The working hours of youth work are unsocial and it was therefore with regret that I felt it best to give up being Assistant to Tim after four/five very good years of being part of a great bunch of lads. I have great memories of the Double in the 2005/6 season, also their spirit which carried them to an unblemished home record in the same season. Although I left the team, my heart was still there, but I suppose the blow was softened by the fact that I have two football groups in my job, all because I know how much football kept me going through those hard times. I look at how some of the kids need football and encouragement as I once did, that is what it is all about, that is why I am there. I am talking with the club to look after the kit for the senior team. I could never leave Dalkey United. I feel I could go on and on about my experiences which are now mostly positive and that I hope to one day write a book about my life story.

To sum it all up Dalkey United has been instrumental in giving me so many happy memories and has been a way of life for me since meeting Frank whom I look upon as my father figure who never judged me and was always very caring towards me. Although I never won anything, any leagues or cups as a player I did manage to win player of the year and clubman of the year. But I have to say that the best experiences I have was when as manager of the Under 14 team the referee's whistle blew for full time when we won both the league and cup.

Finally I knew what it was like to get the winning feeling. I am very proud to have been part of the young men's lives and hope that they get as much out of Dalkey Utd. and football as I have. I really don't know what way my life would have been if it were not for the sanctuary Dalkey United Football Club and Frank gave me. His support and encouragement was timely. It is when I look back and see how football was to give me a passion and an identity that I feel so blessed. The best lesson I learned was that anything is possible, once your mind is open to it. I often wonder about my old team mates like Steven (Steph) Doran, Peter (Pob) O'Brien, John Cavanagh, John McCormack, Dave Fallon, John Sheeran etc. and how they are doing.

I will finish by saying that I am ever grateful for my experiences and for all the memories from my time at Dalkey United. Thank you Frank, Ellen and Family.

Dave Hennessy
May 2008

Lennox Robinson - A Remarkable Person

Lennox Robinson was born in Douglas, Co. Cork on 4th October 1886. He was one of seven children of Emily and Andrew Robinson.

His father was a Church of Ireland minister and when Lennox was in his mid teenage years his father was transferred to Ballymoney in West Cork and he attended Bandon Grammar School.

He suffered from poor health in his young life and following some private tuition in his early years all formal education ended when he was 18 years old. He became an avid reader and two years later he edited a magazine which was published by his family named 'Contributions'.

It was a very appropriate title because for the remainder of his life his contributions to the world of literature and the theatre was recognised internationally.

He wrote his first poem in a magazine 'The Royal Magazine' in 1907 and the following year saw his first play, 'The Clancy Name', a one act tragedy which was produced in the Abbey. He came to the notice of the leading scribes and play writers, W.B. Years and Lady Gregory appointed him manager of the Abbey Theatre in Dublin. G. B. Shaw saw his potential and he appointed him his secretary.

In 1911 he went on his first tour to the United States with the Abbey Company.

In 1913 having been to London with the Abbey Company he left for America again with Lady Gregory as tour manager. On their return the eminent Lady criticised his management of the tour and he promptly resigned from the company.

He went to London in 1914 to direct a play there and returned to Ireland. He went directly to Cork and joined John Redmonds Irish Volunteers to fight in the First World War. He became a Civil Servant and was sent by Sir Horace Plunkett as official librarian for the Carnegie Trust in the Munster area, a position he held until 1924.

At that time Robinson was living in one of Plunketts houses in Dublin, he had been to Dalkey many times and moved into Sorrento Cottage, that beautiful house which lies beside Killiney Bay almost under Sorrento Terrace.

This house became a venue for many of the well known names in the theatrical and literary community, Yeats, A.E. Russell, Shaw, Lady Gregory, Denis Johnston, Lord Dunsany and numberous others became regular guests. They always, weather and

Sorrento Cottage in foreground, beneath Sorrento Terrace, where Robinson lived for many years. Photo taken 1908.

tides permitting, started the evenings by having a swim around the little harbour that still stands on the foreshore in front of the house.

The sloping, terraced banks at the rear of the house were used for performances of plays to entertain the guests. In the course of a discussion with G.B. Shaw one evening over a meal in Dublin, Robinson asked Shaw for directions to Torca Road to see the house that Shaw spent the summers of his youth in and which he spoke about. Shaw responded by saying he would write to him with precise instructions. He wrote the following letter *"I think the shortest way to find the seaside home of my boyhood is to ask the postman where Torca Cottage is."* Dalkey faces Dublin and Howth one-way and Bray Head and the Sugar Loaf the other. The back garden commanded a panoramic view of Dublin Bay, the front Killiney Bay. It was, and is more than halfway up the hill from the sea to the little castle (the telegraph) on top of the hill north of Killiney Hill. It and the group of houses (in my time three) to which it belonged were the highest in Dalkey. To the left of the spectator facing them, at a little distance which may now be filled up with new buildings, was a conspicuous house called Mount Henry.

The nearest landmark at that elevation is 'The Provosts Pump'. A square castellated tower, presumably containing a pump. In my time the heath in front of the cottage and the hill down to the road and the railway was unfenced and unbuilt on: what it is now I do not know. From the railway station you followed the line to the second bridge, turn to the right, toiled up the steep road past Khyber Pass and other romantically named places, turned to the left at the top and walked parting on the welcome level, until you were stopped at Mount Henry. After passing the three, of which Torca Cottage was the third.

If one passes Shaw's Cottage, as it is now known locally and continues for 30 metres or so there is a long pathway or 'Green Road' as it is known about Killiney Bay with a panoramic view of Killiney Bay and the Wicklow Mountains. On a good day it is possible to get a clear view of the Welsh Mountains. On the same walk if one looks across towards Wales, particularly around daybreak on a clear frosty morning one can easily see the lights along the west coast of Wales. If one has enough energy and continues on to the top of the hill overlooking Dalkey Quarry and looks across Dublin Bay to the 'left of Howth Hill', the Mourne Mountains can be clearly visible.

Looking up from the Vico Road towards the 'Green Road' one can clearly see a piece of granite in the shape of a large bird. It was known during my young years as 'The Eagle of Vico'. It was believed for a long time that it was a work of nature. It was established in the 1840's that it was cut out of a piece of granite that lay there, into the shape of an eagle by Des and Tom Cooper, two brothers who lived in a cottage on Ardbrough Road and worked as granite cutters in Bulloch Harbour cutting granite for the building of the inner harbours of Dun Laoghaire.

Lennox Robinson lived in Sorrento Cottage. His talents would be deserving of a book on its own. His love of Dalkey lasted throughout his life. He was over 6'6" tall and after moving from Dalkey to Monkstown he would return to ramble around with his little poodle dog on a lead. Some described him as an austere man but those of us who rembember him would describe him as a shy person. He did not have many enemies and got on well with people with the exception (for a while), of another playwrite - Sean O'Casey. When O'Casey wrote a play - 'The Silver Tassie' both Robinson and Yeats rejected it. He refused an invitation which he received from Robinson to visit him and his wife for dinner in Sorrento Cottage. However when O'Casey returned to Ireland in 1936 for what was his last visit, Robinson invited both of them for dinner to Dalkey. O'Casey would have refused the invitation and wrote later *"I would have refused but Mrs. O'Casey persuaded me to accept the invitation, so we went to see the gulls over Sorrento and indeed, Mr. Robinson and his wife were charming hosts."*

Sean O'Casey died on 18th September 1964 in Torquay and in 1976 his wife Eileen wrote a book about her life with Sean. They were married on 23rd September 1927 at the Church of the Most Holy Redeemer in Chelsea. After years of uncertainty she finally decided in 1971 to spend the rest of her life in Dublin.

A short time after her return she thought of the beautiful house, Sorrento Cottage in Dalkey, where she had such an enjoyable evening with Sean being enterained to dinner by Lennox Robinson and his wife Dolly, back in 1927. She contacted the then owner of the house, told him her story and was invited out with her daughter Shivaun. They spent an enjoyable day talking about the beauty of the place and times long past The house was sold shortly after for £99,000, a record price for that period.

Lennox Robinson was a kind man with a record unparalleled in the history of the Irish Theatre. One of the stories I heard about him was from a Mr. Fintan Delaney, who lived at 3 Ardbrough Road, Dalkey. He and his brother Paddy became friends of Robinson during the years he lived in Dalkey. One morning Fintan was travelling into the city with Lennox on the upper deck

of a Dalkey tram, a butterfly was flying around, Lennox left his seat and spent a considerable part of the journey trying to gently usher the little creature safely out

W.B. with son Michael and daughter Anne, both lived in Dalkey for many years on Leslie Ave. and Rockford Ave. and were truly great neighbours.

through one of the windows. He finally succeeded and as he was making his way back to his seat a fellow traveller asked why he spent so much time ensuring that he ejected the butterfly out through one of the windows. Robinson replied, " I understand the lifespan of a butterfly is 24 hours, I could not countenance the little creature spending his entire life in the top deck of a Dalkey tram."

I believe his action and his response epitomizes the kind, gentle nature of the man whom I and many in Dalkey still remember with affection and admiration.

He continued to work up to the time of his death on 14th October 1958 at the age of 72 years. He is buried in the grounds of St. Patrick's Cathedral in Dublin.

Frank Mullen

Dick Brennan - Snooker and Billiards Star

Dick Brennan was born and reared in St. Begnet's Villas, Dalkey. He started his Snooker and Billiards career in Joe Baker's Snooker Hall over Hick's Shop in Dalkey.

He has had a remarkable record over many years representing his Country in Snooker on 40 occasions and winning 50 Caps for his Country in Billiards. His first victories of note were winning 7 Dublin and District Snooker Championships. He won the inaugural R.T.E. Live Tournament in 1977.

He first became Irish Snooker Champion in 1973. He was runner up in the 1982 Championship. He was successful in East Coast Snooker Championship in 1976 and 1977. Dick won so many titles; it is impossible to document them all in the space available. His snooker victories include the Galway Open and Cork Open Championships. He won 4 International Pro Am Snooker Championships.

Dick Brennan in action on the green baize.

His Billiards career was spectacular representing his Country on 50 occasions. He was All Ireland Open Champion in 1993, 1994 and 1995. He was also the Millennium Open champion. He won over 50 Billiard Tournaments and the highlight of his career was leading the republic of Ireland Team into a reception in Stormount carrying the tricolour to mark the opening of an International Tournament in Belfast, more than likely the first person to carry the tricolour into that Historic Building.

Dick's family also figure in the annals of sporting achievements. His brother Frankie played for Chelsea before returning home to continue his football career with various teams in the borough.

His son Stephen is with Newcastle United F.C. He started playing football with Valeview Shankill at the age of 7.

He joined St. Joseph's Under 11 Team. He won many medals with his club both in Ireland and at various tournaments in Europe. He is certainly a great player having 31 International Caps from under 16 to under 19 levels. He figured prominently in the European under 19 Championships held in Oslo, Norway s few years ago scoring the winning goal against England. He may not have been born in Dalkey but his roots are firmly planted here..

A Tribute to Peter Farrell

On researching the sporting biography of Peter Farrell one is immediately made aware of the statistics and facts, the feats and accomplishments stretching over twenty years or more. And these statistics are impressive by any standards.

Born in Dalkey, Co. Dublin on the sixteenth of August 1922 Peter was one of Ireland's greatest sportsmen. Each year thousands of young people attempt to make their mark in whatever sport that attracts their ambitions. Few become adept enough to become professionals. Of the few who do manage to grace their professions only a small number manage to sustain a full career at the very top. These are the handful who see out their normal playing life and perform to their full potential until their physiology calls time. Peter Farrell was one of that rare breed, a high achiever, a success story.

But to me and no doubt to countless others it was the human side of Peter that made him unique. The modesty, decency and the spirit which he exuded exemplified the true sporting hero. As a schoolboy I assiduously followed his achievements, in Milltown and Dalymount Park and through the Sunday papers when he played in England. And when we became friends in our middle years there were no feet of clay. His hero status was a constant.

So let us look back at the record. The statistics tell us that Peter signed for Shamrock Rovers in 1939 on his seventeenth birthday. Throughout World War II he played for Rovers winning the FAI Cup twice and was runner-up once. He won the League Title twice.

Selected as captain of Eire on his debut, for their first post-War match he played at left half in a 3-1 defeat by Portugal in Lisbon in June 1946.

By now his star was on the rise and the scouts were taking notice. It became inevitable that he would leave Rovers for the opportunity of playing in the highly esteemed Divisions of the Football League. And so in August 1946, Peter and his club and country colleague Tommy Eglinton were signed by Everton in a joint £10,000 deal. Eglington, a diminutive outside left, had played in front of Peter's traditional left-half berth throughout their careers with Shamrock Rovers. They were to stay together for eleven seasons at Goodison Park completing a combined total of almost 900 appearances.

As Everton were relegated in 1951 to Division Two, Peter was awarded the club captaincy. He eventually led them to promotion, as runners-up, in 1954. The previous year had seen the team run Bolton Wanderers close in the F.A. Cup semifinal, losing 4-3 at Maine Road.

Peter played in 421 games in the Football League and scored 14 goals. He played a further 31 games in the F.A. Cup scoring 4 goals in that competition.

He made his last appearance for Everton against Bolton Wanderers in the finalgame of the 1956/57 season. The following October he moved across the Mersey in a £2,500 deal, to become player/manager of Tranmere Rovers once again teaming up with Tommy Eglinton.

In December 1959, at thirty seven years of age, he left Tranmere Rovers and became manager of Holyhead Town and with the assistance of some experienced ex-Everton and Tranmere team-mates he led them to the Welsh League North Title.

Later he returned to Ireland and managed Sligo Rovers and St. Patrick's Athletic.

The post-war period of English soccer was renowned for its austerity and rigour. Professionals in the top clubs were paid £12 per week during the playing season and £10 during the Summer break. Bonuses of £2 for a win and £1 for a draw were not unusual. There were no agents and the player's union offered the barest of protection for its members. The Chairman and Directors of the clubs were demigods with total power over their emplyees so that the players were little more than serfs within the structure of their clubs. Paradoxically the players were being revered by the fans who crammed the grounds on Saturdays. This aberration continued into the 1960's until the wage structure was abolished and players were liberated following a legal battle between the players' union and the managements. But generations of players had failed in being adequateley compensated for their skills and drawing power. Peter Farrell was one of those who had been part of the great soccer circus which brought entertainment to millions of people each weekend throughout the cities and towns of England.

Returning to the Record Book we find that Peter's international career was as illustrious as was his time at Everton.

When he began his international career in 1946 there were in effect two Ireland teams, chosen by two rival associations. Both associations, the Northern Ireland based IFA and the Southern based FAI claimed jurisdiction over the whole of Ireland and selected players from the whole island. As a result several accomplished players around that time, including Peter Farrell, played for both teams.

Peter made seven appearances for the IFA between 1946 and 1949. On November 27 1946 he made his debut against Scotland in a 0-0 draw. Together with Johnny Carey, the great Manchester United captain, Con Martin, Bill Gorman, Tommy Eglinton, Alex Stevenson and Davy Walsh, he was one of seven players who were born in the Irish Free State to play for the IFA XI that day. The draw helped the team to finish runners-up in the 1947 British Home Championships. Peter, during that period of his career, helped the IFA achieve other respectable results including a 2-0 win against a then formidable Scottish team on October 4 1947 and a 2-2 draw with England at Goodison Park on November 5 1947.

But it was his 28 caps which he earned between 1946 and 1957 that made his a household name. It is worth remembering

The Irish team which beat England 2-0 at Goodison Park 1949.
Back (l to r): Con Martin, Tommy Aherene, Tommy Godwin, Tommy Moroney and Willie Walsh.
Front (l to r): Peter Carr, Tommy O'Connor, Johnny Carey, Peter Desmond, Peter Farrell and Davy Walsh.

that in the post war period fewer internationals were played unlike today when players can gain 50 or 60 caps whilst still in their twenties. During the forties and fifties a player who achieved 25 caps playing for Ireland was a rarity and received a specially commisioned statuette. This award became a watershed for an international to achieve and indicative of a long and productive vocation. There was no long substitute list like today and eleven players only turned up to play.

In later years caps can be considered almost as confetti, strewn about on matchdays, as younger hopefuls are tried out for twenty minutes or so. There are warm-up games and managers are free to experiment with footballers who in earlier times would have been very much kept on the fringes. Then, to have been chosen by the soccer establishment to wear the green jersey was the ultimate in recognition. To be chosen twenty-eight times was to hold legendary status. This was the source of Peter's esteem amongst the Irish soccer public.

The international career of Peter Farrell reached its zenith on September 21 1949.

That day an FAI eleven defeated England 2-0 at Goodison Park becoming the first non-British team to beat England at home. Con Martin, the Aston Villa centre half, scored a penalty for Ireland in the 33rd minute and Peter made certain of the victory when he lobbed Bert Williams, the Wolves and England goalkeeper, in the 85th minute.

This was a great period for the English team in general who had the services of such luminaries as Wright, Mathews, Finney, Lawton, Carter and Mannion to call on. For Peter, playing on Everton's ground and in front of many Irish fans who travelled over for the game, it was a most gratifying experience.

The England team of that era had built a formidable reputation through playing friendly matches; they did not enter the World Cup until 1950 when they were humiliated, being defeated by an unknown USA team in the finals in South America. Peter scored again for Ireland in a World Cup qualifier against Finland. His third goal came on May 30 in a 3-2 win over Norway.

The records thus confirms the fact that Peter Farrell played for club and country throughout the full spectrum of his career. Had he been a player of the current generation he could well have achieved a hundred caps, hypothetically speaking and of course barring injury.

The times in which Peter graced the game he loved were in stark contrast to those of today. The post-war era was one of austerity, unemployment and social repression. Soccer was one of the few outlets where those who had jobs could find a touch of glamour and a place of heroes. The game was still a sport and not an industry, as it is now acknowledged. The value system, for better or worse, was different.

The struggle within the game for acceptance, respect and ultimately for survival was as tough, just as it is today. And yet there was a kind of innocence abroad amongst the loyal followers who probably saw their heroes through rose-coloured glasses.

As a boy, standing on grimy terraces, I was aware of the villains as well as my heroes. But they were of a pantomime type, readily recognisable; one knew that they were capable of inflicting pain as if on cue whilst at the same time projecting an aura of innocence. Nothing changes.

With the evolution of television, the product as it is sometimes referred to, seems to have a somewhat altered ethic. The performers on view are now also celebrities. Without doubt there still is great skill and no shortage of drama. Competitions are numerous and the extravagant rewards have meant that the players seem to be more self-absorbed. Incentives are continually on offer from exotic locations for those who are strong enough to survive. I sometimes wonder what Peter would have made of it.

My older brother was a pal of Peter's and in the off-season when he came home to Dalkey, he together with two others played golf in places like Woodbrook and Woodenbridge. They would come back to our home afterwards and I remember the excitement of listening to Peter talking football and touching on games and personalities in his own deferential way without the slightest allusion to his own prominence.

His leadership on the field was manifested by example, honesty and good sportsmanship, rarely playing without that smile which suggested that he knew exactly what he was doing.

He prevailed against the toughest of opponents, never impersonating the methods of the more devious of his adversaries. And when the going got tough he was the inspiration to those around him who may have found that to succumb was the easier option. This transcendence of the roller-coaster ride that the professional footballer engages in was the heart of what he was.

Peter Farrell repesented the very best of what sport offers us and like so many others I am privileged to have known him.

An Admirer

Dalkey Island and Its Martello Tower

A profuse growth of myrtle near a headland on the island of Corsica caused the promontory to be called Cape Mortella. The French had built a circular defensive tower there, as at other sites around the Mediterranean. This one protected an anchorage in the Gulf of San Fiorenzo. In much the same way as the French sent aid to Irish rebels from time to time, so the British responded to a call for assistance from Corsican insurgents, in conflict with the French Government in the Revolutionary Wars in 1793, shortly after the revolution of 1789. On a spring day in February 1794 Lieutenant General Dundas attacked the tower at Cape Mortella with HMS Fortitude, a 74 gun ship of the line, along with HMS Juno, a 32 gun frigate. He expected little opposition when his ships' guns started to batter the tower with their cannon balls.

After several hours bombardment of the tower without any noticeable advantage General Dundas withdrew, indeed his ships were driven off. Fortitude was on fire, Juno damaged and 62 crewmen were dead or wounded from the fire returned from the tower. Later on, when the tower was eventually captured, it was discovered that a small defending force armed with just three guns had been able to conduct a robust defence and inflict significant damage on the well armed attacking ships and their crews. The military were impressed – they strongly recommended to the Government of the day in London that these Martello towers had great value for coastal defence and their construction was vigorously urged around these isles. Nothing happened until 1804 when Napoleon was sweeping all before him in Europe and the invasion of Ireland and England itself appeared to be imminent.

After the passage of the National Defence Act (1804) a Colonel Benjamin Fisher of the Royal Engineers was instructed to start construction of the towers in strategic locations where invasion was thought most likely. Consequently sixteen numbered towers and gun batteries were built between Bray Head and the Liffey and a

The Marello Tower Dalkey Island
Photograph by George Stuart, Goatstown

further twelve on Dublin's north side. Construction started in the summer of 1804 on our tower on Dalkey Island. Communication has always been of great importance to the military but in 1806 it was rudimentary: Morse Code had not yet been invented by Samuel Morse and a semaphore system of using flags meant that each tower was sighted in direct line of vision with its adjacent tower. It also meant from the defensive point of view that their fields of fire would overlap to cover the intervening area of shore and sea.

While the Martello towers in England and those to the north of the Liffey were largely built of brick or rubble, those on the south side of Dublin, including that on Dalkey Island, were constructed of courses of ashlar (square hewn) heavy granite blocks. Dalkey Island, numbered nine, is the largest of the towers (the Martello at Williamstown, Blackrock, and at Sandymount are also larger than the average). It has a gun platform on the roof 34 feet in diameter (the others would have a gun platform about twenty feet in diameter). This larger platform was to accommodate two 24 pounder guns. The usual tower was equipped with just one 18 pounder. The solid iron ball from a 24 pounder had a range of over a mile. If loaded with grapeshot serious damage could be inflicted over a wide arc of sea and shoreline.

As to the tower itself, it is 45 feet in diameter at its base. In outline it is like a squat inverted flower pot, the external wall surface slopes inwards or tapers so that at parapet height it would have a diameter of 25-26 feet. Dalkey Island's Martello was distinctive not alone in being the largest, but it had no machicolation (this is the projecting structure usually over the doorway, supported by corbels, in which there are holes in the floorspace through which missiles could be hurled, hot coals or scalding liquids poured onto attacking forces trying to gain entry through the door and in having – originally – the entry door high in the parapet. Most towers would have had the entrance doorway 10-14 feet from ground level, entry being effected via a ladder which the defending garrison would haul up and house inside the tower. The doorway was situated on the side of the tower away from the open sea and on this side the walls might be only five feet thick whereas on the side facing the open sea - and potentially the direction from which incoming fire would be directed - the wall was eight feet thick. The door itself was a substantial structure of two layers of heavy wooden boards with the exterior covered with sheet iron. The parapet protecting the gunners was a massive affair of granite eight feet deep. The present doorway is slightly above ground level and is a later alteration to the building.

There was one chamber inside which housed the magazine and the gunners' accommodation. The magazine door is of wood but lined with sheet copper. Its hinges were bronze, a copper lock was fitted, bronze and copper were used lest a spark from an iron lock ignite the gunpowder. The ceiling was vaulted to support the overhead gun batteries. In the case of the Dalkey Island Martello the two 24 pounders mounted on the circular platform along with the three guns of the adjacent batteries had a field of fire generally southwards which, along with the Martello Towers at Killiney and Bray, effectively covered the southern approaches to Dublin. Dun Laoghaire Harbour, or Kingstown as it was then, had not yet been built – indeed the gun battery on the end of the east pier was not completed until 1857, after the Crimean War had ended.

Dalkey Island Martello had a detachment of twenty gunners, living in one chamber. It must have been seriously overcrowded with plenty of scope for bickering and argument. They would have been provisioned from Dublin port but there is fresh water on the island, a spring, which the soldiers would have used on a daily basis. Indeed there are three fresh water sources on the island. Across Dalkey Sound, once called St Begnet's Sea, in the village of

Dalkey, The Queen's, a hostelry since 1745 and formerly the Red Crowe, would have provided the gunners in their off duty time with refreshment more to their taste – fortifying ales and grog to help them endure cold nights in the stone tower and battery accommodation. The contractor for the granite built Martellos on the southside, including that on Dalkey Island, was a Mr Ross. He must have had a very busy, energetic, fit and skilful crew of master masons for his sixteen towers along with the nearby batteries were, it is documented, almost ready, by October 1804, only 4-5 months after building work started.

Map of Dalkey and its surrounding areas showing also Muglins
Courtesy of Tom Clarke, Ordinance Survey Office, Phoenix Park.

Master Gunner Robert Larkham was appointed in February 1805 and by June of that year the towers, equipped with guns, were in a state of defensive readiness. The pace of building, in the face of perceived imminent invasion, must have been frantic; but despite that each tower was expertly built to a sound design which for the defensive purposes of the time was state of the art. The cost of the tower was £1,200 – the battery on the island, cost more, £1,800, equipped with three guns, and faced seaward. Each gun was on a carriage which could traverse through an arc of a circle so that its direction of fire could be varied. The building of the battery took place before the tower [were they separate structures or was the battery then installed in the tower?]. Adjacent to the battery was a single storey accommodation house and store room built of granite. The tower and battery were manned by gunners between 1805 and 1886 when the last military personnel were withdrawn from Dalkey Island. By then it is likely that they would have had enough of goat, fried, boiled, stewed or barbequed! In truth they must have spent a good deal of time fishing as there was little flat land on this island of about twenty five acres for sport – football had not yet become widely popular and the game of rugby (which came into being when Tipperary born William Webb Ellis at Rugby School in 1823 during a football game took up the ball and ran with it to the goal line) would only have become popular in the latter years of the occupation of Dalkey Island!

The only other structure on the island is the ancient church of St Begnet. For a long time roofless, it is a remarkable testament to its builders that with all the gales it has endured that it is still standing – and it stands well and proud. The stonework is in good order. It has a small belfry in the west gable, the doorway faces the setting sun with a massive stone lintel of a type typical in the 10th to 11th century. [Is the lintel still in place?] A fireplace was constructed inside the church by the masons working on the battery and Martello tower, who used the ruined church as a place of shelter and probably resided there during the summer and autumn of 1804.

Adjacent to Dalkey Island is The Muglins, a hazard to boats, it carries a conical red and white beacon. It is famous for very little save an event in 1766 when it became the final resting place for two pirates named Zeckerman and McKinley whose bodies after execution in Dublin were hung in chains for all to see. They got what they deserved having taken over a ship and murdered and thrown overboard the bodies of the captain, his wife and the crew. With the wash of the waves the clanking of the chains could be heard from Dalkey itself and was supposedly intended to deter the macho youth of the day from entertaining any thoughts of a career in piracy.

On a happier note the island of Dalkey had an annual ceremony which took place in the late 1700's and which was attended on occasion by up to 20,000 people. A lavish party was held in which a King of Dalkey Island was elected 'Emperor of the Muglins, Prince of the Holy Island of Magee, Elector of Lambay and Ireland's Eye, Defender of his own faith and respector of all others and sovereign of the most Illustrious Order of the Lobster and Periwinkle'. Satirical speeches were made and really it was a joyous annual event, gently mocking the pomp and ceremony which could be witnessed regularly by the people as the military paraded and the establishment showed the native population who was really in charge. There has been in recent decades a reincarnation of the ceremony – a carnival event during which licensed premises stay open until late and their staff work hard to satisfy the terrific thirst of profanum vulgum. The island is inhabited only by goats, other smaller furry animals and birds that seem to thrive and live in harmony.

Okay! Who was St Begnet? A seventh century local saint whose feast day is November 12th, said to be a virgin. Now mind you, according to my St Andrew Missal published by the good monks of the Abbey of St André in Bruges, November 12th is the feast day of St Martin the First, Pope and Martyr who died in 655. After death his body was brought to Rome and his remains lie in the Church of St Sylvester and St Martin. However, in the Parish of Dalkey November 12th belongs to St Begnet!

Dr. Dermot P. A. Stones

At the conclusion of this brief chapter on Dalkey Island and its Martello may I make a plea, as a small voice calling in the wilderness – the island of Ireland has a very rich inheritance of military and defensive engineering and architecture, which as far as I can see is gradually being neglected, falling into ruin and being taken over by nature. It is part of the visible horizon and part of what made us the nation we are today. How can there be such an outcry and protest about Carrickmines 'Castle' when we are allowing the disintegration of what at this point could so easily be conserved and restored? Of course I am talking not only of the magnificent Martellos which dot our coastline (and are found also on Shannon Side) but Charles Fort, Kinsale, Fort Duncannon, sundry bastions guarding Cobh and Cork amongst others. Some work has been done to be sure as at Charles Fort in the 1970s, the Martello at Magilligan Point in Co Derry has been restored and Joyce's Tower in Sandycove is safe for the future, but this isn't enough. In the interests of generations to come, not to speak of future tourism, please let us embark on planned and ongoing restoration with enthusiasm. It would be a good use for public or indeed Lottery funding. We can do this. Sir Edward Lutyen's memorial garden at Islandbridge is a credit to the restorers, after long years of neglect and some vandalism. Please let us as a nation restore and conserve what is an abundant and valuable heritage. A worthwhile spin off would be the employment of masons, joiners, cabinet makers and other craftsmen. The whole nation would be the beneficiaries.

Dr. Dermot P. A. Stones

Dalkey Community Council Limited

One of the most active organisations in Dalkey is the Community Council. Founded in late 1973, it reflects the variety of other organisations operating in Dalkey, e.g. Drama Groups, Residents Associations, Sports Groups, Charities, etc. It has three core principles.

1. To increase community harmony and fellowship.
2. To foster the wellbeing of all the inhabitants of Dalkey without any distinction of any nature whatsoever.
3. To foster facilities in the interest of social wellbeing, health, recreation and leisure.

There are approximately 75 members of the council all of whom are volunteers.

The origins of the council are to be found in the Dalkey Ladies Club in late 1973 when it was decided that a community council was necessary to help bind the diverse organisations in Dalkey into a coherent and vociferous unit to represent the population of the town. A Steering Committe was formed with Mrs. Doris Smyth, as Chairman and Mrs. Judy O'Mahoney as Secretary. The purpose of the Steering Committee was to investigate whether or not there was a need for the creation of a community council. At the time, there were many young families in the area and many of the young mothers were keen to integrate into the town. This led to an enthusiastic effort by all concerned to get things moving. It was also decided to draft a questionnaire and seek the views of the people of Dalkey on what they saw as the purposes of the Community Council. This was circulated to every house in the area and repeat visits took place until the completed forms were returned. Meetings also took place with councils in Kilbarrack and Clondalkin. In the Kilbarrack case, much appreciated help was received from a young Dr. Michael Woods (later a T.D.). The basic concept of the Community Council in Ireland was run on the ideas of Muintir na Tire which, in turn, was started by Canon Hayes in Co. Tipperary in the 1940s.

Following the return of the completed questionnaires an election was held to elect representatives to the council who would be representative of various organisations as well as the geographical areas in Dalkey. A brief mention was published in the Irish Times and this led to a letter from President Erskine Childers, offering to assist the newly formed council in any way he could. Consequently, President Childers formally opened the Community Council at the inaugural meeting which took place in the Sports Centre and more than 500 people attended. A reporter from the Irish Press attended and an article was published together with a photograph The first Chairman was Mr. Peter Northover, Vice-Chairmen were Mrs. Doris Smyth and Mr. Martin Kennedy, Secretry Ms. Mai Kelly, Assistant Secretary Ms. Eithne Dooge, Treasurer Mr. Robin Budd, P.R.O. Mr. Harry Latham, Assistant P.R.O. Mr. Richard Blake. IN the same week as all this was happening, tragedy struck Dalkey with the death in a house fire on Carysfort Road of 11 members of the Howard family. This prompted a call for support to all organisations in the area and helped to establish the Community Council as a worthwhile entity.

Shortly after the beginning of the council, it was decided to publish a monthly

'Newsheet' which quickly became the Newsletter we know today. The first issue was published in April, 1974 and it is clear from the archive copies of these publications that the basic structure of the present council was formed at the very beginning with sub-committees being started for Sports, Planning/Environment, Newsheet, Social Services, Garda Siochána and Cultural Interests.

The new council was most fortunate to get Dun Laoghaire Corporation to purchase Epworth Hall on Rockfort Avenue for the use of the Community Council. However, a subsequent decision was taken by the Community Council to return it to Dun Laoghaire Corporation who subsequently sold it for use as a private residence.

In October 1974, a competition was announced for a new logo for the Community Council. Community events continued much as they do today with many organisations mentioned in the subsequent newsletters, a reflection of the multiude of activities catered for within the area over the years. Among the most popular activities were guided historical walks with Mr. Harry Lathan around different parts of Dalkey.

Ger Coakley

Present Dalkey Community Council
L to R: Maureen Quinn, Danny Merity, Mary Rigney, Carmel Threadgold,
Richard Mooney (Secretary), Ken Dixon (Chairman),
Martine Lavery, Eithne Blake.
Missing from Photo: Rosaleen Callaghan, Gerard Coakley (Newsletter Editor).

First Dalkey Community Council
Back (l to r): J. Mackey, H. Latham, J. Kelly, R. Budds,
R. Blake, R. Lambkin
Front (l to r): E. Dooge, M. Kelly,
P. Northover (Chairman), D. Dmyth, V. Loughran,
M. Kennedy (not incl.)

Brief History of Dalkey United

The following is a history of our club, it is impossible to cover the events of the last 55 years in great detail. It would require a volume of books to deal comprehensively with all the events and all the characters involved over such a long period. During the spring and early summer evenings of 1953, a group of lads from Dalkey would meet almost every evening and spend the hours until darkness fell playing football in the fields under the quarry on Dalkey Hill. The fields were level and clear of any bushes etc. not like they are today. As the summer was ending, Des McWilliams, John Keyes, Tom Roche, Billy Byrne, Barney Kavanagh and Brian Reilly decided under the street lamp at the top of "The

Cup Semi-Final Victory 1954
Back: J. Friel, P. Morris, J. Myler, J. Keyes,
J. Moloney, D. McWilliams, J. Maloney,
V. Dunphy, D. Friel (boy), B. Byrne, J. Walsh,
P. O'Brien, J. Kelly, F. Mullen, J. Doyle, R.I.P.
Front: J Maher, R.I.P., T. Hammond, L. Cooke (on
ground), T. Roach, J. Kavanagh, J. Doyle (boy),
T. Kenny, B. O'Reilly, A. Kavanagh R.I.P.,
N. Murray, J. Dunne (boy)

Flags" to start a football club, and enter the Co. Wicklow District Junior League Division 2. On Thursday nights, the meetings were held in the late P.J. O'Loughlin's garage on Dalkey Hill. They agreed that the new club should be called Dalkey United. The sum of £20.00 was borrowed from M. & Mrs. Dan Friel. A full set of jerseys, knicks, stockings and footballs were bought for £17.15 from O'Hanlon's in Talbot Street, Dublin and everything was ready for the first season

The first unofficial game played was against Ballsbridge and Dalkey won 3-0. At the end of their first season against all the odds, the team qualified for the final of the Co. Wicklow and District Junior Cup

Our First Cup Final

The Club contested its first Cup Final on the 28th May 1954 at the Carlisle Grounds in Bray. The town of Dalkey and the surrounding areas were almost deserted for the game. The opposition was Sandyford St. Mary's, who had at that time years of experience in Junior Football.

The game commenced at a cracking pace and after 15 minutes Dalkey were leading 2 – 1. However with the game drawing to a close, 'the bubble appeared to be bursting', the score was Sandyford 3, Dalkey 2 and Dalkey were awarded a penalty. John Keyes, then 19 years, stepped up to take the

penalty and promptly blasted the ball over the bar, in the general direction of Dalkey town. That appeared to be the end. The Sandyford goalkeeper took the kick out. The aforementioned John Keyes collected the ball direct from the kick out, and with his superb skill ghosted past one defender after another, and from 12 yards out to the right of the goal laid on a perfect pass to Joe Moloney who unleashed a shot. The Sandyford keeper did not see the ball until he turned to take it out of the back of the net, 3 – 3. The kick off and the final whistle came almost simultaneously.

During the week that followed, nothing was talked about in Dalkey, but the forthcoming replay – all the junior press reporters said Dalkey had missed their chance. On the following (4th June) Friday every train that pulled into Bray from 5.30 pm onwards was bedecked with Black and White Flags and Ribbons.

Dalkey attacked from the start and urged on by a bigger following than at the drawn

Tony Hennessey (Capt.) and Jimmy Walshe (Hon. Sec. with League Cup 1960

game, laid siege on the Sandyford goal, but the ball just would not go in. Sandyford took up the running, but the Dalkey rearguard inspired by Jimmy Walsh RIP, DesMcWilliams, Barney Kavanagh and Brian Reilly stood firm.

Pat O'Brien and Billy Byrne were playing the games of their young careers in midfield. The forwards led by Joe Moloney rained shots on Sandyford full backs who were having nightmare games. Tension was at fever pitch and with time and daylight fast disappearing John Keyes was brought down in the penalty area. Brian Reilly at 17 years the youngest player on the field, after several of the 'older' players refused to take the spot kick, coolly placed the ball on the spot, stepped back, sent the

Sandyford keeper to the right of the goal and blasted a low ball into the left hand corner. Incidentally Brian who never missed a penalty played his entire career with our club, a career stretching 13 years. It is hard to understand how 'superstars' who are being paid 40 to 50 thousand pounds a week cannot score from penalty spots. A few minutes later, it was all over. The pitch was invaded and the players were carried shoulder high from the field. The captain, Tom Roche, collected the cup, which was duly filled in the old C.I.E Bar in Bray Station, before its journey to Dalkey commenced. When the train arrived in Dalkey, those who had travelled by other transport and the few who could not make it to Bray were at the railway station to meet the train, which was packed to the doors with supporters. The players were again carried shoulder high down through the town. The cup was filled again in Jim McManus (RIP) Chip Shop for most of the players, and was then taken by the more 'senior' supporters to John Searsons, where it was filled with stronger refreshments. A great night was had by all and the singing continued into the early hours of the following morning.

The Move to Hyde Park

The following Season 1954/1955 was one of the most exciting ever. The team remained undefeated in League, Cups and Shield Competitions until March of 1955 when we lost 3-2 to Sandyford in a 2nd Division Cup Game in Hyde Park.

We had just secured an agreement with Dun Laoghaire Corporation to play our home games in Hyde Park which was then designated as 'an open space'. Des McWilliams, went to meet Mr. Liam Cosgrave T.D. (later Taoiseach) and a few weeks later we had our home ground at a rent of €5 per season. We now pay €600 per season for the lease of the pitch. We own our clubrooms which have the most modern facilities for junior and schoolboy football. Last season we spent in excess of €200,000 on improvements with new dressing rooms, shower rooms etc. which was borrowed from A.I.B in Dalkey.

We won the Wicklow District Senior Cup on Easter Sunday 1955 beating Na Sasairainigh (a long established Bray Club) 1-0 with a goal from Dave Dowdall.

It was a great weekend for football in the area as the late Richie Whelan of St. Joseph's Glasthule won the first of his many Junior International Caps in a match against Scotland in Dalymount Park. Richie was not only a great player but a true gentleman.

The League Championship was won before a packed Hyde Park two weeks later.

Probably the most notable achievement that season was getting through to the Final of the Leinster Junior Shield. Teams from the Province competed in this event. The first round games took place in September and the final the following June.

We had some great victories on our way to the Final. Victories against Shamrock Celtic, Boyne Rovers, St. Lawrence's come to mind. The Semi Final was in Home Farm's ground in Whitehall against Alton United, one of the oldest Clubs in football having won the Senior Cup in the yearly 1920's.

We won 1 – 0 with a second half goal scored by one of the many great centre forwards we have had in our club – Dave Dowdall. Luck ran out however when we were beaten in the final by Malahide United 2 – 0. It was great effort for such a young club. Indeed it was an invaluable experience and Dalkey United became a team that was respected far and wide

throughout Leinster.

The season however ended on a high note. On Whit Weekend Beresford United a team from Liverpool paid its first of many visits to Dalkey. The club was run by friends of the great Peter Farrell who was then Captain of Everton. It was a glorious sunny afternoon in Hyde Park, Dalkey beat our visitors 3 – 2 with goals by John Keyes (2) and Brian Reilly. John was leading scorer that year with 30 goals.

The team then entered the A.U.L Division 2 (Sunday) League and started with a 2 – 2 draw against Reds United at Clondalkin. However, the team soon faced sterner opposition and defeats by Taylor Keith (3-1, Beggsboro (5-1) and St. Kevins (4-1) but success soon followed. The team improved as the season progressed and beat 3-0 Gentex from Athlone before a huge crowd in Hyde Road in the last match of the season. David Dowdall was the leading scorer with 32 goals.

The next season, 1957/58 the Division 2 championship was won and the team was promoted to Division 1 thanks to some heroic performances from John Maher, Frank Bolger, Kevin Smith, Jimmy Casey and others. Summer Tournaments were very popular in those days and Dalkey United has some outstanding successes for such a young club. Frank Bolger was leading goal scorer with 28 goals.

The club formed a second team in 1956/1957 season and joined the A.U.L. Division. Both the 1st and 2nd. Teams continued to make progress in leagues that were then the strongest in junior football.

Dalkey Celtic was founded in the 1955/1956 Season and many outstanding 'local derbies' were played between two great clubs. They were sporting 'enemies' on the field of play but great friends off it. The clubs amalgamated 30 years ago and this event resulted in the pooling of resources that eventually led to the development of schoolboy teams in the club and the building of the modern clubrooms that can be seen in Hyde Park. It was a great decision that was never regretted by all concerned.

Further successes were achieved in the

L to R, Back Row: Ken Kelly, Maurice Cunningham (Capt), Jimmy Walsh, Tony Walsh, Mick Byrne,
Front: Dennis Pender, Jimmy Casey, Charlie Reilly, John Maguire, Mark Hennessey

1959/1960 Season when the senior Team won the A.U.L. League Cup and the Reserve Team won the A.U.L. Division 3 Championship on 13th May 1960. Maurice Cunningham was captain of this team and Matt Campbell was the clubs leading scorer with 37 goals for the season.

The club won the A.U.L Division 1 Title on the 22nd April 1962. The run into the championship was hectic, T.E.K, Bray Wanderers, Home Farm and East Wall were all beaten en-route. In the final game we beat Belgrove 2 – 1 with goals by Arthur Homan and Willie McEvoy in a game in which Dave Knight, John Maher, Brian Reilly and Kevin Smith were outstanding.

We entered the Leinster Senior League in

1964 and went on to have many great victories particularly in the Leinster Senior Cup and the F.A.I. Senior Cup. Epic games under the then new floodlights at Tolka Park against Shelbourne, Drumcondra, Transport, Home Farm during the 1960's and 1970's are vividly recalled and are such a wonderful part of our history. Away victories in FAI Cup competitions against Limerick, Athlone, Cobh Rambl;ers, Drogheda and Swilly Rovers also come to mind. Frank Crawley, Willie Galligan and the famous Benny Henderson managed the teams over this period.

The club reached the quarter final of the F.A.I. Senior Cup in 1966. They played Waterford, then one of the leading clubs in the Country and although, we had most of the play Waterford scored the winning goal by one of the games leading players Alfie Hale a few minutes from time.

In the following years we were beaten 1 – 0 by Transport in the Semi Final of the F.A.I. Intermediate Cup and 2 – 1 by The Workmen's Club in the Semi Final of the Metropolitan Cup.

Yes, the late sixties through the seventies were exciting years by any standards. Players such as Dave Knight, George English, John Maher, Hughie McCann (still very much involved) Joe Kelly, Fran Byrne, Billy Kane, Kevin Smith, Brendan Martin, Colm Molloy, Maurice Ledwidge, Jimmy Mooney Peter Montgomery, Dave and Eddie McDonald made wonderful contributions to those games.

In 1974 we won the F.AI Intermediate Cup by beating Rialto 2 – 1 at Tolka Park. The club was managed at that time by Tommy Maguire and both goals were scored by Gerry Wildes who went onto a great career with Shelbourne – the League of Ireland and was the first player from the club to play in the European Cup.

League of Ireland B Division
In 1968 we became members of the League of Ireland 'B' Division and we continued to play in the Leinster Senior League with our second team and erected floodlights over our training area inside the road railings which we continue to use up to the present. Initially everything went smoothly and our team continued to improve in the League of Ireland. However, the organisation deteriorated and the clubs like ours who did not have teams in the Senior Division of the League were treated very unfairly. It was not unusual to arrive at an away venue as far away as Waterford, Dundalk or such places and find the grounds closed and no official of the club present to explain why the fixture was not being played.

We had no means of redress, no action was taken by the League and the travelling expenses were considerable. Not withstanding these problems the club continued to improve, we won the League Cup for the Blackthorn Trophy in 1975/76 and 1976/77 Seasons.

In the 1977/78 Season we were determined to become the first club to win the Cup for 3 years in succession. Every effort was made by all involved to achieve this objective, players trained as never before under the direction of our Manager the late Mick Dalton whose contribution to the club over many years was immense.

We reached the Quarter Final, we were drawn to play away against Dundalk. Keeping in mind the fact that we were dealing with the most incompetent and unprofessionally organised league that we have been involved with in our history, the events detailed here were mind boggling. Reflecting back as I write, I cannot find a logical explanation.

On the Friday night prior to our game with Dundalk, that outstanding personality, a

A.U.L. Div. 1 Champions 1961-62
Back: J. Mullen (Chmn.), J. Maher, R.I.P.,
K. Smith, D. Knight, F. Byrne, C. Molloy, J. Kelly
(Trainer).
Front: F. Mullen (Ass. Sec.), M. Lewidge, M.
Hennessy, B. Martin (Capt.), A. Homan,
J. Kelly, B. O'Reilly.

true gentleman of immense integrity and Manager of Dundalk, Mr. Jim McLaughlin rang our chairman to know if we would agree to postpone the game. It was dreadful weather and he said that he was sure that the pitch would be unplayable the following Sunday.

It was the depths of winter and with snow, sleet and gales almost all sporting events were postponed that weekend. We readily agreed to a postponement. Dundalk as was their responsibility duly notified the referee, linesmen and the league and we awaited notification of a date for the re-fixture.

Many weeks later Hugo McCann and I both read in newspapers that the league had made the draw for the semi-finals and that Dalkey's name was not included. The club notified the league that we had not played the Quarter Final match, we were informed that the Semi Finals were going ahead the following Sunday and that was the end of the matter. Dundalk were informed that unless they played the match they would be expelled from the competition.

The club then placed the matter in the hand of our two legal friends the late Mr. Martin

Management Committee 1961.
Back: Joe Mullen, Tom Ross, Chairman,
Pat Flynn, James Kelly, Ed Keenan.
Front: Frank Mullen, Jimmy Clyne,
Sam Richardston, Larry O'Toole,
Jimmy Walsh, Hon. Sec.

Kennedy S.C. and Mr. Colm Condon S.C. who kindly offered to help us following a well publicised dispute that eventually ended as we headed to The High Court. The league decided to declare the result of the semi-finals null and void. We beat Dundalk and went on to win the trophy by beating Bohemians in Dalymount Park.

Following our victory we immediately resigned from the League of Ireland and am pleased to say that we never regretted the decision.

Paul McGrath

When Paul McGrath joined Dalkey United in 1978 it became immediately obvious that he had a great career ahead of him. Although he was young he showed a level of maturity that was away above his age.

The club was fortunate to have people who because of their long involvement in the game could identify a player of exceptional ability quickly. Among those in the club at that time were Johnny Dunne, Tommy Cullen and the Vice President Billy Behan,

whose son Terry also gave great service to the club. At a very early age Paul, through Billy Behan who was a lifelong friend of the great Sir Matt Busby was destined for Manchester United. Unfortunately as the planning of his move to Old Trafford was at an advanced stage, Paul became seriously ill. His problem was totally unrelated to the well publicised problems that he endured in later life. It was however necessary to postpone his move to Manchester United and he spent a lengthy period in and out of hospital. The illness lasted for a couple of years during which time he received great help from Dalkey United and great encouragement from Sir Matt and Billy Behan who consistently made it clear he would be welcome in Manchester if his health recovered sufficiently.

First Dalkey Utd. Schoolboy Team to Win a League
Championship.
Back: S. Reilly, C. Murray (Ref.), P. O'Neill.
Middle: J. McCormack, P. Leonard, C. Snoddy,
R. Fitzpatrick, L. O'Hegarty, B. Mullen, M. Russell,
B. Olden.
Front: M. Ryan, J. Sheeran, J. Reid, E. Newbanks,
J. O'Neill, C. McCabe

A few months after he resumed playing football with Dalkey United Sir Matt and Billy suggested that he should test his strength for a trial period with a League of Ireland Club. Several League of Ireland Clubs including Shamrock Rovers, Bohemians and Home Farm were contacted and Paul's circumstances were outlined, they showed little or no interest. Eventually St. Patrick's Athletic were approached by Dalkey officials and it was explained to them that Sir Mat and Billy Behan had suggested that Paul should have a trial period with a League of Ireland Club. If he got through satisfactory he would be signing for Manchester United. It was further explained that Dalkey United did not require any transfer fee and it was agreed that any money forthcoming from Manchester United should be invested for Paul's future.

His period of just a few short months in the League of Ireland was so successful that he won Player of the Year Trophy in 1979.

While Dalkey United and their officials were away on a football tour in Germany Paul was brought to Old Trafford and he signed for United for a salary which was less than that which he was earning in Ireland and a signing on fee which was disgraceful. Many different stories have been written about this period of Paul's career some of them so incorrect that they border on being fictional. I reiterate that when Paul left Dalkey United he did so on the understanding that only he would benefit financially when he signed for Manchester United. Such was not the case and such is life.

Paul without doubt was one of the best players that Ireland ever produced. He came to our club as merely a boy, I remember the day well and he became one of the great central defenders of all time. I recall the great names who played in that position over the last 60 years, our own Jackie Carey and Charlie Hurley would figure in anyone's list of the top ten. Billy Wright and Neill Franklin of England, George Young of Scotland, John Charles of Wales, Ockwick of Austria, Santa Maria of Spain,

Socrates of Brazil and Franco Baressi of Italy would be the remainder on my lists. There is no doubt in my mind he would be as good if not better than most of them. He was certainly more versatile and could excel in either fullback positions or centre field. There is one aspect of his professional career that always amazed those who were close to him during his time with Dalkey United. That was, that none of his managers ever realised his potential as a

Dalkey United Schoolboys 1979-80
Back: Finbarr Flood, Brian Gallagher,
David Hennessy, Barry Mullen, Peter O'Brien,
Ollie Barry, Kevin Kerr,
Conor McCabe, John Kavanagh,
Front: David Moran, John Sheeran,
Colm Carrigan, John McCormack,
John Cavanagh, Derek Kavanagh.

centre forward/striker. On numerous occasions when Dalkey would be struggling in a game if Paul was pushed up front he would swing the game around with some glorious goals. Paul has experienced the good life and the tough side of it, he will always be remembered as one of the most outstanding footballers that Ireland ever produced and that is hopefully how most people will remember him.

I will always remember him as the young lad with the large head of hair who came out into the big world after a young life in several orphanages. It was a world that he so often found difficult to handle and at times still does.

My dad recalled during one of his many good periods, a few years after his career ended he was with him in the Gaiety Theatre when that most talented of performers, a genius in his own right Phil Coulter, spotted him in the audience and stopped his show to pay a tribute to Paul. He ended his few words by saying, "he was the only sports person I knew who transcended the popularity boundaries of the game he graced for so long". Paul got three standing ovations which he richly deserved.

He is on record as stating that the highlights of his career were the European and World Cup Finals.

During his time in Dalkey United he was constantly an inspiration to all those around

Dalkey United U11's Cup Winners 1989/90
Back: T. Burke, B. Mullen, D. Forde, N. McCann,
A. Bowman, C. Crangie, C. McAteer, A. Cahill,
P. Maher, B. Allen, M. Power.
Front: B. Delaney, A. Archbold, J. Gleeson,
D. Conroy, J. O'Reilly, R. Conroy, M. Boots,
D. Kenneddy.

him and some of his displays will remain in the memory forever of those who were involved in the club during his years there. Paul's courage during the period when he was recovering from illness was unique and everyone not just in Dalkey United but throughout the football world wished him well. When he first came to Dalkey United the club arranged accommodation for him with Jimmy Hammond and his wife Anne. The Hammond family had a long relationship with the club and 'Jem' s brother

Teddy was a prominent member of the very first team that won the cup in 1954 and the double of League and Cup in 1955. Teddy was following in the sporting traditions of his brothers George and Nicky who were accomplished players. Nicky was a member of the famous 'Dr. Wrights Old Boys' team who caused such a major shock by winning the keenly contested Summer

Dalkey Utd. Schoolboys 1983
Back: John Byrne, Rory Campbell, John Flynn,
Front: David McCann, John Byrne,
Joseaph Madden

Tournament in 1949 in Sallynoggin.

Paul's first job was a roofer for the Hammond family who have been involved in the roofing business for generations. He later went to work as a Security Officer for Michael Fenton who owned C.P. Security and turned out to be a wonderful help to Paul in so many different ways.

His display during his years with Dalkey were superb, he played in defence, centre field and up front from where he scored some great goals.

Paul writing in the club's Golden Jubilee Brochure said, 'I was so lucky to have joined Dalkey United as a young lad starting out on a career in football. I have been fortunate to have had a wonderful career that has given me such joy and comfort and so many wonderful memories. None of this would have been possible were it not for the help and kindness which I have received from the first day that I joined the club from those involved in it. The organisation of my testimonial by the club was

The Brilliant Young Footballers from the Fifties 30th Anniversary Get Together.
Back: Joe Maloney, Johnnie Dunne, Ned Cooke, Tom Roche, Frank Mullen, John Keyes, Brian Reilly.
Middle: Ted Hammond, Nick Keyes, Des McWilliams, Barney Kavanagh, Hugh Magee, R.I.P.,
Front: Billy Byrne, Pat O'Brien, Liam Cooke, Jimmy Walsh, R.I.P.

incredible. I never deserved such a tribute, and it was almost beyond belief. Their kindness knows no bounds and in good times and bad they have been of incredible help to me'.

It was the most successful testimonial ever organised in which the entire committee of the club were involved for over a year. The large contributions made by National Lottery, Denis O'Brien and Ged Pierce were the foundations for the financial success which culminated in over 45,000 filling Lansdowne Road for his testimonial game.

We were close to Paul during his entire career and my father has often been asked what was his greatest game. He has absolutely no hesitation in saying that his display against Italy in the World Cup Finals in The Giant Stadium in New Jersey, when Ireland beat Italy 1-0 was his greatest ever. His display that day ranks with the great displays of Tommy Godwin when Ireland beat England 2-0 in Goodison Park on Wednesday, 21 September 1949 when Peter Farrell scored the second goal. It also is in his opinion compares favourably with Johnny Giles display on 1st November 1959 when Ireland beat Sweden by 3-2. Sweden had been runners up to Brazil in the world cup the previous year when Johnny scored that glorious goal in the 'School End' at Dalymount Park and Liam Brady's display in the defeat of Brazil by 1-0 on Saturday 23 May 1987 when Liam scored the winning goal in the Havelock Square End of Lansdowne Road – truly golden moments: in the history of Irish Football.

Our growing recognition was further enhanced by schoolboy and senior teams visiting and playing in tournaments in what was then known as West Germany at the beginning of the 80's. This recognition was consolidated when the Dutch Senior National side used our new facilities for training prior to their World Cup match against the Republic of Ireland in October 1980.

Although the trophy cabinet may not have been as full as previous times there were reasons to celebrate in the May of 1983 when a Dalkey United Senior Team managed by Joe McCann and skippered by Peter Gough won the Tommy Vaughan Cup by a scoreline of 1 – 0 over Park Villa at a packed Red Cow ground, the winning goal coming in the 10th minute of extra time scored by a jubilant Maurice Mulville. Managers deserving of notable mention over this period were Don Tierney, Adrian Cairns, Jack Beirne, Joe McCann, Wes

McDonnell, Mick Power, Dave Kane, Essie Carolan, Dan O'Toole and Matt Britton.

Our other soccer connections saw us entertaining Kirkwood Soccer Club from Delaware in the USA and several high profile friendly matches culminating in the 40th anniversary exhibition match at Hyde Road against Millwall F C in July of 1993. Another success was in 1998 when we won the Liam Dodd Cup beating Tymon Bawn 1 – 0, the winner coming from the instinctive Johnny Orange after being setup by Bernard Rowe, to the delight of Manager, Jack Beirne.

In 2003/04 the senior team led by Dan O'Toole won promotion to the Leinster Senior League to Div. IA In 2006/07 the senior team managed by Matt Britton won Division 1 of the League, a truly remarkable success.

We have indeed been fortunate to have had numerous people down through the years who give of their services voluntarily up to and including the present day. Without the help of so many it would not be possible to continue. After 55 years it would be unfair to mention names. Suffice to say that the level of assistance has been unique.

List of Honours

Senior Teams

1953 – 1954	Co. Wicklow and District Cup Winners
1954 – 1955	Co. Wicklow and District League Champions and Senior Cup Winners
	Leinster Junior Shield Runners Up
1956 – 1957	A.U.L. Division 2 Runners Up
1957 – 1958	A.U.L. Division 2 Champions
1959 – 1960	A.U.L. Division 3 Champions
1961 – 1962	A.U.L. Division 1 Champions
1962 – 1963	A.U.L. League Cup Runners Up
1965 – 1966	Quarter Finalists in F.A.I. Senior Cup
1968 – 1969	Semi Finalists in F.A.I. Intermediate Cup
1973 – 1974	F.A.I. Intermediate Cup Winners
1975 - 1976	League of Ireland Blackthorn Cup Winners
1976 – 1977	League of Ireland Blackthorn Cup Winners
1977 – 1978	League of Ireland Blackthorn Cup Winners
1982 – 1983	Leinster Senior League Vaughan Cup Winners
1997 – 1998	Leinster Senior League Liam Dodd Cup Winners
2003 – 2004	Leinster Senior League Division 1B Runners Up
2006 – 2007	Leinster Senior League Division 1A Champions

DALKEY UNITED

First Game Played Sunday 20th August 1953

Line Out

Paddy Thorpe

Nick Keyes   Ned Luby

Billy Byrne   John Maher   Des McWilliams
Brian O'Reilly   John Keyes   Joe Maloney
Liam Cooke   Tom Roche (Capt)

Others who played in 1st season:
Pat O'Brien   Hughie Magee   Vincent Mulligan   Andy Kavanagh
Teddy Hammond   Barney Kavanagh   Jimmy Walsh & Martin Kelly

Paddy and Marie Thorpe

The late Jimmy Walsh R.I.P. with John Maher R.I.P. on way to Wembley 1964.

*A Year Later
Tom Roche, Barney Kavanagh, Joe Maloney, Des McWilliams*

Schoolboy Football

Many people regard football as a religion so it was somewhat appropriate that the old 'Laundry Field' hockey pitch in Loreto Abbey Dalkey provided the venue for the first Dalkey United schoolboy team in September 1976.

The playing surface could never have been described as a billiard table but that did no prevent our Under 11 team from winning the league title in our inaugural season in the now defunct South County Dublin League, also known locally as 'The Monkstown League'.

The religious theme continued when we briefly moved venue to St. Joseph of Cluny School, Killiney and soon after entered additional teams into the Catholic Youth Council (CYC) League.

Our period in this league was extremely successful and our teams secured a total of 11 trophies in a four year period commencing in the 1978/79 season and also moved to playing matches on the main club pitch in Hyde Park.

This was an era that preceded Euro '88, Italia '90, 'the Celtic Tiger' and Sky Sports. The game of association football during these years did not attract the significant amounts of money that it currently does at all levels.

It was therefore, an ongoing challenge to maintain and develop our schoolboy section and enormous credit is due to Joe Dowling RIP, Des McWilliams, Joe Cullinane, Hugo McCann, Maurice Cunningham, Sean Thomas, Finbar Flood, John Kavanagh and many others for their fantastic efforts during these years.

During the summer of 1989, local advertisements on the formation of a new Under 11 team attracted sufficient numbers for two teams under the guidance of Bob Allen and myself. This season reached a successful conclusion with victory over St. Mary's, Sandyford in the South County Dublin League Cup Final on a deserved score line of 2-0.

Although the 1990s heralded the dawn of a new era for Irish football on the international stage, Dalkey United failed to add any further schoolboy honours to their collection. However, in the latter part of this decade the club made a significant decision that would greatly influence the direction of Dalkey United going into the new millennium.

The town of Dalkey and surrounding areas was experiencing a rapid growth in young families and the club moved to devote significant effort and resources into attracting some of these young children into our schoolboy section. Progress both on and off the pitch has followed at a rate that not even the most optimistic would have predicted at the time.

With all our teams now competing in the EBS South Dublin Football League the initial breakthrough came in the 2002/03 season with the somewhat modest return of Under 8C League Runners Up. However since that season our schoolboy teams have enjoyed an unbroken run of delivering honours at most age groups and in all competitions.

Among the highlights of many successes were our Under 13 team, managed by Niall Coleman winning the league on an unbeaten run in the 2003/04 Season. A further notable achievement was recorded in the 2005/06 Season with our Under 14 team, managed by Tim Galvin and David Hennessy securing a league and cup double.

A rapid expansion of a schoolboy section in any football club requires solid structures. In this area, we are fortunate to have a vibrant Academy Section feeding young players into our Under 8 teams each season.

Our Academy Section was originally the idea of current schoolboy manager, John Thorne. It commenced some years ago with modest numbers but now caters for in excess of 50 young members between the ages of 4 and 8 in twice weekly training sessions.

Another landmark was achieved at the commencement of the 2007/08 season when, for the first time in the history of Dalkey United AFC, we fielded at least one team in all age groups from Under 8 up to the oldest group of Under 17.

Given the above landmark, it was perhaps appropriate that the 2007/08 season also heralded the announcement of a significant sponsorship deal with Pierse Contracting. This generous arrangement is worth €40,000 to the club over a three year period and allows all teams in Dalkey United AFC to be kitted out to a standard that befits the current standing of the club.

This is compounded by the fact that the Management Committee of the club has decided to withdraw from Intermediate Football and concentrate all its efforts on Schoolboys and Schoolgirls football from the start of the coming season (2008-2009)

Barry Mullen
July 2008

List of Honours

Schoolboy Teams

1976 – 1977	South Co. Dublin Under 11 League Champions
1978 – 1979	C.Y.C Under 11 League Champions
	C.Y.C Under 11 Shield Winners
	C.Y.C Under 13 League Champions
	C.Y.C Under 13 Cup Winners
1979 – 1980	C.Y.C Under 12 League Champions
	C.Y.C Under 12 Cup Winners
	C.Y.C Under 14 League Champions
1980 – 1981	C.Y.C Under 13 League Champions
	C.Y.C Under 14 League Champions
1981 – 1982	C.Y.C Under 13 League Champions
	C.Y.C Under 14 League Champions
1982 – 1983	Dalkey Festival Tournament Winners (Youths)
1989 – 1990	South County Dublin Cup Winners (Under 11)
2002 – 2003	South Dublin Football League (SDFL) Under 8C League Runners Up
2003 – 2004	SDFL Under 9B League Champions
	SDLF Under 13 Div 2 League Champions
2004 – 2005	SDFL Under 8 Premier League Cup Winners
	SDFL Under 9 Major League Champions
	SDFL Under 12 Marie O'Reilly Cup Runners Up
2005 – 2006	SDFL Under 9 Major League Cup Winners
	SDFL Under 10 Major League Cup Runners Up
	SDFL Under 11 Paul Steward Cup Runners Up
	SDFL Under 14 Div 2 League Champions
	SDFL Under 14 Premier League Cup Winners
	DDSL Under 12 Div B1 League Winners
2006 – 2007	SDFL Under 8B League Runners Up
	SDFL Under 8D League Champions
	SDFL Under 8 Catherine O'Farrell League Cup Runners Up
	SDFL Under 9C League Champions
	SDFL Under 9E League Runners Up
	SDFL Under 14 Div 2 League Runners Up
	SDFL Under 16 Premier League Champions
2007 – 2008	SDFL Under 8 Div 4 League Runners Up
	SDFL Under 8 Major 2 League Cup Runners Up
	SDFL Under 9 Div 3 League Runners Up
	SDFL Under 9 Div 5 League Champions
	SDFL Under 11 Premier League Cup Runners Up
	SDFL Under 17 League Cup Runners Up

Back to the Sea the Story
of Mrs. Audrey Topping

Mrs. Audrey L. Topping was a well-known and very respected figure in Dalkey for a long number of years.

She cut a commanding figure both in physique and a wonderful head of hair. Local gossip had it that her hair turned to grey after her experience of being saved from the R.M.S. Leinster which was sunk by a German submarine in 1918.

The Leinster was a forerunner to the mail boats or the Sea Link Ferries that sail between Dun Laoghaire and Hollyhead every day.

The R.M.S. Leinster

Many lost their lives on that awful day. The firemen who where facing defeat in the 1st World War had no compunction about blowing up passenger ships alleging that they were also transporting arms and explosives.

She was also known for her love of nature, she would never cut a branch from a live tree or pick wild flowers from the 2 acres of land that surrounded her house – Rocklands, Harbour Road, Dalkey. The gardens stretched down to the sea where she had a private harbour in which she had her daily swim all through the year.

She was noted for her love of animals and usually had at least a dozen dachschunds all of which had the freedom to roam around the grounds.

All the neighbours children and me spent many happy days in our childhood climbing trees, riding around the grounds on her two donkeys or just playing in the large summer house on the side of her garden. If you misbehaved you would be imperiously dismissed but after a week or so you would be reprieved and all would be forgiven. Around 1943 Jack Doyle rented Rocklands from Mrs. Topping and lived there with his wife Movita for some time. He rented one of the small houses that faces the sea in Sandycove as one walks up to the Forty Foot, just before The Joyce Museum.

When she was moving her personal belongings to Sandycove my pals and I helped her because she had been so kind to us when we were younger.

During Jack Doyle's tenure in Dalkey he certainly livened up the town and was a very funny man to meet on the streets or at Bulloch Harbour where we swam a lot in those summers of our youth. We did not understand that he would have partaken of significant amounts of drink. He never looked to us to be drunk but we learned in later years of the amounts he consumed on a daily basis.

Mrs. Topping returned to Rocklands before the end of the War and lived there until circa 1951 when she died after a short illness. She let it be known that she wanted to be buried at sea in the vicinity of where the Leinster sank, from where she was rescued.

Friends of hers arrived in large numbers and on a sunny summer Saturday afternoon the largest flotilla of boats ever assembled at Dalkey bore her remains out to the Kish Bank where the final prayers were read by the late Canon Collins from St. Patrick's Church almost across the road from Rocklands where she lived for so many years and gave so much happiness to so many young people.

Her final wish was granted and her remains were consigned to the deep in a lead coffin.

Patrick J. Kavanagh
July 2008

The Gorgeous Gael and The Dalkey Connection

Dalkey United A.F.C. Yearbook 2003/04

Down through the years, Dalkey, for various reasons, has attracted a significant number of well-known people.

Famous film stars, writers, singers and personalities have, from time to time, marked their presence in Dalkey for varying periods of time. Shaw, Joyce, Cusack, Newman and Parnell immediately come to mind. The number of well-know people, both nationally and internationally, who currently reside in Dalkey and obviously enjoy the beauty, and at most times the tranquillity of the area, is significant.

Jack Doyle and his lovely wife Movita.

In the summer of 1943, two of the best-known stars of screen and stage of that time arrived to live in Dalkey and settled in Rocklands on Harbour Road. During these dismal wartime years, Jack Doyle, "The Gorgeous Gael", and his stunningly beautiful, American-born wife, Maria Louisa Castaneda, certainly took Dalkey by storm. Maria Louisa was known to her family as Mavie but was universally known as the film star Movita.

"Jack" Doyle was born in Cobh on 13th August 1913. He was the first son born to Michael and Anastasia Doyle. He weighed in at 14lbs. He was christened Joe. The Doyles were a well-known boxing family and Jack's grand-uncle had been a British Forces Boxing Champion.

Michael Doyle was a merchant seaman but two serious accidents rendered him incapable of working. He injured himself in a fall at sea and he was discharged from the navy. He got a job in a local quarry but lost his left eye as a result of an accident in the quarry. It was very difficult to find employment in Ireland during these years but Stacia, like so many mothers in those days, was very resilient and she became the main breadwinner in the family, working in local farms and houses.

Joe, meanwhile, was growing into a well-built child. When he was twelve years old, he was nearly 6ft tall and weighed eleven stone. Where schoolboys gather, fights often occur and if Joe was around he was never challenged as he had developed a name for himself by seeing off lads much older than himself with a snappy right uppercut. His idol during those years was the World Champion, Jack Dempsey.

When Joe joined the Irish Guards he became known as Jack Doyle. He gave his age as eighteen, two years older than his correct age, and succeeded with his application. He had failed to join the Free State Army by giving the wrong age.

When he enlisted as an Irish Guardsman, he was 6ft 3ins and weighed in at around thirteen stone. At sixteen years old, he had all the natural attributes to become a great boxer. He was a beautiful soprano and had a wide repertoire of old Irish and Scottish songs. This talent made him instantly popular when the singsongs started in the barracks at night.

Jack got involved in the various boxing tournaments in the armed forces. Despite his tender years, he was an instant success, defeating opponents, a lot of whom had built up formidable records of victories. He won fights with such ease, often knocking his opponents out in the first or second round, indeed regularly in the first minute of the fight. He emerged a firm favourite to become the youngest ever armed forces heavyweight champion.

After a couple of years, he was in a position to give support to his family in Cobh, in what was a very impoverished period in our history. He bought them a beautiful house in England, where they settled. He attempted to buy himself out of the Army. His Commanding Officer, Col. Pollak, would not agree, at least not until he represented his regiment in the Armed Forces Championship. He was determined to have a champion in his regiment. He was not to be disappointed, Jack, representing the Irish Guards, became heavyweight champion on 19th February 1932. He was then discharged from the Army. During his Army career, he fought thirty fights and won thirty, all but one by knockouts.

Some of the leading managers of the day were keen to sign him on contract, although he had not yet reached his nineteenth birthday. Dan Sullivan became his manager. He won his first fight by a knockout in thirty seconds. Dan was known as a very clever manager.

Jack won his next three fights in the first round and he then fought the experienced Scottish champion, Bobby Shields, in front of a packed Anfield, the famous home of Liverpool FC, on 21st July 1932.

The vast majority of the crowd were Irish and they went crazy when Jack delivered his now famous right hook in the first round, poor Bobby had no change of beating the count.

He had fourteen more fights before the

Brian Watters and Pat O'Shea of the Commodore Hotel Cobh.

Second World War broke out in September 1939, which, in effect, was virtually the end of his boxing career. He fought twice in Dublin in 1943, winning one and losing one. While making a great name for himself in his boxing career, he also became a big box office attraction as a singer in the concert halls and theatres of England. He cut nine records, all of which were successful.

He also starred in two movies and socialised not just with the stars of screen and stage but also with members of the Royal Family. He was, in fact, the biggest name in the London social scene during the pre-war years. It was widely reported that he had a romance with a certain princess. One thing is irrefutable: wherever he travelled to, Britain, Ireland or the USA, huge crowds turned out to greet him. He was known and admired right across the whole spectrum of society.

He met and married Movita, and during the time he lived in Dalkey, he certainly lived the high life. It was a regular occurrence for him to travel with an entourage from Larkin's Pub, now Finnegan's, to the leading hotels in the city, where he spent money at an incredible rate.

Movita and he drew full houses in all the towns where they sang in Ireland during those wartime years. His heavy drinking and lifestyle did not impress Movita and eventually she left him and went back to the UK, later returning to the US, where she married Marlon Brando.

Jack's drinking brought him down so low that he ended up living in an abandoned car in Dublin City. He did, however, maintain respectable appearance, having his clothes cleaned by friends in the Wicklow Hotel, who also let him use the hotel to wash and shower.

In 1947/48, he became friendly with a Nancy Keohe, who had some friends in show business. Despite his sad state, with her help, he succeeded in changing his ways and commenced rebuilding his career as a singer and writer.

In 1949, he applied to the British Boxing Board of Control for his boxing licence to be restored but was refused. It was the correct decision, as his fitness to box had radically deteriorated due to his heavy drinking and general lifestyle.

Throughout the 1950s and 1960s, he continued to sing to crowds, not in concert halls but in pubs in London, Manchester and other cities where large number of Irish emigrants lived.

Nancy continued to live with him until the summer of 1976, when she left him never to return. He continued to drink. This time there was no Nancy Keohe to save him from self-destruction.

He lived rough on the streets or in laneways of London. He was truly down and out: no money, no friends and no hope. He was found dying in a laneway and taken to hospital on a freezing cold night. He died a few hours later in St. Mary's Hospital in Paddington on 13th December 1978. When the news reached Cobh, it was rumoured that the plans were to bury him in a pauper's grave in London. This was not true as two of his brothers were arranging to have him buried in London, where his parents were buried.

His Cobh friends got agreement from his brothers to bury him in Cobh. Amongst those friends were Pat O'Shea, proprietor of the Commodore Hotel, formerly Chairman of Cobh Ramblers and a great friend of our club, who travelled extensively with us around Europe supporting Ireland with a great sponsor of our club, Brian Waters, a Cobh native and former owner of Maxwell's Chemist, Castle Street, Dalkey.

Pat and Brian also helped to arrange and cover the cost of the funeral, which travelled by train to Liverpool by boat to Dublin, where large crowds turned out to pay their respects, with a special Requiem Mass in Merchants Quay, Adam & Eve Church. There was another Mass in Cobh where large crowds again turned out for one of the biggest funerals ever seen in that famous old town.

The Dalkey connection continued to the end. His remains were taken to Cobh Cathedral, which was built of Dalkey granite. The funeral was one of the largest ever seen in that beautiful old town. A wonderful tribute to a man who brightened the lives of so many during those dark war time years. How sad that his colourful life ended in the dark, lonely streets of London.

Frank Mullen

St. Patrick's School

The Parish School opened in 1870 being housed in part of the Lodge & Parochial Hall built in 1868 by Charles Leslie JP. An inscription gives the construction date over the Lodge doorway. The building comprised the present Lodge and stage area of the Hall. It was not until early this century that the hall was extended to take in the area occupied by the present two senior rooms.

The firs records of 1st December 1894 showed a registration of 30 pupils (12 boys and 18 girls). It was on that date that the school was first registered with the Educational Authority and given the number 14647. Up to then it was a local Church School supported by parochial subscription.

The school began as a one-teacher school and remained so until the 1950's. In the 1920's to the 1950's there was one large classroom taking in the present two senior rooms plus the stage area. Heating came from an upright coal stove half way along the vast wall of the room. There were outside toilets in the area now occupied by the passageway and cloakroom. Mrs. Armstrong was the teacher who was later succeeded by Miss Florrie Armstrong.

Rev. J.D. Murray

Rev. F.C. Young

Canon J.F.D. Williams

Rev. R.B. Rountree

school numbers diminished to around 115 but has since increased and stabilised at about 130 pupils.

In common with other National Schools a Board of Management was formed in 1975. This has been a very successful development and the Board have run the school very efficiently since that date.

The School has had a very high academic standard in recent years with a number of pupils achieving scholarships and good reports at secondary level.

Later with pupil numbers increasing to well in excess of 200 plans were made to build a new school for up to 8 teachers. A site was offered in the nearby grounds of Charleville but was never realised and many of those involved went on to found the 'Dalkey School Project' Primary School in Glenageary. Thereafter the Discipline and behaviour in the school under the present Principal, Mrs. Gertrude Clinton and assistant staff is excellent.

The PTA, have been very successful in developing extra curricular activities for the pupils such as remedial help, and also in the area of sports such as hockey, football, basketball, cricket, tennis and rounders and 'small' games activities for the younger pupils. The PTA have also provided the school with a great deal of extra equipment and teaching aids projectors, recorders, photocopier etc.

At present there is a 'New School Development Committee' negotiating with the Dept. of Education for the construction of two new classrooms over the existing two classrooms in the main school building and to remove the prefabricated buildings which is now nearing the end of its expected and useful life. In this development it is intended to provide a purpose built school while also providing separate adequate accommodation and facilities for the use of the parish. With these developments to look forward to and the continued dedication of teachers and parents the successful future of the school is assured.

St. Patrick's Church of Ireland
Anniversary Brochure 1993

The History of Dalkey Church

On 26th September 1991 the parish of Dalkey celebrated the 150th anniversary of the opening of the Church of the Assumption of the Blessed Virgin Mary.

The celebration was not confined to that one day. It lasted a full week and had a double purpose. Firstly it was to give thanks to God for a century and a half of prayer and worship in the Church in Castle Street.

Secondly, it was to mark the completion of the massive programme of restoration, during which the old building was completely renovated and prepared for another century and a half of Christian worship.

Dalkey Parish is mentioned in the earliest diocesan records of the See of Dublin. The old church of St. Begnet in the graveyard opposite the present church is claimed to date back to the seventh century. Cill Beagnait was in fact the ancient name of Dalkey.

Church of the Assumption of the Blessed Virgin Mary

In mediaeval times Dalkey, 'The Town of the Seven Castles' was a bustling port. Local historian, F.M. O'Flanagan, in an article on Dalkey published in the Dublin Historical Record in 1941/42 gives details of the castles. Two of the castles still stand, Goat's Castle, which is now the Town Hall and across the street Archibold's Castle.

Mr. O'Flanagan identifies four more castles as follows: Dungan's Castle opposite Kent Terrace; Wolverton's Castle at Webster's corner of Ulverton Road; House Castle at the rear of a grocery shop called Murtagh's and Black Castle between St. Patrick's Road and Maxwell's Pharmacy. He thinks the seventh castle was probably Bulloch Castle. The town was important enough to hold seven fairs each year and to contribute two hundred men of arms for the defence of the Pale when required.

In subsequent years the importance of Dalkey declined, probably due to the development of Dublin port. The Rev. Edward Hogan in his Description of Ireland in 1598 tells us that the 'close of the 16th century marks the disuse of Dalkey'.

The Start of Modern Dalkey

An old tombstone in the graveyard of St. Begnet's Church gives a clue as to the beginning of the development of 'modern' Dalkey. The tombstone commemorates the shipwreck of the Prince of Wales packet in November 1807. This tragedy, together with the sinking of the transport Rochdale with the loss of 380 lives led to a public petition for a safe harbourage to be built on the coast between Dublin and Dalkey.

The Act of 1815 called for 'the erection of an asylum harbour and place of refuge at

Dunleary'. Building commenced in 1816 and the granite for the harbour came from the quarries in Dalkey Hill. This venture led to the growth of Dun Laoghaire and subsequently Dalkey as residential districts.

The Need for a Church

With the general increase in population, helped by the influx of 600 quarrymen and their families. Dalkey's Catholic population had increased greatly by 1838. In that year John D'Alton, the historian of Co. Dublin, said 'the city itself is running into this little village that a few years since presented but the humble hovels of fishermen and stonecutters'. He gave the population as '1,402 persons of whom 1.290 were classed as Roman Catholics'.

Dalkey was at this time part of the parish of Monkstown. In March 1840 Canon Sheridan, the parish priest of Monkstown called a meeting of the inhabitants of Dalkey. At the meeting it was decided that a church should be erected in the town. Two hundred pounds was collected at the meeting. A site was decided upon and was leased from Mr. Thomas Connolly. In later years his son, Canon Connolly, parish priest of Harrington Street donated the land to the church.

Building and Dedication

The Catholic population was poor and the Church was a simple building. It was smaller than the present Church. It consisted of the present nave and was built about thirty feet back from Castle Street. The main door was facing the street and the altar was at the far end, where the gallery is now.

It is ironic that the men who had spent thirty years hewing granite from the quarries could not afford granite for their own church. The walls were made of stone, pebbles, mortar and earth which was plastered over. For all that, their church was just as precious to the people of Dalkey as any grand cathedral.

An early engraving.

Loreto Abbey

The same year of 1841 saw the coming of the Loreto Sisters to Dalkey. Mother Teresa Ball rented Bulloch Castle and set up a school for poor children there. Mother Ball a Dublin woman, had originally entered the Order of the Institute of the Blessed Virgin Mary in York.

She established a house in Rathfarnham in 1821 at the request of Dr. Daniel Murray, coadjutor bishop to Dr. Troy, Archbishop of Dublin. The house was called Loreto House after the home of the Holy Family, and this was the start of the Loreto Order which would become a household word throughout Ireland and all five continents.

The renting of Bulloch Castle was meant only as a temporary arrangement. The following year she began building a convent on a beautiful site beside the sea. She herself was responsible for the design of the building, which was opened in 1843. The Abbey in Dalkey, unlike the Church, was built of 'unexcelled Dalkey granite'.

Apart from its outstanding role as a convent and a school, its beautiful situation made it a holiday and convalescent home for Loreto sisters from all over the world. When Mother Ball was dying in Rathfarnham she asked to be moved to Dalkey, where she died peacefully on 19th May 1861.

Developing Parishes

Meanwhile the new Church in Dalkey was becoming firmly established. In 1846 its first resident curate was appointed, Father James Fitzpatrick.

The parish structure in the whole Dun Laoghaire area gradually changed and developed as the population grew. After the death of Canon Sheridan in 1862, the parish was divided. Father James Cavanagh was appointed parish priest of Kingstown and Monkstown.. Father John Harold was appointed parish priest of Glasthule, Dalkey and Ballybrack. He died in 1868 and was succeeded first by Canon McCabe and then in 1880 by his brother Father George Harold who was parish priest of Glasthule, Dalkey and Ballybrack until his death in 1894. The Harold Schools in Glasthule and Dalkey are a fitting tribute to the Harold Brothers and their dedicated services to the people of the locality.

It was during this period that the church in Dalkey was considerably enlarged to accommodate the growing population. The handsome tower and belfry was erected at one end, together with the gallery and organ. The organ was a fine two-manual instrument designed by the eminent Dublin organ builder, John White.

Dalkey as a Parish

After the death of Canon George Harold in 1894, Ballybrack was made into a separate parish and Archdeacon Murray was appointed parish priest of Glasthule and Dalkey. On his death in 1927 Dalkey was separated from Glasthule and made into a parish in its own right.

Since being made a parish, Dalkey has had six parish priests. Canon Jones was appointed the first parish priest in 1927. He was succeeded in 1931 by Canon McGough, who was parish priest at the time of the centenary celebrations in 1941. He died in 1943 and was followed by Father Michael Boylan, who was here for less than three years. He was transferred to Iona Road parish in 1945 and was replaced in Dalkey by Father Paul Rafter. Father John Meagher succeeded Father Rafter in 1967 and remained parish priest until his retirement in 1985 when Father Forristal, our present parish priest was appointed.

Father Meagher's eighteen years as parish priest can perhaps be used to illustrate the kind of dedication and commitment which has characterised all six parish priests. He reconstructed the sanctuary of the Church in accordance with the liturgical requirements of Vatican II. He organised new classrooms in the Harold Boys' School. On behalf of the parish, he presented the land near the Church where the tasteful development for the old people's houses was built. He laid out the car park which benefits the town as well as the Church. Father Meagher obviously cherished his years in Dalkey, as he chose to live out his retirement in the parish he had served so long.

Reflection on 150 Years

The anniversary celebrations give an opportunity to commemorate not just the Church itself but the priests and people of the parish who have worshipped in the church for over 150 years.

All we know about Patrick and Catherine Lambe is that they were the first couple to be married in the Church in September 1841 and that, according to the Church records, they subsequently had three children who were baptised there. But as we celebrate we can think about them and about all those parishioners who over the years came to the parish Church to be baptised or absolved, to receive the Eucharist, to be confirmed, to be married, to be mourned; and we can give a thought to the priests who ministered to them.

We, the parishioners and priests of today, are a living link in a chain of worship in our Church which stretches back for a hundred and fifty years and stretches forward, with God's help, 'till time and times are done'.

First published 'Memorial Booklet in Sept 1991 to commemorate the 150 Anniversary of the Building of Dalkey Church. Compiled following research by Una Neiland and reproduced by the kind permission of the current P.P Fr. McDonagh.

Moran Park - Paddy Moran

Dublin was a city of mourning on Monday, 14th March 1921. The sadness that engulfed it spread throughout the country particularly south of the city through Blackrock, Dun Laoghaire, Dalkey and Bray.

If it was possible the sadness was probably more profound in the village of Cresna not far from Boyle, Co. Roscommon for it was there that Paddy Moran was born in March 1888. After all the years that have passed I wonder how many who walk through Moran Park in Dun Laoghaire know why the park was dedicated to the memory of Paddy Moran in 1961.

There was a large crowd present when Moran Park was opened in 1961 but it could not compare with the 40,000 plus who gathered in the vicinity of Mountjoy Jail on that bitterly cold morning from five o'clock onwards when Paddy Moran and his close pal Thomas Whelan along with four of their colleagues Patrick Doyle, Frank Flood, Thomas Bryan and Bernard Ryan were executed in that jail allegedly for their part in the Bloody Sunday, November 21, 1920 assassination of fourteen members of the British Secret Service. Moran and Whelan maintained their innocence right up to walking to the scaffold to meet their doom. The Irish Independent of Thursday, March 15, 1921 under the heading 'A City of Tragedy' described the scene – Dublin was a city of tragedy yesterday morning – a centre of mourning, a city of the dead – when between 6 am and 8 am six Irishmen, some of them merely boys, yielded up their young lives on the scaffold within Mountjoy Prison.

No factory whistle was heard, no chime of bells – the only tolls being that from churchyard or steeple calling the faithful to worship. No clang of tram, no roar or rattle of car or motor, no rumble of trains, no sound of human activity disturbed the solemn silence that hung heavily over the entire city.

All avenues of appeal were explored, the Dun Laoghaire Branch of the National Union of Railwaymen pleaded with their M.P through their head office, to obtain a Royal Prerogative of Mercy for Moran, the plea failed. He was a Barman in Lynch and O'Briens Pub which stood beside where Shaws and E.B.S. are now in Lr. Georges Street in Dun Laoghaire, almost from when he came to Dublin in 1909.

Paddy Moran

The Roscommon Herald reported on Saturday, 12 March 1921 that a reprieve had been refused and that 'very strong opinions were entertained in Dublin and Kingstown as to his innocence and that prominent residents made vigorous efforts to have him reprieved".

Moran was tried for his complicity in the assassinations. Despite evidence in his favour he was found not guilty of manslaughter but guilty of murder. One British soldier identified Moran from a group of 60 people who had been arrested. He said he saw Moran near the scene of one of the murders outside 119 Baggot Street. He swore that he could be sure because he identified the time by the chime of the bells at nearby St. Stephens Church. The Rector of the Church gave evidence that no bells rang in St. Stephens Church at the time of the incident due to a fault on that particular day. A corporation official gave evidence of seeing the accused outside McFees shop Lr. Georges Street near the crucial time.

It was alleged also that he travelled from Dun Laoghaire through Blackrock town in a car on route to the city approaching the time of the shootings. A Tramway Inspector, a DMP Constable and a Sgt. Connelly who were on duty in the town gave evidence that no car passed through the town when they were on duty between 6 am and 9 am – A shopkeeper gave similar evidence.

The Irish Independent of 11 February 1921 reporting on the trial when analysing the evidence as given from witnesses by Counsel for the Defence of both Moran and Whelan wrote "what excuse can be made for the scandal of the sentence of Whelan and Moran, whose defence, had it been in an English Court would, we dare say, have shattered the prosecution". The evidence of identification was so weak, that a jury would be certain to disagree with it and the evidence of an alibi, together with the simple and sincere denials of the prisoners was so strong that there was no other course for fair minded and logical men, than to acquit on the capital charge".

It went on "we do not beg these men's lives we demand them. In England they would not have been doomed to die. Do they want the tide of unabiding hate and an unfailing memory to flow so deep between their people and ours, that its dark waters will never

subside. If they do not, these men must not die, and the hand of the hangmen must be stayed in Ireland".

The only person caught in the act on that Sunday morning was Frank Teeling. An escape was organised from prison and arranged by Moran and Teeling along with Ernie O'Malley and Simon Donnelly. It involved inside help from friendly prison officers and after four failed attempts to cut a bolt on a gate it finally succeeded but Paddy Moran refused to go as he felt that he would never be convicted that he would let down the honourable people who were giving evidence to refute what was undoubtedly perjury evidence by the state witnesses.

As O'Malley later stated he and his comrades tried to warn Moran that irrespective of the evidence he would be hung but Moran would not change his mind and stayed. He was found not guilty of manslaughter but guilty of murder and sentenced to death as was Thomas Traynor and the other four men.

Both men spent their last days in peace with themselves protesting their innocence to the very last moment. On the day before the executionConor Waters, the Prison Chaplin, Fr. McMahon and the Rev. Dr. Dargan attended to their spiritual needs.

The Evening Mail on the day of the executions reported that "having heard mass and received the last sacraments showing amazing courage they asked Conor Waters to deliver their final messages. Paddy Moran who with Whelan vigorously protested his innocence said to send his love to his family and loved ones. He was so reconciled to his fate that he expressed the hope that a reprieve would not come; for he said he could never hope to be so prepared to meet God again.

Thomas Whelan who spoke to the Canon after his colleague said "give my wife and sons my love. Tell them to follow and never surrender. Tell them to pray for me and I will always pray for them. Tell them I am proud to die for Ireland".

The two men then joined in the singing of the hymns which they could hear from the crowds outside the prison walls and walked calmly to their deaths at 6 am.

The last of the six Frank Flood and Thomas Bryan were executed at 8 am.

The executions took place between 6 am and 8 am, it was a bitterly cold morning with light regular snow showers falling during those early hours. This did not prevent the thousands present in the roads and streets from kneeling and praying aloud. Churches all over Dublin held early masses and bells tolled from approx 5 am.

When the last executions had taken place the snow had stopped the morning stars had faded away there was no more time for praying or weeping. There was no public transport which did not start again until midday so the crowds made their way either on foot, bicycle or whatever.

All businesses remained closed until 2 pm. This was agreed with employers and employees days before the executions throughout the city and numerous other parts of the country. Businesses in Co. Roscommon closed for the entire day. The sadness that engulfed the country, was so profound in Dalkey and particularly Torca Tennis Club which had its courts in Darcy's fields on Ard Brugh Road. Paddy Moran was a regular visitor there. His girl friend Bernie O'Connell was a prominent member and a good tennis player. She lived on Dalkey Hill and was distraught and broken hearted by the loss of the man she loved so much, she never got over her trauma. She, like the country at large, maintained he was innocent and never had another love affair during her lifetime. She died in 1971 aged 73 yrs.

Paddy Moran had quite a number of friends in Dalkey and many of them were alive and well when Moran Park in Dun Laoghaire was dedicated to his memory in 1961. I spoke to many of them on that day and they were consistent in their tributes to him and their respect for his memory.

Frank Mullen

Select Stores Dalkey

Paddy and Margaret McCabe started their fruit and veg shop in 1959. Originally the building was divided into three shops, which included Gilbeys wine merchants and a butcher on the Railway Road side. Paddy and Margaret expanded the business by first buying Gilbeys and then the butcher's shop. This left them with a substantial business premises and room for them to live upstairs with their five children, Brian, Leo, Hilary, Mairead and Oliver. Paddy was a great supporter of many voluntary groups within the town and served for many years on the Harold Boys School Development Committee. Sadly, Paddy died in 1980, leaving Margaret to run the store and bring up their children. Hilary, Leo and

Brian helped their mother through the 80's and 90's which were tough years.

In 2000 Margaret retired and Oliver returned from his travels in Australia and America with lots of ideas leading to the transformation in 2004. Leo runs McCabes' Oil, fuel merchants, Hilary still works part-time and Mairead runs Select Hampers.

Now Select Stores is also a Café and Juice Bar using only fresh fruit and vegetables. Oliver has trained as a dietary counsellor and can help you with their variety of organic whole foods and supplements. You can also buy ecological cleaners, refilling bottles in order to reduce recycling. They also have an extensive range of natural skin care products.

Now you can enjoy an ambient busy atmosphere with sounds of smoothies and juices being produced freshly from lots of fruit and vegetables. Eat at the salad bar produced by Blazing Salads or take it away.

The aim is to provide you with the optimum nutritional guidance with the odd joke and giggle so it's not too serious.

Oliver McCabe

Oliver McCabe, Select Stores

Memories of Jack Doyle

Spending all of my childhood near the sea on Coliemore Road, many of my after-school hours were spent combing the rocks from Bulloch Harbour to The Ramparts on Vico Road – mostly for firewood but occasionally, particularly during the war years (WW2), I would come across some interesting pieces of flotsam, many of these provided by the MV Bolivar when it foundered on the Kish Bank. But that's a story for another day.

It was on these rock explorations that I first caught sight of the late Jack Doyle. It was as I passed one of the many splendid houses whose gardens run all the way down to the sea that I noticed an Adonis figure of a man running down the garden of 'Rocklands' towards the beach carrying a beautiful woman on his shoulders. Spellbound, I watched as they dived into the sea, laughing and splashing, realising at the same time I was watching the legendary Jack Doyle and the equally legendary actress known as Movita who, talk had it, were staying 'somewhere in Dalkey' for the Summer. The house 'Rocklands' was owned by a Mrs. Topping, a colourful character, often seen out walking with at least 10 german dachs-hunds. The same lady who, it was said, had been a survivor of the MV Leinster when it was sunk by a German torpedo and indeed had held her son afloat until rescue arrived. I was to see the fabulous couple again during that Summer as they frolicked on the beach and felt privileged, for a short time, to bask in the glow of such colourful people.

The next time I encountered Jack Doyle was in much more mundane circumstances. I was on a No. 8 Dalkey Tram when he, Movita and another couple boarded it. When the conductor came along to collect fares, Jack flashed a large £5 note for payment, a lot of money at the time for fares that went in penny increments. The conductor refused to accept it as it would have meant him having to part with all his loose change, and the result was an exchange of angry words which was eventually calmed when one of the couple in Jack's company paid the fares. I did not realise then I was witnessing the sad, drink induced, decline of a legend.

But Jack's beautiful singing voice was still intact and the last time I saw him in Dalkey was when he gave a concert in Dalkey Town Hall. I was one of the young lads who could not afford the entrance fee and had to be content with hanging around outside the door to watch and listen. We were there when at the interval, Jack came out and pocketed some or all of the takings before adjourning to Arthur Duffy's pub, known as 'The Queens' Hotel, next door only to return for the second half 'fully nourished' for his attempts to emulate the Great Caruso's feat of reaching notes high enough to break glass, and to us standing outside listening to this wonderful voice, it seemed as if he had fulfilled his wish.

Many years later, working in England, like many young Irishmen of that time, I passed a dishevelled character on a London Street whose frame and faded good looks looked familiar. He had passed when I realised with sadness and shock that the remnants of a once great figure had crossed my path once more and probably for the very last time.

Pat O'Brien
14 August 2008.

'Ms Camogie' calls it a day

Sile steps down after 22 years spent in the top job in her code

She held the top spot of the country's largest female sporting body for 22 years – a tenure surpassed only by GAA head honcho Liam Mulvihill who vacated the Croker hot seat last year.

But despite this the recently retired Camogie Association Ard Stiúrthóir Sile de Bhailís is largely unknown outside of camogie circles preferring to leave the limelight to presidents like Liz Howard and Miriam O'Callaghan.

"I never had a public profile. It isn't in my nature. I like to work in the background". Explains the true Blue "Dalkeyite".

Credit

Despite this reticence, Sile can claim a huge part of the credit for the current healthy position of the game which passed its centenary year in 2004.

Participation levels have jumped to more than 100,000 since Sile took up the position in January 1986.

Sponsorship income has grown substantially, a Strategic Plan is in place, the game is played in some "shape of fashion" in every one of the 32 counties, the Association now has a full-time staff of four officials in Croke Park and a network of eight development officers throughout the country.

Her love affair with camogie began in her native Dalkey where she still resides. "My father Gerry Wallace introduced me to the game. Like my grandfather Jem Fox, he was a stilesman in Croke Park. I used to sell programmes outside the grounds.

"I played there a few times before playing for Dublin as County Finals used to be played in Croke Park in the 1970's and 80's. I won an All-Ireland Junior medal with Dublin in 1972 and captained the team in the senior final in 1976 when Kilkenny beat us by a point."

The opposing captain that day was Mary Fennelly who would go on the become

Ms Camogie Sile de Bhailís

Camogie President during Sile's time as Ard Stiúrthóir.

The Cuala club enjoys a special place in her affections. "I won an All-Ireland before I won a medal with the club and that was when we won the Senior B championship in 1985. John Bailey – former Dublin GAA Cathaoirleach was the coach."

During her playing days with Cuala and prior to that Naomh Mhuire and Dalkey Mitchels, in common with every other club, all games were played in the Phoenix Park.

Mentor

"We used to meet up in town or in Dun Laoghaire and get the bus to Islandbridge. Matches started at 11.00 a.m. and continued on the hour every hour until about 4 o'clock in the Summer time. Doirin Golden's (current Dublin senior mentor) father Mick was the groundsman and he hung the nets and lined the pitches.

Everyone knew everyone else and we all had our own patch of the field. You could be playing, umpiring, refereeing – anything!"

The club has often been a welcome refuge for Sile during difficult times in the job. "There have been times when things were frustrating and my outlet was to go to the club and go training and hit the sliothar all over the place".

The much heralded integration project between the Camogie and Ladies Football Associations and the GAA seems to have ground to a halt. But Sile remains opti-mistic: "I believe that under new GAA Director General, Pauric Duffy, that it will gather new momentum.

"At club level, it's more or less completely integrated. We need to work more at county board and provincial levels.

The celebration of the Association's centenary in 2004 brings back great memories. "I was blessed to be part of it. It brought together everyone and it gave the game an injection that was needed at the time."

Welcome

Sile leaves the main stage happy in the knowledge that no matter where she goes in the country the welcome mat is always on the doorstep.

"I go with a sad heart but also knowing that the Association is in great hands."

A Local School

The Wicklow People of Saturday 19th January 1901 reported that "on the previous Sunday (13th January) the Parish Priest blessed a new school on Porter's Rd. Dalkey. The school was opened for the admission of boys the next day, the 14th January 1901. The school was erected as a memorial to the late Canon George Harold P.P. A teacher's residence was also built on an adjoining plot. His Grace the Archbishop had sent a donation of one hundred pounds".

Perhaps a clarification of the above report would help. The priest was Rev. James Canon Murray who had succeeded George Harold as Parish Priest of Dalkey/Glasthule which was a single parish at the time. They became separate parishes in 1927. George Harold had died on the 13th January 1894. He had an older brother called John, who had been P.P. in 1863 of Glasthule, Dalkey, Ballybrack, Cabinteely and Little Bray which was all a single parish at that time. John died in 1868. He spent most of his time as P.P. building St. Joseph's Church in Glasthule. He was buried in the Church of the Assumption Dalkey. A slab there commemorates this. In 1880 his brother George became P.P. of Dalkey, Ballybrack and Glasthule. Following his death in 1894 the parish was split in two, Dalkey/Glasthule and Ballybrack/Cabinteely. This was the parish arrangement when Harold opened. Slabs commemorating both the Harold brothers are also to be seen in Glasthule and Ballybrack churches.

Porter's Rd. is now known as St. Patrick's Rd. The school Harold Boys' was a two-roomed red-brick building, which you can see now on that road. The entrance hall was the small building jutting out from the main building at the front. At the back was a yard, clay covered with an outdoor toilet and a fuel-shed. Over the entrance door at the front was an inscription which read

Harolds School 1932-33
Back: B. Byrne, P. Kane, –, D. Smyth, W. Redmond, S. Hickey, T. Kielty (teacher)
Third Row: S. Cunningham, J. Farrell, –, –, J. Murphy, K. Byrne, M. Keogh –, B. Young.
Second Row: –, T. Smyth, –, J. Mitchell, –, –, P. Farrell, C. Redmond, Howard
Front Row: J. Banahan, D. Blower, –, Flood, R. Brown.

'HAROLD MALE NATIONAL SCHOOL 1901'.

A new classroom was added to the rear over twenty years later. The physical building remained like this up until the 1960's. Due to increased numbers of pupils at this time two new classrooms, toilets, cloakrooms and an office were built using grey cement blocks! This can be seen now to the north of the original building. In the early 70's, again due to increased pupil numbers a pre-fabricated classroom was erected at the back of the school. It was used for about ten years and then removed. Brendan Moloney, a parent and friend of the school knocked down the toilet and fuel-shed in the 1970's and even though they hadn't been used for years it ended a link with the past. The external appearance of Harold has remained, as can be seen today.

The interior of the school however has changed quite a bit over the years. When the school opened in 1901 the classrooms were "heated" by open fires in each room. This was followed with storage heaters when the new section was added in the 1960's. Then by oil-fired central heating in 1990 and today it has a gas fuelled system. Venetian blinds were a very decorative item in the 1960's extension but the original windows had no covering until the 1970's when parents purchased them. The entrance hall at the front was no longer used after the 1960's extension provided a new front entrance and it was used as a place to put discarded school materials. But in 1990 it finally became what it is today - a staff-room! The cloakrooms, which were also a 1960's addition, were converted in the 1990's into computer and special-education rooms. The largest classroom from1901 is now a general purpose room. All of these changes cost lots of money and the parents and the D.E.S. provided this, which has changed the Harold of 1901 into a modern school today.

So much for the building! What made the school a success over more than a century were the parents, pupils and staff. In the case of Harold up to the 1970's, parents had little involvement except providing the pupils! For every pupil who attended Harold and for the teachers also many incidents and stories were told over the years. I've been told of some which occurred before my time in Harold. A well loved teacher there was Peadar O hUallachain. An old lady used to come in each morning before the arrival of the pupils to light the fire in the rooms. When she met Peadar she always said "Good morning Mr. Hooligan"!. Diarmuid O hAlmhain who was Principal form the 1940's to 1971 had

a Gaelic household. He told the story himself that one day he was working in his garden. A person passing his gate with a dog didn't know Diarmuid was inside the hedge. Diarmuid's dog growled at the neighbour's dog and the person outside said "Come away outa there, that auld dog only knows Irish"!. After an election in the 1960's which used the slogan "Let Lemass lead on", the school got many of the posters afterwards to use as class posters. After pictures were drawn on the blank sides they were tacked to the windows. Passers-by noticed a picture of Sean Lemass with the slogan mentioned promoting a certain political party along the windows to the front of the school. They were removed in haste!

A picture of Canon Rafter hung in the office for many years. While he never "interfered" in the running of the school, at Christmas a large box of Lemon's Pure Sweets was sent for distribution to teachers and pupils! A Christmas box maybe was the point!

The first Principal was James Waldron and I would think the only English person to hold the post in over 100 years! He died suddenly in 1914 and Bernard Hughes succeeded him. I met his daughter, a nun, who visited the school in the 1980's and was living in Australia. I thought it would be easy to get teachers' names from past times but it's nearly impossible! There are no lists or information after 1920. I know Hugh Leonard, a past pupil, mentions in articles teachers he had experienced in his time there. All pupils' names are listed in the different registers for the past 107 years. Maybe the names of teachers aren't as important as what they contributed to the Dalkey community over the years. A man whose name is synonymous with Harold was Proinsias O Maolain - Frank Mullen.

A native of Sallynoggin he spent over forty years teaching there of which the last thirteen years were as Principal. He was a very talented man but if I had to choose two things for which he gave his all they would be choirs and Gaelic games. With Diarmuid O hAlmhain they had school choirs singing on Radio Eireann in the 1950's. The time and effort given was for the love of music and an interest in children's education. He excelled at training teams in Cumann na mBunscol competitions. From the 1950's onwards his teams won finals in both codes in Croke Park. It was only in the early 1980's when I took the school teams and attended Cumann na mBunscol meetings in the Teachers Club in Parnell Sq. that I realised what a legend this man was. Many teachers there asked me about him and told of playing against his teams. We were very fortunate to win a hurling final in Croke Park in June 1984 which was when he retired. The following September I continued with a team in the football competition and Proinsias came to a couple of the matches. But suddenly and sadly he died in October. To honour him, Cumann na mBunscol renamed the competition we were taking part in as Corn Ui Mhaoileain. With his help from on high we reached the final in Croke Park the following December. We won and his wife Mairead presented the cup to us. It's a very special memory.

From the 1970's onwards parents became involved in many different ways in school-life, and I realised how important the school was in the community and its life.

Were there stories from my time? Of course. On one occasion the school-keys disappeared. Every class went searching. After more than an hour, a very wise person lifted the cover on the toilet cistern and there, sitting on top of the ball-cock was the set of keys! On another occasion the school was contacted by the manager of Quinnsworth. In those days when a glass bottle was returned you got a deposit returned. It seems Quinnsworth stored these returned bottles at the back of the store. Pupils discovered this and they took plenty of bottles and walked in the front door and collected numerous deposits. It ended with the manager's complaint! In June, when the sixth class were leaving, throwing eggs was popular for a time. Eggs past their sell-by date were also stored at the back of the supermarket. This time it was the teachers begging the manager to change this custom! In corporal punishment days, a stick belonging to a teacher disappeared at lunch-time. Many years later the culprits confessed that it was thrown on to a train going to Rosslare from the bridge on Ardeevin Rd! And so on, and so on!

I hope the few things mentioned here paint

Sean O'Gormain

a little picture of a school that is part of the Dalkey Community. I can't imagine the town without a school called Harold.

Sean O Gormain.

Brief History of 17th Dalkey Unit St Begnets Troop Catholic Boy Scouts Of Ireland now 17th Dalkey Scout Group Scouting Ireland

Last year 2007 was the centenary celebration of the first ever Scout camp which took place on Brownsea Island and this year is the centenary of the first Scout camp in Ireland. Many changes have taken place in our movement throughout these years. There were two associations at the time C.B.S.I Catholic Boy Scouts of Ireland and S.A.I Scouts Association of Ireland. We were affiliated to C.B.S.I. About 20 tears ago the Boy was dropped from the name and more recently our two associations have joined together to form one organisation for the country now called simply S.I or Scouting Ireland. Our scout group was formed in 1927 and has continued since giving the joy of scouting to many thousands of boys and girls. We hope to be around for many more years to come. Our first meetings in 1927 were on Wed and Friday evenings and were held in the Harold Boys School on St Patricks Rd Dalkey. The first Scout Leader was a Mr Quigley who lived on Railway Rd Dalkey.

Over the years we have had many meeting places such as Stables on Convent Rd (where the new shops are now). The taproom of the Town Hall Dalkey (now the heritage centre), the chaplain at that time was a Fr Carney who used to hire the main hall one night a week and assembled a boxing ring and all the scouts like it or not were given gloves and put into the ring, red ears and black eyes were not unknown. He also taught many a Scout to swim in the little Harbour of what was then the Cliff Castle by placing a rope noose around a scouts waist,this was attached to a wooden pole and in you jumped! We also met in the stable at the back of Swales yard which is now (Our Ladies Hall) we had one room downstairs and a ladder up to the loft. we also used Epworth Hall on Rockford Ave but since June 1976 we have had our own den at the top of the football field on Hyde Rd, thanks to a huge amount of hard work by Parents and Leaders at the time.

Opening of the Scout Den in 1977.

The equipment we use has also changed a lot over time. The Group did not own much until 1946 when there was a lot of Army surplus gear for sale. For Three Shillings (which took a long time to earn) you could buy a large button Poncho or Army cape. They would keep you dry in bad weather and became your groundsheet which we slept on in camp with two old Army blankets and six big safety pins from which you would make an envelope bed and unless you got this right your feet would get very cold at night. We also had a few old Army Bell Tents which had quite a lot of holes in them so instead of counting sheep at night to help you sleep you could count the stars. Nowadays we use lightweight Dome Tents easy to put up and pack away and can handle all weather conditions. We use Mummy Sleeping bags with hoods and lie on thermo rests or carry mats to insulate you from the cold. We wear breathable waterproof raingear and boots, fleeces to keep warm, LED torches to see at night with and GPS to find our way. The equipment may have changed but the scouting ideals and activities remain very much the same as when the organisation was formed. We still camp and hike,do our mapwork, cook on fires and sit around campfires at night singing songs and telling yarns. In scouting we make friends for life and we try and instil in our Boys and Girls to be a friend to all,to love our country, be kind to animals, look after our environment, to show respect for other peoples property and help all who need it.

As well as our own green land we have camped in many different places and countries over recent years such as England Scotland,Wales,Belgium,Holland,Luxemb ourg,Germany. Last year we had a group of 70 away camping high in the Swiss Alps in Kandersteg which was an amazing experience.

Members of the Scout Troop 1930.

We have four Sections in the group Beavers 6-8 Cubs 8-11 Scouts 11-15 Ventures 15-19. All our sections are mixed and we have 130 children in the group. This year (2007) we had 40 Scouts and Ventures off to Homberg in Germany camping for two weeks and 30 cubs are off to Gurteen in Tipperary for one week.

Members of the Scout Troop 2008.

Thanks must be given to all the parents past and present who have helped and supported us in many many ways over the years and hopefully well into the future, to the residents of St Begnets Villas who have allowed us to carry on Scouting, our many friends in Dalkey and all our scouts past and present and last but not least we must remember all those men and women who have given great service as Leaders and have worn the "Blue and Gold" since 1927 and continue to do so. Without you we would not be here. New members are always welcome and especially new Leaders are always needed to help give Scouting to all, our aim is to help all young people to become good citizens of this country or wherever they may go.

You can catch up with our activities and photos, apply for membership, enquire about being a Leader on our website dalkeyscouts.ie

Martin Ellard
Group Leader
July 2008

Built with Dalkey Granite

In 1857 Bishop William Keane was appointed Bishop of Cloyne. The fastest expanding parish under his control was Queenstown which was the new name of Cobh, Co. Cork. He soon realised that there was an urgent need to build a Cathedral and he set up the necessary structures and committees to plan the project.

On 10th November 1867 the draft plans submitted by Architects Pugin and Ashlin of South Mall, Cork were formally approved by the Building Committee.

An integral part of the plans were that the stone to be used to build the exterior of the Cathedral was to be Dalkey granite which had been used successfully in the building of Dun Laoghaire Harbour. It was to be used with cutstone dressing of Mallow Co. Cork Limestone.

All the granite was cut in Bulloch Quarry and transported to Cobh by sea.

On 25th April 1868 Bishop Keane dug the first sod on the agreed site which was on a hill overlooking the town and on 25th July 1868 he laid the first stone.

In March 1915 the last scaffold surrounding the spire was taken down and the building was virtually completed.

The Cathedral of St. Colman was consecrated on 12th August 1919. It stands majestically as a landmark to the skill and expertise of all those who worked on the building of it and in recognition of the quality of Dalkey granite.

Frank Mullen

Cobh Cathedral, Co. Cork
built with granite from Dalkey.

Mick Holden (1954-2007) - Remembered

Mick sadly passed away prematurely, aged 53, in 2007. He is a local sporting legend, having won a senior All Ireland football medal in 1983 with the Dubs. He represented Ireland in Australia in the Compromise Rules series in 1986. He was a dual All Star in hurling and football. He captained his local club, Cuala, to one of their three Dublin senior county hurling championships (1989, 1991 & 1994). His sporting achievements go on and on.

Mick was born, bred and died in Tivoli Terrace, Dun Laoghaire. He was third in a family of six children – P.J., Vinnie, Mick, Helen, Margaret and Jo – to his Kilkenny born parents, Tom and Josie. He was educated in St. Joseph's School, Tivoli School, Tivoli Road and later at the Christian Brothers in Eblana Avenue, Dun Laoghaire.

At the age of 18, he went to New York where he worked for two years in construction. On his return to Dun Laoghaire, one noticed his physical development. He had also honed his social skills.

Back home now, he took up his first job which brought him into contact with many families in the local community. He was the Royal Irish insurance agent for Monkstown, Sallynoggin and Glasthule. He later managed the 'Rainbow Rapids' water slides in Dun Laoghaire Baths. He went on to manage and direct his own company, Cuala Property Management. Mick had a very good sense of life/work balance and always found time for a fag and a pint and whatever else might be going on.

His sporting career took a big turn when Kevin Heffernan selected him to play full back in the 1979 Leinster Senior Football Final. From then until 1985, he was a permanent feature on the Dublin football team. His blonde head and distinct gait distinguished him on the field of play. (It also won him many admirers off the field.) However, it was not his good looks that he will be remembered for.

Mick Holden will be remembered for his 110% heart and commitment he gave every time he went on the field. He never wanted to let his side down. He had great leadership qualities. He had the ability to inspire his teammates. He had huge honour and integrity and an unquenchable spirit. In short, he never gave up. As a Dub, he won the admiration of the country when he picked his team mate, Barney Rock, up from the ground and told him to get on with the game – rather than lying down injured.

Mick Holden in action for Dublin.

Mick was a great man to have in a dressing room. He had the ability to relax himself and his teammates, no matter how big the occasion. However, once he crossed the white line, it was straight down to business. He was teak tough. His bravery cost him serious injuries, most notable the loss of his finger. He had it surgically removed over the Christmas period to ensure that he wouldn't miss a match!

Mick always had a sunny aspect to him with a roguish eye and a happy smile. One could write a book on the Mick Holden stories. On the day of his funeral, the huge crowd paid testament to his popularity – each person with their own Mick Holden story.

During the height of his football career he was crowned King of Dalkey. This was the height of his political career, but with the help of his election agents, Harry Roberts and his brother P.J., I'm sure he could have made Taoiseach.

His inter-county career finished in 1985. He spent 9 months in Australia after the Compromise Rules series. He settled down to married life and had two children, Jodie and Patrick. Mick's mother died in 1986 and his father passed away in 2005. Mick crossed over in 2007.

His inter-county football career dominated his middle years, but it was when he returned to his roots, Cuala, that he got most satisfaction. He played in three successful hurling championship finals despite having only four fingers on one hand. His bravery and commitment was never more clearly exemplified than in a Leinster club semi-final replay. Mick lined out to play despite having taken the sliotar full in the face, smashing his nose, from none other than the famous Tony Doran of Wexford and Buffers Alley, the previous Saturday.

He comfortably moved into management and coaching. He demanded the high standards he had given himself. Drawing on his knowledge and experience, it was clear that Mick was a gifted coach. It is a great regret, that he will not have the opportunity to fulfil his potential in this area.

To meet Mick, as he walked along a Dun Laoghaire street or was sitting comfortably at a local bar, was one of life's pleasures. His shy smile and quiet greeting was an introduction to great, easy and enjoyable company. Never comfortable in the limelight, Mick was a quiet man with strong views. An engaging storyteller, he had many great stories and anecdotes – and nobody could tell them better than him. Like all great storytellers, he was a good listener and observer of life. He interpreted life and communicated his views through these yarns and stories. Mick possessed a genuine humility and wore all his great sporting achievements very lightly indeed. He had a great ability to relate to a wide range of people of all ages – he never lost his common touch.

If you were going to war, or to a party or just for a pint, you would want Mick Holden with you.

Mick Holden loved his kids, his partner Bernie, his fags and pints, his hurling and his friends and family. He loved life. His spirit of fair play and personal integrity will keep him forever in our hearts.

Mick's great achievement is that he is loved as much after his death as he was during his life.

As dheis De go raibh a anam dilis.

Vinny Holden

Happy Memories of the Shops in Dalkey 50 years on

Icame to live with my husband in Dalkey almost 50 years ago. I have some wonderful happy memories of the shops in Dalkey in those far off days. As I think back over the years I believe that while a lot of the shops have changed, the staff working in them are and always have been friendly, helpful and courteous. I remember as a young mother I could leave my pram and baby outside McLoughlins shop at the corner of Coliemore Road and go into Dun Laoghaire or to have a little time to myself in the town. Betty Holmes and Anne Lynton who worked in McLoughlins would keep an eye on the pram and indeed they often had more that one pram to look after as other mothers availed of their kindness.

The Mother and Baby/Father and Son Shop at the corner of Castle Street and Patrick's Road was a great place to shop. It carried such a wide range of stock including their renowned hand smocked children's dresses at a reasonable price that there was no necessity to go to Dun Laoghaire or Dublin to buy clothes.

Maxwells, H.C.R. and Fillers Chemist Shops were as good as any doctors surgeries. If any of the children were unwell or had any minor accident Mr. Kennelley and Mr. Chambers never failed to give the children the successful cure. When I got what they believed was the correct treatment for the children it never carried a health warning or a long list of possible side effects. One thing they all had in common was that they all cured their ailments. Mr. Tim Kerins who has a chemist shop in Castle Street for many years certainly lives up to the high standards set by his colleagues of a different generation.

Finlaters, where Eurospar is now situated was the original 'local supermarket' in those days, as I believe it had been for many years. Mr. West looked after the bacon counter. Miss Furlong was in charge of the vegetable counter. Miss Maggie Dowling looked after the cash office which overlooked the entire shop floor. There were no cash registers on any of the counters, all of the items purchased were paid by the staff member pushing a sales docket with the tendered cash into a type of cup

L to R: Johnny Dunne, Paddy McGrory and Peter Butler

which was secured onto a carrier socket on a wire which was at arms length above the counter. This was propelled along a wire by the assistant pulling a lever, to the cash office and the change was returned by a similar method to the appropriate counter. It was a large store in the context of shops of that time, it was fascinating to see the young babies lying in their prams watching the containers criss crossing along the wires at speed along the length and breadth of the shop.

Gemmas Newsagents shop which was closed just recently was owned by the Heneghan family. It was the only newsagents, stationery in Castle Street. In my early years in Dalkey Mr. Heneghan ran the shop assisted by his son Peter who was a very quiet and kind young man and who tragically lost his life in a traffic accident on 20th September 1966. I will never forget the shock we got when on our way to Mass that beautiful autumn Sunday morning. Robert Boland who was a great pal of Pat Heneghan was selling the papers outside Gemmas shop which was closed. He told us the tragic news and the town went into a state of shock. Pat took over the running of the shop and he was assisted over the years by several kind people. I recall some of the names, Kathleen Livingstone, Margaret Dowd, Miss McKenna, whom I believe had their family shop for many years where the Ulster Bank now stands. Mrs Henegan also worked there. All of them gave a great service over the years. It was where we bought our daily papers and I often treated myself to $\frac{1}{2}$lb box of chocolate mallows.

Derek McDonald and Eddie Doyle outside Doyles Butchers, the only butchers shop left in Castle St.

Castle Street

During those years it was safe to send the children down the town when they got older to get little messages as we called the goods in the shops. They would arrive home with the messages and with the change having been wrapped up in paper by one of the people who served them.

Mary Newport who had a little grocery shop beside Dave Langans Post Office where Don Giovani's Restaurant is now was another favourite shop. She sold groceries and vegetables which came daily from Wexford. She married one of the Donnelly lads from Dalkey Hill and after some years they moved down to Wexford where they set up their own business.

Mr. White's shoe repair shop at the back of a sweet shop across the street from Joe Dowd's shop which also sold sweets, minerals and ice cream. Noel and Kathleen Byrne run an excellent fruit and veg shop there now.

A shoe repair shop since the early 1930s. The art of hand stitching shoe repairs is carrd out by Willie Clegg

Paddy McCabe had the vegetable shop on Tubbermore Road. He was a very kind and gentle person. He built up a great business and nothing was a problem for him. He died at a young age and left his wife and five children. I will always remember him in his beige shop coat and at Christmas he could pull out bundles of small pieces of paper from his pockets and get details off one of the pieces with the customers name, details of the order including the size of the turkey the customer required.

Mrs. McCabe was a wonderful woman she continued to run the business and look after the children most of whom are now involved in what is a thriving business with great credit due to them. Paddy would be proud of their success.

Donal Hick and Bernie Ferguson of Hicks Pork Butchers who have been trading in the town for over 60 years.

The Golden Gift Shop beside the old Tramyard which was owned by Mrs. Flood was and still is an interesting shop to browse around and buy little presents to suit every requirement.

The two butcher shops in Castle Street were Brian Dunnes which was in fact part owned and managed by his brother Johnny for some years before I came to Dalkey. Johnny was a great character and when he was not in the shop I would go up to Grimes Butchers where Eddie Doyle has an excellent butchers shop today. Mr. Hammond from Sallynoggin looked after the place at the time.

After Mr. White retired I would go to a cobblers shop which still trades today. It is situated beside the old Tramyard. I believe along with the Banks and the Chemist Shops it is trading as the same business since the early 1940's.

Mick Byrne had a lovely fish shop at the end of the town near McDonaghs. There would be a queue outside it on a Friday morning for fresh fish, which was similar to the queue that would be outside Hick's on a Saturday morning. Mick also died at a young age and his wife Mary continued the business ably assisted by her son Alan. Kathleen Larkin who worked there for years often told the story of Paddy Quinn arriving in the shop to buy a "Bunny". He had just arrived home from one of his round the world sea faring trips and had spent many hours in the various pubs which liked to welcome him home as he would be financially sound for a few weeks. After several requests to Kathleen to explain what he wanted, he replied, "excuse me Kathleen but I want to buy a f- - -ing rabbit".

On that funny note I will finish my short account of some happy memories of my early years shopping in Dalkey and the happy lifetime spent with special people and great characters that make Dalkey the fascinating place that it is and God willing will remain.

A happy housewife, mother & Gran
Ellen Mullen

The Prefab Bungalow on "The Green Road"

As one goes through a gap in the cul-de-sac at Mount Henry on Torca Road, one enters a quiet beautiful walk, high above the Vico Road. It is not particularly well known except for regular walkers of Killiney and Dalkey Hills. It is one of the most beautiful "roads" in the entire area of Dalkey. This is known as the "Old Green Road" – it is still mostly carpeted with velvety short grass and is reputed to have been laid out for the same George of England after whom Kingstown was named, to drive and admire the view.

Mrs. Chippendell Higgin of Killiney Castle bought a model bungalow and had it erected there and often used it to dispense hospitality to her guests in these ideal surroundings.

Rare plants and trees which she had planted may still be seen near the site.

In the Black and Tan War it was used as a Head Quarters by the local I.R.A. and again by the Republicans in the Civil War, when it met its end in flames at the hands of Free State Troops. Those who examined it at the exhibition could have had little idea of the strange future in store for its timbers!

Extract from Vol. IV No. 2 December 1941 – February 1942 Glimpses of Old Dalkey by F.M. O'Flanagen

Saint Begnet, Patron of Dalkey and Dalkey Island

Feastday – 12 November

Becnat daughter of Colmán son of Áed is listed in the eleventh-century pedigrees of Irish saints as one of the saints of the people known as Dál Messin Corb. Dál Messin Corb ruled over large parts of north and mid-Leinster to the eight century AD when their authority was confined to the Wicklow Mouintains. St. Kevins of Glendalough was the most famous saint belonging to Dál Messin Corb and medieval lists of Irish saints suggest that Becnat was regarded as one of familia Coemgeni 'the family of Kevin' and that her churches in Dalkey were subject, therefore, to the monastery of Glendalough. The personal name Becnat is interpreted as being either a feminine form of Bec 'small' or a name consisting of the Irish words bec 'small' and nat 'lady, woman'. Other female Irish saints and heroines have similar names, including Bláthnat and Damnat. Becnat daughter of Cían of Munster appears in the literature as mother of the saint Finán Cam, founder of the church of Cenn Étig (Kinnity, Co. Offaly). The place-name Cell Becnatan, Kilbegnet, survives throughout the country as at Kilbegnet, barony of Ballymoe, Co. Galway, Kilbegnet, barony Potnahinch, Co. Laois and a townland of Kilbegnet in the parish of Kilgorman, Co. Wexford. Becnat of Dalkey's feastday of the 12th November is recorded in the late medieval Book of Obits of Christchurch Cathedral, Dublin.

Dr. Edel Breathnach,
Micheál O'Cléirigl, Historian,
Institute, U.C.D.

Ruin of St. Begnets Church on Dalkey Island.

Drama over the White Rock and Killiney Strands.

The summer of 1955 was one of the best of the last century and the days of July and August were ones of uninterrupted sunshine from dawn to dark.

During that glorious summer my pals and I developed the habit of doing swims along the shore from Coliemore Harbour to the Vico Bathing Place (known locally as 'The Ramparts') or from there to the White Rock and back. When we were swimming at Bulloch we would swim to the forty foot and back to Bulloch. On the days we spent at Sandycove and the Forty Foot we would swim close to the shore to Dun Laoghaire pier and back.

I swim all year in the sea, summer and winter (weather permitting) and thankfully I still have the health and strength to enjoy these swims with friends 53 years later during fine summer days and this year a group of us completed the Dalkey Island Swim.

Friday, 15th July 1955 was one of those beautiful days. In the early afternoon the late Tony Dempsey, Patsy O'Farrell, Paul Barry and I set off from 'The Ramparts' to swim to Sorrento Point on a very slack low tide. We were on our way back enjoying the swim at our ease, we were approximately 60 to 80 yards off shore when one of the lads saw a small plane flying very low off The Green Road which runs along Killiney Hill over the Vico Road. The plane came in low by the trees of Killiney Wood over the White Rock towards Killiney Strand.

It appeared to be heading towards the White Cottage which were very popular tea rooms on Killiney Beach. We knew almost instantly that it was in serious trouble. The thoughts of it crashing on the crowded beaches of the White Rock or Killiney were frightening and too awful to contemplate.

During these days every train that came into Killiney Station was packed with people going to the beach and with the tide so far out the crowds would be greater.

Suddenly the plane swung to the left and immediately started to regain height as it headed out to sea. We thought a tragedy had been avoided and someone said the pilot had been brilliant. No sooner had the comment been made when the plane stopped in midair and dived down into the sea. It appeared to miss some yachts nearby but we could not be sure from the distance that we were from the scene.

I recall we were very shocked by what we had seen but remained calm and swam back to the bathing place.

The large crowd there were convinced that the plane would have missed the swimmers in the water off the beach.

A group of us got dressed and decided to go to the beach, we climbed over the railway wall and walked along the tracks to Killiney Beach and onto the strand. People were leaving the beach in their droves and quite a few were very distressed.

It took some time to find out if there were many casualties and then it was apparent that the passenger in the plane had been killed and some swimmers had helped to put the pilot into a rowing boat and bring him ashore. The Dun Laoghaire Life Boat with another launch which I believe was from the Irish Lights Depot in Dun Laoghaire arrived at the scene.

There is a sandbank off the beach and swimmers were diving down to try to locate the plane, an hour or so after our arrival the wreckage was discovered and it was towed ashore by one of the large launches that had arrived from Dun Laoghaire. Some Irish Army planes were also searching the area for other survivors. It was established that the person who was killed in the crash was a Mr. Beatty who was a Barrister who lived in Pembroke Road. They were a well known legal family. His unfortunate mother and father were on the beach when his body was taken to the beach. His mother collapsed and had to receive medical attention. If memory serves me correctly his Dad was a Judge.

The pilot of the plane for whom a lot of praise paid to him for his successful efforts to avoid crashing into packed beaches was Enda McLoughlin of Sandymount, who was a member of the Western Training School in Celbridge, Co. Kildare.

Although it was fifty three years ago the memory of that dreadful afternoon remains vividly in my mind.

Frank Mullen
May 2007

The Story of Cricket in Dalkey

IT may come as a surprise to many, but the game of cricket holds a firm place in the sporting annals of Dalkey.

In fact it stretches back almost 150 years, with the Irish Times of Thursday May 16th 1861 announcing the formation of 'The Dalkey Cricket Club'.

In the flowery prose of the time, the notice read:

"This club has just been formed, and promises to attend to its members much sport during the present season. Mr Burke, of Dalkey, has kindly granted them permission to play in one of his very fine fields situated in the locality. Arrangements are being made for having two meetings of the club each week".

Although the club would play its first home games that year, the Irish Times also carried a report of a game involving a team from Dalkey in the summer of 1860.

The game took place in the Phoenix Park on Saturday August 4th, with the Eagle Cricket Club providing the opposition. They were to prove too strong for Dalkey's fledgling side, winning by 118 runs, although a report in the following Wednesday's paper remarked that: "For Dalkey, Mr. A. Carpenter batted well, and the round-hand bowling of Mr. Goddard was difficult to play".

Goddard took eight wickets in the two-innings match, while W. Preston claimed seven. Carpenter was the only Dalkey batsman to make it into double figures, scoring 18 in their first innings.

Goddard was to prove the hero of Dalkey's first recorded home match on Friday July 9th, 1861, when he literally took the biscuit with 12 wickets against Garibaldi.

Seven of those wickets came in Garibaldi's first innings and he also held on to three catches as the visitors were rolled over for 81 as Dalkey went on to claim victory by nine wickets.

We can't be sure if Goddard celebrated with a drink, although Henry Sproat advertised in that day's paper that a dozen bottles of Pure XX Porter were available from his emporium at Glasgow House in Glasthule for a mere three shillings and sixpence.

He may even have saved his few shillings for the following day and went to see "The Renowned Prima Donna, Mademoiselle Parepa" perform at the Sussex Hall in Kingstown at half-past two.

Either way Goddard was back in fine form the following Tuesday, although his ten wickets were not enough to save Dalkey against "An Eleven of Sandycove" as they suffered a home defeat.

The local derby must have brought in the crowds, with The Irish Times of July 11th noting "The batting of Messrs W Wiley, H Graves, and H West, for their respective sides, was much admired (even by the fair sex)".

Although it is hard to pin down when the demise of Dalkey Cricket Club came, it is likely that it happened towards the end of the nineteenth century, when the growth of the Gaelic Athletic Association resulted in cricket clubs all over the country dying out as football and hurling grew in popularity.

It wasn't the end of cricket in Dalkey, thanks to the arrival of an unknown Englishman, Wilfred P Toone, to the village in 1904.

Toone founded Castle Park School after paying a sum of £4,070 for the castle and 34 acres and his love of the game is best summed up by former pupil Morgan

Dockrell, when he states that cricket "was his religion".

Toone would hand over the school to Donald Pringle in 1938, while the wooden cricket pavilion was opened in 1940.

Both Toone and Pringle are celebrated in the school crest, while Toone's son Geoffrey would go on to act alongside John Gielgud and Laurence Olivier in the Old Vic Theatre Company. He is probably best known to modern audiences for playing Lord Ridgemere, owner of the stately home where Delboy and Rodney Trotter drop the vintage chandelier in one of the funniest comedy sketches of all time.

Many students left Castle Park with a fine grounding in both education and cricket. Donald Pratt would even go on to captain Ireland in the sport, winning ten caps in the 1960s, during which time he scored half-centuries against Scotland and New Zealand.

Cricket still flourishes at the school, while the ground also plays host to Taverners cricket matches during the summer, with both The Dalkey Archives and a team from Fitzgerald's Pub in Sandycove using the facility.

Of course James Joyce is associated with Fitzgerald's and we will leave the last word to the author, who wrote so beautifully about this most wonderful of games.

"And all over the playgrounds they were playing rounders and bowling twisters and lobs. And from here and from there came the sounds of the cricket bats through the soft grey air. They said: pick, pack, pock, puck; little drops of water in a fountain slowly falling in the brimming bowl."

Emmet Riordan
A Native of Dalkey and
cricket correspondent of The Irish Times

A cuppa that's healthy enough for Gwyneth

Although in use since ancient times, Cupping for many made its debut a few years ago when Gwyneth Paltrow turned up for a New York film premiere in a low cut dress revealing a selection of unusual circular bruises.

Not unlike love bites, they were the after-effects of a type of alternative therapy called cupping. Commonly used for thousands of years in Traditional Chinese Medicine, the practice of placing heated glass cups on the skin along the meridian lines to promote the movement of blood, qi (the body's internal energy) and lymph system was first documented in the oldest recorded medical text book, Ebers Papyrus - dating back to Egypt in 1550 BC.

Since then cupping has been used in one form or another in all cultures from England to Tibet, Greece to Siberia, the Aborigines to the Islamic nations.

Today, it is most often used in conjunction with acupuncture and tuina massage, a traditional Chinese form of massage.

One such Chinese medicine practitioner working with cupping in this way is Rabie Dine, of the Dalkey Oriental Clinic 17 Castle St., Dalkey.

A Chinese medicine praciticiner, he and his herbalist father before him use cupping for a variety of ailments, from colds and flus to pain relief. "Cupping is a method used to encourage the flow of the blood, the qi and the lymph system. Traditionally this dry cupping was done using glass cups heated with a naked flame and then placed on the skin but due to the risk of burning and thanks to modern technology we now use hard plastic cups with little pumps to control the degree of suction created," he says. So once, I've got over my disappointment at not having tiny fish bowls anchored to my body, Rabie diagnoses me by asking questions, observing my tongue and taking my pulse. With the story of one of his patients, a man in his 70s who was barely able to walk with arthritis finding enough relief in 10 sessions that he's now out

mountain climbing, Rabbie explains: "I commenced treating him and after five

Niamh Hooper, Health Writer Irish Independent

weeks of two sessions a week with approval of his GP, who was kept informed of his progress, took him off all his prescribed medication. It had not been necessary for him to take any prescribed medicaiton since Thursday 25th October 2007 and his is now walking the hills and mountains free of all pain. He expressed a desire to visit me once a month to ensure that there were no signs of any relapse thankfully there are no signs to date.". "Another patient has been suffering from severe pain in the left leg for 3 months. The complaint had manifested itself quite suddenly. The person played golf very regularly but had reached the stage of being unable to play and was severely restricted in movement. He was the subject of considerable medical investigation and was taking a lot of prescribed pain killers to no effect.

I commenced treatment and after 3 sessions he was waking 300-400 yards and after 5 sessions was playing eight holes of golf without any pain. The improvement continued and following a further 3 sessions was playing a full round of golf. There has been no reoccurence of the pain and is golfing several times a week." Rabbie makes sure there is total interaction between the patients GP and himself, if the patient so desires and the treaments are covered by the leading medical insurance companies. I'm looking forward to having my tight shoulders and back ache sorted out.

Lying face down on the bed, Rabie places the first of about 10 cups on my upper back and shoulders. And then he adds a further 10 on my lower back. It's an odd sensation of increasing tightness as more cups are added but I'm happy enough to stay like this for the required 15 minutes. As the skin beneath my cups doesn't become particularly dark in colour, it's clear I have no deep-seated blood statis and that my condition wasn't too severe. (True) Understandably, an area of my right shoulder which was dislocated and broken a few years ago was slightly darker but is still nothing to be concerned about.

"Lots of people, many of them golfers, come in with frozen shoulders but all that's really going on there is stagnation. Once we get blood flowing so it can nourish the area, the stagnation dissipates. If I move the cups and create a suction for the whole area by sliding them with a little oil, people find it can take only five to seven session to

relieve the condition," he says.

Since cupping began, all types of cups have been used all over the world, from animal horns to shells, brass, ceramic, bamboo, tin, bronze to rubber cups. Whether the vacuum is created by placing the base of a buffalo horn on the skin and sucking the air out through the opening at the tip before a nimble tongue fills it with a wad of dried grass or it is created by inserting a lighted cotton wool ball dipped into a small globe

Rabie Dine, Chinese medical practitioner.

of thick glass before placing it on the skin, the principles of cupping remain the same. The creation of a vacuum causes the skin to be sucked up into the cup and this encourages the flow of fresh blood to the area, the flow of Qi and lymph thus clearing local stagnation. As blood can be drawn into the small blood vessels just below the skin, it may cause purple marks that look like bruises. Some argue they are not in fact bruises, but are pathogenic factors brought to the surface to be expelled.

This can be felt first hand with colds and flus. When the glass cups are lifted, apparently a whip of chilly air is released where it has literally been drawn from the body. "The easiest and fastest way of relieving a cold, especially in children is with cupping. By stimulating points between the shoulder blades it pulls the cold from the inside out."

Verdict:

Cupping for me was an unusual sensation with the skin feeling tingly and tight. Afterwards I felt less tension in my shoulders and in general although to give it a real try I know I would need to have pronounced symptoms for which it is recommended. Having lasted the test of time, I feel there must be something in it.

*Cupping is usually done in conjunction with acupuncture and tuina. For a 45-minute session with Rabie Dine costs €55. To make an appointment call 086 404 9688.

The Facts:

The practice of cupping is believed to have been used as therapeutic procedure to draw to the surface any irritations, such as stings long before evidence of it was documented. Hippocrates, known as the father of modern medicine, recommended it for the treatment of angina, menstrual ailments among others. The action of suction is one that we use instinctively when you think about it. As a kid when you jammed your finger in a door, you sucked it to soothe the pain away. Various types cupping exist; primarily they are wet cupping in which a tiny incision is made into the skin and blood is drawn off and dry cupping – the subject of this week's therapy.

Dry cupping is said to be particularly useful in the treatment of musculo-skeletal aches and pains, conditions such as asthma, colds and flu, digestion, sciatica, menstrual pain and other blood conditions.

It is important cupping is carried out only in a clinical environment by a registered practitioner.

The Evidence:

Beyond its use in Traditional Chinese Medicine for thousands of years, cupping has been described as the "most popular medical method practiced by the majority of people in Syria". In a recent report in the Arabic News, a Syrian medical team lead by heart surgeon Dr Ahmad Takreiti conducted a series of studies on 300 patients, both male and female. It found when cupping was applied to the upper back, between the scapula for three minutes, positive therapeutic results were reported in the treatment of heamophilia, lymphoma, migraine, gout, asthma, rheumatism and certain chest complaints. Another study conducted by St George University in London found that cupping stimulated significant differences in the level of pain, range of movement and well-being experienced by patients with knee problems.

Niamh Hooper
Health Writer, Irish Independent
First published in Irish Independent 10th
December 2007

My Famous Old Hometown

Dalkey is a famous town, a unique place. Many stories have been written about it through the centuries, both in a serious manner and in jest, some of them exemplary in their own ways.

It has a truly long and varied history, much of it well documented, particularly over the last four to five hundred years. One of the most interesting publications that I have read was James J. Gaskin's "Varieties of Irish History," which was published in 1869. While it does not dwell exclusively on Dalkey, it gives an interesting account of how it was perceived almost one hundred and forty years ago.

Gaskin describes Dalkey as follows: "Dalkey, a beautiful picturesque spot, a fashionable watering place." Most people who are familiar with the town in this, the 21st century, would express similar views. He goes on to describe it as a "a rising and prosperous township, where peace and harmony prevail in its municipal councils – health abiding Dalkey woos the sigh of the southern gale with so much effect – Dalkey with its pure and salubrious atmosphere, limpid springs, holy wells, religious educational institutes and gorse crowned hills on one of which is perched a Danish Ruin – Dalkey within half an hours drive from the Irish capital, with its historical associations, lead mines and well arranged baths. Dalkey where marine treasures and villas of rural beauty with their appropriate Irish names, are securely Dalkey."

Another writer of that period, J. Sheehan, who used the non-de-plume "The Knight of Inishowen" in one of his columns in The Comet Newspaper, a popular publication of the time wrote: "They tell me that nobody insures their lives around Dalkey for fear that they should pay the amount of their life policy three times over in premiums; in fact, they say that very few people die about this part, at least in Dalkey at all."

A local scribe known as "Sir Lucius" wrote: "Most assuredly, the people about this favourite spot along the shore and on the rocks and on the hills that encircle the sea live to a patriarchal age. When they go off at least, nobody seems to know what they died of. At all events, they go off gently and easily."

View over Dalkey showing my Grandfathers house in the foreground

This comment was certainly an appropriate description of my own grandfather, Michael Mullen, who was born at Ard Brugh Road on Dalkey Hill on 4th August 1867. His ancestors on his father's side came to Dalkey from Rathmichael in 1794 and on his mothers side the Fox family came from Rathmichael in 1796. They were stone cutters and his grandparents and granduncles worked on the cutting of the granite for Dun Laoghaire Harbour, the Inner Harbours and the Sea Walls along the railway lines, most of the granite for the latter two was cut in Bullock and the foreshore to Sandycove. One of his granduncles, Kevin, was killed when he fell from a ledge cutting granite in the Bullock Quarry area.

My 1st Team.
My Dad, my Mam, Eileen, Michael and Myself.

My mother was born in Kilimor, Co. Galway on 14th November 1903 and she was a wonderful mother, a great cook and like all mothers of my young days always seemed to have plenty of time to provide goodies for our pals who would come into the house. My father, also named Michael, was born at 4 Ardbrugh Road on 8th August 1896. My Dad was a barman in Quigley's, later McDonough's and then became a bin man and road sweeper with the Council. I recall when I was very young asking my dad why he had to go out to work around 5.30 on Christmas Mornings. He told me that he had to have the streets clean early on those mornings before people started coming to first mass. He also worked early on Sundays and Bank Holidays. He explained that he got paid overtime for doing the work and it was important during those bad times to earn as much as he could to help to buy food and other essentials for the home.

Another question I put him was why he always wore his Sunday suit when he was going to his Union Meetings some evenings after work. He told me that it was respect for his union that he dressed well for the meetings. He was deeply involved in trade union work and was a great supporter of James Connolly and Jim Larkin. I recall he asked me if I would like to go to Jim Larkin's funeral, I told him that I would. He gave me a note to say I would not be in school the following day and I remember going into the city on the tram with him and some of his friends including Tom Thomas, Jimmy Reilly, Bill Hannah and others.

He remained friends of the Larkin family and when he died in 1956 I was moved to see members of both the Larkin and Connolly families at his funeral.

These two incidents left a lasting impression on my young mind and had a profound influence on my future life. I always enjoy work and never understood the meaning of "the Monday morning feeling". I spent 26 years of my working life in the Garda Siochana which I joined on 12th November 1959. The first two years of this in Dun Laoghaire. In November 1961 I was involved with a small group of colleagues in organising a protest meeting at the Macushla Ballroom in Dublin to improve our conditions of service.

On the night before an order was given to every member of the force by the authorities that attending the meeting would result in disciplinary action being taken against them and if the organisers were identified they would be dismissed forthwith.

Conditions were so bad that we decided we had not much to loose and that we would go ahead with the meeting hoping that a coulple of hundred would attend, over 1,000 turned up. Support for the movement spread countrywide and many meetings were organised. Within a week or so numerous members were disciplined and most of the committee were sacked. Chief Superintendent Dan Devitt, called to my house on a Sunday night and told me he believed that I was a leading member of the committee. I made no comment. He told me that the Government had accepted an offer to mediate from the Archbishop of Dublin, John Charles McQuaid and he asked me to meet with the Archbishop. I replied that without prejudice to myself I would oblige. He then accompanied me in a patrol car to the Archbishops residence in Kiliney and left me outside the gate. For a few moments I felt a little unsure of myself. During those days the Archbishop was a very powerful figure and as I was walking up the driveway in the darkness to the hall door I suddenly remembered my dad had told me some years earlier that if I ever got involved in trade union work and found myself negotiating with the Archbishop to be very careful of him as he had broken a promise to him and his colleagues over some dispute in the 1930s.

That recollection gave me the confidence that I needed, the discussions went on until 4.00am with no progress. I walked back to Dalkey. The following day I was asked to attend further discussions which went on late into Monday night. I then contacted the Minister for Justice, Charles Haughey, and he agreed to talk to me in confidence. I have kept that confidence until now. We met and he asked me what would settle the dispute. I told him in detail and he said it would be settled speedily on the condition that I never mentioned that we had met. It was settled after a further short meeting with the Archbishop, my colleagues got their jobs back, all disciplinary actions were dropped and following the setting up of a committee a Representative Body for Guards was formed and most of our demands were met.

I was involved in representative affairs for the remainder of my career both part-time and full-time. I received invaluable advice and assistance from a lot of my Dads old trade union friends. I received great satisfaction over the years and obviously had some frustrating experiences also. I subsequently became Dublin Area Chairman, National Vice-President and President.

Barry, Geraldine with baby daughter Katie, self in Royal gear, Ellen and Aideen.

One of my most satisfying achievements was setting up the Garda Medical Insurance Society along with Mick Conway, John O'Brien and others, it is now recognised as being the most comprehensive medical insurance company in the country. I introduced the concept of Neighbourhood Watch to the authorities. In the early 1980s I failed to convince management of the force of the advantages of setting up a modern welfare service, a post traumatic counselling service and other such institutions that would have helped members of the force and their families.

I subsequently got so frustrated with the entire organisation in the Garda Siochana that I took a career break, started my own Insurance Brokerage company and that effectively ended my career in the Gardai.It was the most satisfying and self-fulfilling decision I have ever made. I have to say that the vast majority of An Garda Siochana are decent honourable people.

My dad also grew vegetables in plots of land between Dalkey Avenue and Cunningham Road and on the Firm Bank which is situated between Dalkey Avenue and Hillside as one walks past Dalkey Park. It is the bank on the right which leads down to the railway bridge on Barnhill Road. Larry Doran is the only one with a plot there today.

Like so many fathers of those times he cut turf on Glencree often leaving Dalkey on bicycles between 5 and 6 a.m. on Sundays to cycle to the bog returning at 9 or 10 p.m. after a long days work. He would say it was easy coming home as it was all downhill. If the summer was good (as they all seemed to be back in those times) he might succeed in cutting two loads of turf. He would sell one load and the proceeds of the sale would help to pay the school fees for my brother, my sister and myself when we were in secondary schools.

Aideen with husband Stephen, Cameron and Niamh.

One of the early memories I have of being with my dad was another occasion that had a significant influence on my life. Neighbours in those days as they are to a great extent in present times, help each other in times of sickness and death and celebrate happy times together. One of the

kindest families who lived on Leslie Avenue (and there were many) were the Wilmott's, yes the family of our beloved "King Larry", when Mr. Wilmott died his remains were taken to St. Patrick's Church on Harbour Road. As was the custom the men carried the coffin in turns into the church. As we were walking towards the church door I was holding my Dad's hand behind the remains, a man said to him, "Mike you cannot go in there", I was surprised at this remark. My Dad said he was good enough to enjoy life with him as a close neighbour; his church is good enough for me to go into. We went in and the man who spoke to him followed us as did all the crowd who were standing outside.

I have been fortunate to have travelled extensively around the world whether on business, through sport or on holidays. I have never had any difficulty in going into a place of worship regardless of what denomination it happened to be to pray for a short time in peace.

Daddy died suddenly walking to first mass with me on Sunday 5th August 1956. He was sixty years old and he was a great loss. A couple of weeks after he died I was walking along Castle Street on my way to the football club with Paddy Carroll (Junior) when a man approached me and told me he had great respect for my dad whom he knew well. He said if I ever needed any advice or help to contact him. He became a true and sincere friend, my confidant and the father figure in my life. He subsequently became Chairman and Vice President of Dalkey United. He was Michael Hayde. When he died on 25th January 1987 I felt his loss profoundly for a long time. I felt it was another father figure gone from my life.

My dads sisters Nora, Alice and Kathleen were also born in the same house on

Ardbrugh Road. I recall when on holidays from school playing across the road in the field under the east quarry of Dalkey Hill when my Aunt Kathleen who was a great cook, would bring us into the house and give us homemade cakes and lemonade, homemade fudge was a delicious treat in those days also. This sort of invitation was a regular occurrence on the hill. The beautiful houses and cottages at the rear of O'Loughlin's grocery and off licensed shop (Lockey's) at the top of the flags were homes where the doors were always open and we were given cakes, sandwiches and other goodies. The Byrnes, O'Reilly's and Wallace's lived for generations in those houses and their families are there to this day. I recall Stella Dowse who died this year approaching her 100th birthday and who lost two brothers in the Second World War. She and her family lived in Ardbrugh Villas for almost her entire life and were great neighbours.

Our old family home is no longer there; a beautiful modern house "Ardan" stands on the site today. The Delaney's house and grounds are also gone. The houses of Ardbrugh Close are on the site. Darcy's house and fields where the Torca Tennis Club functioned for many years from the latter part of the 19th century to the 1930's is the site where the houses of Dalkey Rock now stand. Children played in Darcy's fields when there were no cattle there but this ceased following the collapse of part of the cliff on Halloween Night in 1947.

I remember very vividly the numerous hours I spent during winter evenings in my grandfather's house in front of a large turf fire as he spoke of events, then long passed, which he remembered and happened during his life. His recall up to a few weeks before he died was remarkable, listening to him was akin to reading history books. While he told stories of people going to and

coming home from the Boer War, the First World War including his brother Joey, he never spoke about the events of 1916 or the War of Independence, probably because the family's involvement was such that he preferred not to dwell on that period. I discovered later that people who went through those difficult years were reluctant to talk about their experiences. Joey served in the two World Wars and I asked him one day how he survived both wars and with a smile on his face said "drink" and then he explained that he was a Quarter Master Sergeant in charge of food supplies and was always well back from the frontline.

My granddad along with my dad instilled into my young mind an interest in sport and history that have been very important to me as I enter the autumn of my life.

My Grandad in his eighties at old ruin on top of Dalkey Quarry c. 1950

Those evenings which I spent with my granddad before the turf and log fires are such wonderful memories, which can be best described by the great Sigerson Clifford in a lovely poem he wrote of his memories of a similar bond with his own grandfather thus:

My grandfather tendered the turf fire
and leaning backward into legend spoke

of doings old before quills inked history
I saw dark heroes fighting in the smoke

I see the wise face now with its hundred
wrinkles
and every wrinkle held a thousand tales

Ah! I should have put a noose about the
throat of time
and choked the passing of the hobnailed
years
and stayed young, always shouting in the
hills
where life held only fairy fears.

Granda with myself, my dad, sister Eileen and
brother Michael. c. 1944

Barry and his wife Jan with Cian and Amy.

The long lives of people living as described in Gaskin's excellent book was in some simple way a reflection of the way my grandfather lived.

A couple of years before he died, when he was approaching ninety years old, he contracted a bad flu. If memory serves me correctly, it was "The Asian Flu", he was attended by Dr. Fitzpatrick of Coliemore Road, Dalkey. He recovered quickly and told me that the last time he was treated by a doctor was in 1904 when he and some friends went to Glasgow to see Celtic play Rangers. Later that evening he was knocked down by a tram while walking to the Dublin Boat and he spent a short time in hospital in Glasgow. He apparently did not suffer any after effects and spent the next fifty years or so of his life without requiring any medical attention.

Gaskin also described Dalkey as "a fitting home for convalescents" quoting I believe the immortal words of Dalkey born poet and musician John Dowland, who was born in 1563 and died in 1626, in describing Dalkey said it was "a place where smiling spring its earliest visit pays and parting summers lingering bloom delays".

There is a mosaic in Sorrento Park dedicated to Dowland's memory. The park, which was left in trust to the people of Dalkey by Lady MacDonald in 1894, is a truly beautiful place with its panoramic views of Dalkey Island, Killiney Bay and the Wicklow Mountains.

These words are as true today as they were when they were written all those years ago. If one walked around the roads of Dalkey, particularly through Sorrento Road, Vico Road, Dalkey Avenue, and adjoining roads in late November into December, one can see the departing year's leaves on many trees. The approaching spring buds and blooms can be seen on the aforementioned roads and adjoining gardens in mid January. It can be a most exhilarating stroll on mild mornings during these winter weeks to see very visible signs that spring and summer are on the way.

Some friends whom I swim with in the seas around the Forty Foot and the Vico all the year and regularly walk around some of the roads referred to say "they often get the feeling that summer never really ends". Daft as it may sound I fully agree with their opinion.

My great friend and mentor Michael Hayde.

Thomas Moore was born on 28th May 1779 over a shop in Aungier Street in Dublin, where his father had a grocery and spirit store. He died on 26th February 1852 and was a regular visitor to Dalkey particularly in his younger days before he went to Sloperton Cottage in Wiltshire, England. He married in 1812 and lived in the cottage until his death. He lived for periods in Paris where he wrote a lot of his works. He paid many visits back to Dublin with his wife and family. He had 3 daughters and 2 sons all of whom predeceased him. He lived in lodgings in 17 Rue a Ajou Paris and from there published a monthly journal of stories, songs etc. In the October of 1820 issue he wrote, it is only within these few years I have begun to delight in the charms

inanimate nature, the safest as well as the purest passion. [Extracts from Poetical Works by Thomas Moore published by Routledge & Sons London in 1884]. This story is given credence when the Knight of Inishowen (John Sheehan) in writing about Dalkey and its beauty speculated that Thomas Moore could have been thinking about Dalkey when he wrote: -

How dear to me the hour when daylight dies,
And sunbeams mealth along the silent sea,
For then sweet dreams of other days arrive,
And memory breathes her vesper sigh to thee.

And, as I watch the line of light, that plays
Along the smooth wave t'ward the burning west,
I long to tread the golden path of rays,
And think 'twould lead to some bright isle great.

Yes, Dalkey is a town steeped in history and although somebody decided in recent times to call it a village, it is still a beautiful place to live which has expanded but still held its character.

As one of Dalkey's, indeed one of Ireland's, most eminent writers Hugh Leonard points out elsewhere in this anthology "Dalkey is not only a town (or a village) but a suburb" and remarkably, it wears both descriptions with ease. As the latter, it is consciously a part of the world outside; as the former it looks after its own affairs, it is self-contained, a shared community in every sense. Most important of all, it has retained its character and is most proud of its eccentricities".

I could not imagine myself living anywhere else. I have so many happy memories, my childhood days, and going to school with my sister Eileen and my brother Michael in Loreto National School where my dad went and my children and grandchildren have secured their early education. I have fond memories of our teachers there, Miss Kelly who lived with her sister on Corrig Road, Miss Regan from Dun Laoghaire. Mother Celine and Mother Felicita. I recall moving onto Harold Boys School where we were thought by Pronsias O'Maolain (a cousin) Peadar O'Hulachain and Dermot O'hAllanin. All of these contributed in a very important way to any success I attained in later life.

My mum as a young woman at home in Galway.

I consider myself lucky to have had wonderful grandparents and parents all of whom have passed on.

One cannot survive and be happy without loyal and trusted friends and thankfully there are many in Dalkey, some of them life long friends. I have been involved with Dalkey United since its formation in 1953 and have a life of happy memories, of great people who have been and presently are involved in the club.

Geraldine and her husband Tim the parents of Katie, Conor, Caoimhe and Ellie. Our son Barry, his wife Jan and their children Cian and Amy. Aideen and her husband Stephen their little girl Niamh and her big brother Cameron continue to give us great happiness and love. I believe that there is nothing like the laughter and banter of chil-

dren around a house to make one feel good and young.

I live close to my brother Michael, his wife Peg and their children Declan, Niamh and Michael, their respective spouses Pam, David and Stephanie and their children all of whom have provided great support over the years.

Geraldine with husband Tim, son Conor and daughters Caoimhe and Ellie

I have wonderful memories of the summer holidays swimming in the White Rock, the Vico Bathing Place, Bulloch Harbour and the Forty Foot. I have so many happy memories of growing up and having lived all of my life in this lovely old town that it would be impossible to numerate them all in this story.

I have been blessed with having a wonderful wife, Ellen whom one of my aunts described her as "a nice girl but she is from the country" i.e. a runner into Dalkey.

Ellen the mother of our three loving children Geraldine, Barry and Aideen, has been a tower of strength and support to me in everything that I have achieved or tried to achieve since we first met. My hope is that God will give us the health together to cotinue to enjoy the love of our family, the company of our friends and carry on the work I do for the club that has been a life long passion for me, Dalkey United and my favourite old hometown.

Frank Mullen

Leabharlanna Poibli Chathair Bhaile Átha Cl
Dublin City Public Libraries

Dalkey - My Hometown

My hometown of Dalkey
Is heaven to me.
From Craggy high cliffs
To fast flowing sea.

To pause in the Village
On the hill.
One gets a strange feeling
That time has stood still.

Stone craftsmen of yore
Brought our granite to life.
Building cathedrals and piers
Which still give delight.

Our sportsmen and writers
Of worldwide renown.
Always speak highly
When they talk of their town

Our sons and our daughters
Now roam far and wide.
But their hearts still belong
Here in Dalkey, their Pride.

When strolling its streets
As seasons pass by.
We seep in its beauty
Beneath a soft moving sky.

There's no place on Earth
So like heaven to me.
Just leave me in Dalkey
'Till called home to Thee.

Frank Mullen

Castle Street 1944 with No. 8 Tram in background.
l to r: Murt Dempsey, Frank Mullen, Johnny Egan on Jack Thomas Milk Cart.

Kings of Dalkey

First Winners of the Heineken Cup
for Inter Pub Football Tournament 1987
L to R: Jim Forde, King Larry, Bill Brown, Seamus Sheeran,
John Cleary (Capt.), Mick (Digger) Dalton Manager R.I.P.

Cuala Ladies celebrate Tug of War victory with King Frank

King Liam with happy children at Hyde Park

King Johnny Dunne presides over senior citizens party.

King Norman in Royal Court.
L to R: Jimmy McGlone, Jack Fitzpatrick,
King Nornam Judd and Fred Somers

King Jack Dalton 1991

Guinness Dalkey Grand Priz
King Mervyn with Rev. Fr. Des Forrestal P.P. and
Rev. Ricky Rountree, St. Patrick's C of I lead off the
competitors on a practice lap.

Enjoying the Festival over the years

Disaster

Determination

Success

Boat Tayto at Bulloch 1952
Steering Ged Pierce Snr., Frances, Patsy and
Anne Pierce in bow port side Ged Pierce behind him
Kathleen Nolan

A Happy Baby

Betty and Tom Doherty R.I.P. at
a Dalkey United Function

Phylis Hayden, Sonny Hayden, Frances McCann, Hugh McCann

One of Dalkeys Great Characters
Robert Boland

Fionnuala Eithne, Maurish Duggan, Jimmy Duggan R.I.P.,
Des Beirne, Kathleen, Deirdre

Children enjoying Festival Games.

James Archibald, Dalkeys Great Marathon Man with some loyal fans.

And they are off!

Dalkey Inter Pub Tournament 1971

Colamore Hotel
Back: W. Long (manager), P. Lambe, D. Lambe, - Joe (Jumbo)
Curtin, M. Mullen, P. Byrne, Frank Crawley (Ref.)
Front: – – Bobby Moore, – Michael Fanning.

Searsons Team
Back: M. Hayde (manager), N. Sweeney, D. Seavers, S. Golding,
J. Dunne, T. Quinn.
Front: P. Mathews, J. Mooney, G. Hick, B. Taylor, L. Cooke,
P. Connolly

Finegans Team
Back: E. Russell, M. Newbanks, – – , J. Healy, P. Davis,
D. Finnegan (manager)
Front: M. Hayes, B. Cruise, P. Byrne, R. Boland, H. Byrne

Cuala Under 12 Football Team 1985
Undefeated in both Football and Hurling for the entire season
Back Row: Gavin Martin, Donal Farrell, Declan Corry, Bill Gleeson,
Cian Crowley, Karl Boylan, Simon Carroll, Dermot Farrelly,
Dave Sheeran, Shane Crowley, Tommy Kelly.
Front Row: Monty Murphy, Ger Ecker, Frankie Hayes, Eoin Devlin, Rian Kelly, Derek Cahill,
Conor Magee, Tommy Byrne, Darren Summers, Dara Kennedy

Happy Fishermen from left Jimmy Kelly, John Cunningham (Chairman), Shay McLoughlinn,
Vinnie Mulligan, Tony Wallace

Keeping the children entertained.

Keeping the children entertained.

Dalkey Swimming Club 1945
Back Row: Ursula Maguire, Joe O'Rourke, Jimmy Duggan, Dick O'Hanrahan, Alexan Kennedy, Paddy Duggan, Jimmy McGilton and sons, Gus Farrell, M. Murray, McDermott, Jimmy Byrne, Sidney Foley, Middle Row: Nora Kennedy, Noreen Kennedy, Celia O'Dowd, J.J. Kennedy, Peggy Kennedy child, Maurish Duggan, Vera Smyth, M. McGilton, Suzan Atkinson, Tommy Kavanagh, Cyril Murray, Johnny Keane. Front Row: McGiulton, Tony Duggan, Maguire, Harry Byrne, Tony Kelly, Blair Murray, Tom Ross, Joe Quirke, Kevan Dowd/

King Liam Silke with the late President Hillary.